Adventures in Playmaking
Four Plays by Carolina Playmakers

The Playmakers Theatre. First state-owned theater in America to be devoted to the making of a native drama.

ADVENTURES IN PLAYMAKING

Four Plays by Carolina Playmakers

Edited by

John W. Parker

The University of North Carolina Press Chapel Hill

To my wife

DARICE JACKSON PARKER

CONTENTS

ILLUSTRATIONS

INTRODUCTION: *Fifty Years of*

Playwriting in a University

The special occasion for the publication of this volume of full-length plays is the celebration of the fiftieth anniversary of The Carolina Playmakers. It will really be the fifty-first season of playmaking at The University of North Carolina at Chapel Hill—the dramatic organization having been founded in the fall of 1918. But a decision was made several years ago to wait until we had actually concluded fifty years of activity before marking the event. Mankind, in our part of the world at least, has set this pattern in reckoning his age. We are only following that custom, but with this variation: instead of limiting ourselves to one day of recognition of the fact of age, we are electing the whole succeeding year in which we can evaluate the past, take stock of the present, and plan for the future.

The appearance of this collection of plays is only one facet of the festival events of 1968–69. In 1969, The University of North Carolina Press will bring out a history of The Carolina Playmakers written by Walter Spearman with the assistance of Samuel Selden. The entire season of major and studio productions has been carefully selected with the anniversary year in mind. We expect a number of former Playmakers, now in professional theater, to return to join us in making the productions more distinctive by their participation as performers, writers, directors, and designers. Throughout the year, several nationally known leaders and commentators will participate in panel discussions of the state of theater arts in the United States and abroad, and exhibits will be on display. The climax of the year's celebration will be the spring homecoming to which some five thousand Playmaker alumni have been invited.

Why were full-length plays instead of one-act plays selected for this volume, since the initial reputation of The Carolina Playmakers was based largely upon the writing and production of one-act plays by student authors? And why these particular plays?

First, other editors, during this fifty-year period, have made the country conscious of the original dramatic work done here at The University

of North Carolina by bringing out several collections of plays molded in
the short form: *Carolina Folk Plays* (*First, Second,* and *Third Series*),
*The Lord's Will and Other Plays, Folk Plays of Eastern Carolina,
Alabama Folk Plays, Mexican Folk Plays, Carolina Folk Comedies,
American Folk Plays,* and *International Folk Plays.* And although a new
collection has not appeared in two decades, perhaps those in print will be
representative enough, for the time being, of almost a thousand one-act
plays (listed in the Appendix) which were written here and first produced on our stage.

Second, our original plays in the full-length form are considerably
fewer in number than the one-acters. One reason for this, of course, is
that students are usually not with us long enough to experiment, with
any confidence, in this longer, more complicated form of playwriting.
For years, many of our graduate students have elected to submit a long
original play in lieu of the traditional research thesis as a part of the
requirements for the master's degree program. But most of these plays
are, as early exercises in the full-length form, stageworthy only to a
limited extent, and only a few more than forty have actually been produced by us. Fewer still have been included in a season's major bill for
a paying audience. None of them, so far as I know, has been published.
Therefore, it seems to be altogether fitting for the selected best of our
work in the full-length form to be recognized on this anniversary occasion.

As to why these particular plays were selected for inclusion in this
volume, I gladly recognize the fact that I was guided by advice from a
Playmakers' staff screening committee and by members of The University of North Carolina Press. We agreed that the plays had to represent
the best of our writers' work in this form; they must have been produced
for the first time by The Carolina Playmakers; and they must be chosen
from various periods of our fifty-year history. And so it came about that
we finally selected these four plays: *Singing Valley,* a romantic comedy
of Mexican village life, by Josefina Niggli (1936); *Spring for Sure,* a
musical play of the Smoky Mountains, by Catherine McDonald and
Wilton Mason (1950); *A Little to the Left,* a comedy of the Banana
Republics, by Brock Brower (1959); and, *The Battle of the Carnival
and Lent,* a drama of the Middle Ages, by Russell Graves (1967). The
first is a thesis requirement play by a graduate student; so is the second,
with musical collaboration by a former student; the third had a special
student as author; and the fourth play was written by a member of our
staff. All of the plays proved to be stageworthy, and it is our hope that
other theater groups will now find enjoyment in producing them.

Grateful mention should be made here of the teachers of playwriting in the Department of Dramatic Art, who inspired and worked so diligently to assist the successive generations of student authors:

Foremost, of course, was Professor Frederick H. Koch (Proff—without quotation marks or a period, to all who knew him—a term of endearment contracted not from "professor," according to the late Archibald Henderson, his colleague and great admirer, but from "prophet"). It was Proff Koch who devised the term "folk play" in referring to the early nature-oriented, regionally connected plays of his students. And it was he who yearningly, yet confidently, liked to paraphrase Walt Whitman at every opportunity: "Expecting the main things from those who come after."

Later, collaborating with Proff Koch as instructor, was Samuel Selden. They made a wonderful combination—Koch with his infectious optimism and Selden with his respect for detail and technique. During this period Professor Selden gave us the first of his many books which would eventually cover all the arts of the theater—this one, *An Introduction to Playwriting*.

Also in these middle years, Paul Green returned to the campus from Hollywood and joined our staff as consultant to writers who were primarily interested in the full-length play form. And as enrollments in the playwriting courses grew, Professors Harry Davis, Kai Jurgensen, and I were drafted to serve as advisors—first to the beginners and later to graduate students writing long plays to fulfill thesis requirements. For two seasons each, Lennox Robinson, noted Irish playwright, and Walter Pritchard Eaton, well-known New York drama critic and retired teacher of playwriting from Yale University, were members of our staff as special consultants and lecturers.

Professor Thomas M. Patterson became the principal teacher in the writing division of our dramatic art program in 1950. Under his leadership we have seen the student writer drift away from the "folk idea" as a motivating factor and rebel against the constrictions of the well-made play. Following trends set earlier in France and England, we have had the usual number of avante-garde pieces, with carefully concealed plots, with protagonist and antagonist sometimes becoming one, and with story line and dialogue drawing heavily upon the audiences' imagination and interpretation. Some of them have been interesting and stageworthy experiments; others have not.

It is pleasant to recall the years I have served on this teacher-of-playwriting team—since the late thirties, in fact. Mostly I have conducted the courses in the summer sessions and acted as adviser to thesis playwrights during the fall and spring semesters.

Perhaps a word may be said here, too, about the title of this book,

Adventures in Playmaking. I hope it is applicable and provocative, but it did not originate with this editor. Its coinage, so far as I know, goes back to our very early days when Frederick H. Koch, founder and first director of our organization, made use of it to label an illustrated lecture he gave at the beginning of each school year to dramatic art students, Carolina Playmakers, and friends. It always seemed to me to be a particularly appropriate name for the inspiring and enthusiastic tale he told of our beginnings and accomplishments to whatever period of our history it· happened then to be—accompanied by lantern-slide photographs of former productions and of people who had been associated with us as actors, writers, directors, and whoever came to mind in embellishing his story. It was really an adventure! He made it seem so, anyway. Mr. Koch also used the phrase for chapter headings in several of his books; and I, myself, borrowed it once to entitle a brochure concerning our work in playwriting. So, inasmuch as "Adventures in Playmaking" can conceivably be regarded as a kind of family property, I presumed to use it again—in loving memory of Proff Koch—and because I think it is appropriate for this book on this occasion.

JOHN W. PARKER

Chapel Hill, North Carolina
January, 1968

SINGING VALLEY

by Josefina Niggli

A scene from *Singing Valley,* by Josefina Niggli. Originally produced by
The Carolina Playmakers in 1936.

THE AUTHOR: *Josefina Niggli*

Hailed in her native land, shortly after the publication of her volume of one-act plays by The University of North Carolina Press, as "Mexico's national playwright," Josefina Niggli was born in Monterrey, Nuevo Leon, the only child of a prominent glassware manufacturer. Her father was of Swiss lineage. Her mother, of Virginia ancestry, was well-known as a concert violinist and leader of an all-girl orchestra which toured the United States extensively around the turn of the century and prior to her marriage.

Young Josefina was tutored at home, principally by her mother, before leaving for high school studies in San Antonio, Texas. There, in a second home established by her mother and maternal grandmother—with her father making frequent visits from his base of business operations in Monterrey—she continued her education at Incarnate Word College. It was in this sheltered but artistically stimulating environment that she first became attracted to writing. Several poems and short stories, written at this time, have since appeared in various magazines and anthologies.

Miss Niggli enrolled for graduate study in dramatic art at The University of North Carolina at Chapel Hill in the summer of 1935. Under the guidance of Professor Frederick H. Koch, noted teacher of play-writing, and his associate, Professor Samuel Selden, within the next two years she wrote a colorful series of one-act plays reflecting the lives of her Mexican people. All of these plays were originally staged by The Carolina Playmakers; several of them were included in tour bills; and all of them were published by The University of North Carolina Press under the title *Mexican Folk Plays*. The author laughingly recalls that her father was influential in establishing her reputation as a writer throughout Mexico by insisting that copies of this book be placed in all railway lounge cars. (He was a stockholder in several railroad companies —and a valued shipper.)

During her program of graduate studies in Chapel Hill, she wrote, and the Playmakers produced, her first full-length play, *Singing Valley,* which is included in this volume. It is a story of home-longing and pride of origin, both on her part and that of her characters, told in a light, ro-mantic style with occasional bursts of intense poetic feeling. A few months later saw the production of her second long play, *The Fair-God,* reflective of a much more sophisticated element of Mexican society and a more glamorous period of national development.

In the World War II years and shortly thereafter, Miss Niggli was an instructor in dramatic art on the Chapel Hill campus and that of its sister university at Greensboro. During this period she was particularly active in radio writing and production. Many of her scripts, written for NBC International, were broadcast to Latin America in Spanish and were a vital contribution to cultural relations in this hemisphere. Since then, her television scripts have enjoyed popularity in Rome, Paris, Toronto, and Sydney.

Her three novels have been equally well received: *Mexican Village* won the Mayflower Society Cup, presented annually for the best novel by a North Carolina writer; *Step Down, Elder Brother* was a Book-of-the-Month Club selection; and *Miracle for Mexico* was a recent Christmas best-seller. Out in Hollywood, MGM based one of its early technicolor films, *Sombrero,* on several of Miss Niggli's stories. She assisted in the adaptation.

After intermittent periods of association with the Old Vic School in England and the Abbey Theatre in Ireland, Miss Niggli returned to this country where she now heads the Department of Drama at Western Carolina University at Cullowhee. Her most recent book is *New Pointers on Playwriting,* published by The Writer, Inc.

PREMIÈRE PLAYBILL CREDITS

Singing Valley, by Josefina Niggli, was originally produced by The Carolina Playmakers, on July 15, 1936, in Memorial Hall, Chapel Hill, North Carolina, under the direction of Samuel Selden, who also designed the setting. Costumes were designed by the author and executed with the assistance of Grace Barlow. Make-up was under the supervision of Hester Barlow.

THE CAST

DOÑA BECA, *a great lady of the valley* . . . Jessie Langdale
DON RUFINO, *Mayor of Abasolo* . . . . . . Joseph Feldman
FATHER ZACAYA, *the village priest* . . . . Don Watters
DON PABLO, *the Civil Judge* . . . . Wallace Bourne
DOÑA AMPARO, *his wife* . . . . Jo Humphries
ESTER, *Doña Beca's niece* . . . . Hester Barlow
CONCHA, *Doña Beca's daughter* . . . . Fowler Spencer
DON ANTONIO . . . . Robert Finch
GUADALUPE (LUPITA), *Don Antonio's daughter*
. . . . . . Jane Rondthaler
ABEL, *Don Antonio's son* . . . . Alfred Barrett
CARLOS BALDERAS, *a candy vendor* . . . . . Willard Miller
FERNANDO PEREZ, *a news reporter* . . Bedford Thurman
JULIO ROMERO, *Don Pablo's son* . . . . . John W. Parker
PEOPLE FROM THE VILLAGE . . G. W. Tidd, Betty Barlow,
Eleanor Patrick, Lois Latham, Naomi Cunningham, Bruce Higgins

SCENE AND TIME

The patio of don Antonio's home near the town of Abasolo in the Santa Catarina Valley, in the year 1935.

ACT ONE: Ten o'clock of a March morning.
ACT TWO: Half-past five of an afternoon in June.
ACT THREE: Three-thirty o'clock in the afternoon of December 12, the day of Our Blessed Lady of Guadalupe, patron saint of Mexico.

ACT ONE

Most patios are the heart of the house, filled with tables and comfortable chairs, and always flowers set about in gay pots. But DON ANTONIO LOZANO *has been in exile for over twenty years, and this patio looks deserted and unlived in. The back wall is cut into two parts by a gate opening on the right (the gate itself has vanished), and a barred window seat on the left. The house entrance in the left wall is a door with a low stoop in front of it. On the right, the solid wall is broken by a niche that should hold a holy figure, but it is empty now. There are no flowers. For furniture there is a bench near the house door, and a stool near the right wall.*

As the curtains open, we see a group of people. The important man in the windowseat (his hat tipped to the back of his head, his bright red bandana neckerchief doing its best to outshine his pink shirt), has greasy hands and a too hearty manner. He is forty-five, and his name is DON RUFINO. *In direct contrast to him is the much older priest, standing in the patio opening and gazing out across the valley.* FATHER ZACAYA *has known enough sorrow to have gained the wisdom of gentleness. The Civil Judge,* DON PABLO, *sitting on the bench, is a bird-like man who covers a warm heart with a brusque manner. He is definitely afraid of* DON RUFINO. *Next to him sits his shy wife* DOÑA AMPARO, *clutching a parcel, wrapped in newspapers, to her bosom. But it is the forty-year old widow, dressed all in black, called* DOÑA BECA *by everyone, who really dominates the group. Born to be a manager, she is now superintending the cleaning of the house. At the moment she is standing on the house step, arms folded, head high, glaring inside.*

DOÑA BECA (*calling sharply*). Dust, girl, dust! Don't just flick your cloth over the furniture.

ESTER (*in a plaintive voice from the house*). But, Aunt Beca, I am dusting. The furniture is too old and worn. There's no polish in the wood.

DOÑA BECA. Give me no excuses. Every morning I ask God, "Why, Blessed Lord, did you give me this worthless chit for a niece?"

DON RUFINO. All these young people are worthless now-a-days.

DOÑA BECA (*whirling on him*). No more worthless than you!

FATHER ZACAYA. Now, now, no quarrels, with Antonio coming home at last.

DOÑA BECA. True words, Father. And as for you, Rufino Gonzalez, you'll have to step back now. Gossip says that Antonio has more money than you'll ever own, for all your goat flocks.

DOÑA AMPARO *(with awe)*. Think of Antonio Lozano having money. And he with only this house to his name when the government sent him into exile.

DON PABLO. He didn't even own a donkey. The lowest beggar owns a donkey.

FATHER ZACAYA. But he had the courage of his convictions! I well remember him standing on a soap box in the middle of the plaza daring to defend the federal government when all the world had turned rebel.

DON RUFINO. Courage! Pah! Finding a gold mine is not a matter of courage. It's a matter of luck.

DON PABLO. I wish we had such luck in this valley.

DON RUFINO *(angry)*. And perhaps you don't like the way I handle the affairs of this valley?

DON PABLO *(quickly)*. Indeed, I was saying nothing against you.

DOÑA AMPARO *(nervously)*. All the world knows you've been a good mayor.

DON RUFINO. I made you Civil Judge, and I can unmake you . . . like that! *(He snaps his fingers.)* Let me remind all of you that the gold in this valley is stamped with the shape of goats . . . my goats.

DOÑA BECA. Not any more. Antonio is bringing a new kind of gold. . . .

DON RUFINO *(snorting)*. Pah! I am a traveled man, me. I've been from the southern tip of Yucatán to the northern town of Eagle Pass, Texas; and out of my wisdom I say: all these golden men are alike. They heap their glittering coins together and clutch them tightly to their bosoms. If you think you're going to catch one glimpse of Antonio Lozano's gold . . . ha! I laugh at your ignorance!

DOÑA BECA. This brilliant Rufino can tell the angels how to crochet their wings.

DOÑA AMPARO *(almost in tears)*. Please, Beca, don't make trouble . . . not today.

DON RUFINO *(laughing sarcastically)*. Do you think I can be injured by a woman's cackle?

DOÑA BECA. Cackle is it? I'll fry your ears!

DON RUFINO. As the devil said to Brother Saint Michael. And you know what happened to the devil.

FATHER ZACAYA. Enough of this!

DON RUFINO. I speak my mind when I please, and as I please.

FATHER ZACAYA. Not in my presence! I am still priest of this valley.

DON RUFINO. Only as long as it pleases me to have you stay.

FATHER ZACAYA. Do you dare speak against the Church?

DON RUFINO (*blandly*). And I a good Christian? I was merely speaking of having you sent to another parish . . . which you well know I can do.

DOÑA BECA (*triumphantly*). Not if Antonio doesn't want him moved!

DON RUFINO. I'm warning you. Don't put too much trust in this Antonio Lozano. He's been gone from this Valley since 1913. It is now 1935. . . . (*To* DON PABLO.) How many years absence, my good Civil Judge?

DON PABLO. Twenty-two years.

DON RUFINO. Precisely. Twenty-two years. He has roamed the world. He has found gold in Australia. And now, suddenly, with all that money . . . does he go to Paris? Does he go to New York? No. He comes here, to this valley . . . to our valley. Why? Have you asked yourselves that question, eh? He, who could buy sacred Rome . . . why does he come to our poor little corner of the world? (*He looks triumphantly at them. They glance perplexedly to each other.*)

FATHER ZACAYA (*uncertainly*). This is his home.

DON RUFINO. After twenty-two years? He'd lose himself between the plaza and the church.

DOÑA BECA. Old friends . . . old memories . . . the house where he was born. . . .

DON RUFINO. This tumbled down place? And he used to fine hotels? As for friends and memories . . . of my wisdom I tell you: gold knows no friends, and has no memories.

DOÑA BECA. Antonio is different! You speak with a foreign mouth. . . .

DON RUFINO (*sullenly*). I've lived here fifteen years. I am the elected mayor of Abasolo. . . .

FATHER ZACAYA. What are fifteen years? This valley is very old. Why, the first Spaniards came here in 1539. . . .

DON RUFINO. Give me no history, good Father. That is in the past . . . it is finished . . . done with. . . .

FATHER ZACAYA. Is it, indeed? Then let me remind you of the proverb: He who comes to this valley and drinks of its water, will stay here forever. . . .

DOÑA BECA (*triumphantly*). That is the true answer, Rufino Gonzalez.

Antonio is a child of this valley. His first ancestor came here in the seventeen hundreds . . . and he returns like a swallow to his nest, bringing his children with him.

DON RUFINO *(disgustedly)*. Woman's logic!

DOÑA AMPARO. I can't believe Antonio has two grown children. What did his letter say, Beca? Are they both boys?

DOÑA BECA. The oldest is a girl.

DON PABLO. What a pity.

In the distance a train whistles.

DOÑA BECA. But the youngest is a boy.

DON PABLO. Better the youngest than no boy at all. A man needs immortality . . . his name passing on to generation after generation.

DOÑA AMPARO. I wonder if the train has arrived yet?

DON RUFINO. Arrived and gone. I heard it whistle as it left the station.

DOÑA BECA. Saints be with us! And we here not doing a thing!

FATHER ZACAYA. Now, daughter Beca, don't get excited. There isn't anything for us to do until Carlos Balderas brings them here from the station.

DON RUFINO. Carlos Balderas indeed! What a welcoming committee. You wouldn't leave it to me to do it properly with a band and fine speeches. Oh, no. You had to roost here like chickens on a roof while Carlos Balderas . . . that candy vendor . . . meets them at the station.

DOÑA AMPARO. But Carlos sings so well.

DON PABLO. He will give them a fine welcoming song. . . .

DON RUFINO. One man moaning on the wind . . . when I could have been making an elegant speech!

CARLOS *(singing very faintly, off left)*.
　　　　The four cornstalks are left all alone
　　　　On the ranch that is my own.
　　　　The house that's so tiny,
　　　　So white and so shiny,
　　　　Is left very sad.

DOÑA BECA *(excitedly to* FATHER ZACAYA). Do you see them at all?

FATHER ZACAYA *(shading his eyes and peering down at the train)*. Not even the ears of the horse. But that is Carlos singing.

CARLOS *(his singing comes nearer and nearer.)*
　　　　There's no deer on the mountain-side gray.
　　　　Everything is faded today.

For no birds are flying,
The roses are dying,
Since I've been away. Ay-yah!

DON RUFINO *(disgusted)*. Now there is a happy ballad to welcome a man home.

DOÑA BECA *(starting toward the house, calling)*. Ester! Devil take that girl! Ester! Come out here! (ESTER *runs in from the house. She is a shy, pretty girl of eighteen in a neat pink skirt, a white blouse, and a shawl over her shoulders. Behind her is* CONCHA, *also about eighteen. She wears lavender instead of pink, and flirts with every man from five to eighty.)*

DOÑA BECA. You, daughter! What are you doing here?

CONCHA *(pouting)*. I wanted to see don Antonio come home, mamá.

DON RUFINO. She wanted to roll the eye at Carlos Balderas.

DOÑA AMPARO. Concha is engaged to our son, Julio. Concha would not roll the eye at any other man.

DON RUFINO. She rolls the eye when she asks for the salt.

DOÑA BECA. Keep your tongue away from my daughter. And you, Concha, behave yourself. *(To* ESTER.) Did you get all the floor tiles washed?

ESTER *(nervously)*. I needed kerosene to make them shine, but I didn't have any. No one told me don Antonio was arriving until this morning. . . .

CONCHA. La! He's only a man. He won't notice floor tiles.

DOÑA BECA. Antonio's daughter is not a man.

DOÑA AMPARO. Antonio with a daughter. How wonderful. *(Holding up her parcel.)* I brought her a little present. It isn't much, because I didn't have time to make anything really elegant, but I think she'll. . . .

DOÑA BECA. If you crocheted it . . . it's a masterpiece.

FATHER ZACAYA *(excitedly)*. I see them! The carriage is almost here. *(He hurries through the gate and off left.)*

DOÑA BECA. You two girls stand against the wall. Don't get in our way. *(The girls, hand in hand, obey her.)*

DOÑA AMPARO. I do hope she'll like my present.

DON RUFINO. It's more important that Antonio like the goat-business.

DOÑA BECA *(snorting.)* The devil is shaped like a goat. And you call yourself a good Christian.

DON RUFINO. I'll be in heaven before you! Saint Peter will say, "We want no woman with a sharp tongue here!"

DOÑA BECA. Let me tell you, Rufino Gonzalez. . . . (FATHER ZACAYA *enters from the house in time to interrupt them.)*

FATHER ZACAYA *(sharply)*. Will no one greet our old friend?

As DOÑA BECA *swings around in confusion,* FATHER ZACAYA *steps aside and* DON ANTONIO LOZANO *enters. His American clothes do not look well on his peasant body. But his children are born of city ways.* LUPITA, *very modish, inclined to be sulky, about 21, follows him. With her is* ABEL, *a pleasant young man who has been dominated all his life by both his father and sister. Everyone is looking at* DON ANTONIO *as he faces* DOÑA BECA, *and no attention at all is paid to the last arrival,* CARLOS BALDERAS, *whose candy tray swings from his shoulders. He, alone, is intent on* LUPITA. *There is dignity in him, and something else . . . a kind of private enjoyment of the world around him.*

DON RUFINO *(importantly)*. As mayor of Abasolo, it gives me true pleasure to welcome you back to. . . .

DOÑA BECA *(pushing* DON RUFINO *aside)*. Get out of my way, you fool.

She and DON ANTONIO *stare at each other, remembering shared memories. Then they fling their arms about each other in the traditional Mexican embrace.* DON PABLO *and* DOÑA AMPARO *sweep down on them, and they, too, embrace* DON ANTONIO *while* DOÑA AMPARO *weeps noisily.* DON RUFINO, *disgusted, retires to the window seat.* LUPITA *superciliously notes the emotional display.* ABEL *quietly "eye-flirts" with* ESTER *and* CONCHA *who giggle silently together, and* CARLOS *still watches* LUPITA *with an amused smile.*

DON ANTONIO. My friends. My old friends.

DOÑA BECA. You've not aged a day. Not a day.

DON PABLO *(loudly blowing his nose)*. We've missed you, Antonio.

DOÑA AMPARO. I never thought I'd live to see this day.

FATHER ZACAYA. We must not forget that Antonio brings us a beautiful gift . . . the gift of his children.

DON ANTONIO. Indeed. My little family. My girl is named for our Blessed Lady of Mexico: Guadalupe. We call her Lupita. And the boy . . . I named him for my old friend Father Zacaya. . . . He is Abel.

LUPITA *(impatiently)*. You sound as though we were pet dogs. (DON RUFINO *laughs, but the others frown at her disrespect.* CARLOS *smiles and nods thoughtfully.*)

DON ANTONIO *(trying to smooth an awkward moment)*. Eh, Lupita has the blunt nature of her blessed mother, dead these fifteen years. My children, this is doña Beca of whom you've heard so much. . . .

ABEL *(moving forward eagerly)*. Are you the one who threw water on my father when he serenaded you?

DOÑA BECA. That was my dear father. Antonio sang under the wrong window that evening.

FATHER ZACAYA. You must learn our language, my son. Here one does not serenade . . . one sings the rooster.

LUPITA *(dryly)*. How very quaint. (CARLOS *suddenly laughs aloud. Everyone looks at him. He smilingly shrugs his shoulders, and they all look again at* DON ANTONIO.)

DON ANTONIO. And these are my two good friends don Pablo and doña Amparo. . . . *(To them.)* I heard you were married after I left.

DOÑA AMPARO *(proudly)*. Pablo's the Civil Judge now . . . a very important man.

DON RUFINO. Because I made him important! *(Moving forward to face* DON ANTONIO.) I am Rufino Gonzalez, mayor of Abasolo, at your service. *(He bows grandly.)*

DOÑA BECA. Mayor he calls himself. The truth is, he owns all the goat flocks in the valley, and we need him for his money. . . .

DON RUFINO. Deny, if you can, that I am a practical man. *(To* DON ANTONIO.) I've been a good mayor, and I've kept out of the valley every man who might spoil it . . . or seek to change it.

DON ANTONIO. Then you don't approve of progress?

DON RUFINO. I believe in our simple ways. I hope, señor, that you don't plan to change anything.

DON ANTONIO. I have . . . let us say . . . certain plans.

DON RUFINO *(glancing around at the group)*. Interesting . . . very interesting. My office is always open to suggestions. Whether I approve of the suggestions is another matter. And I think you should know, senor, that nothing happens in this valley without my approval. Nothing.

DOÑA BECA *(sharply)*. Pay no attention to this . . . this foreigner, Antonio.

DON RUFINO *(yelling)*. Foreigner! I've been here fifteen years.

DOÑA BECA. Fifty years, and you'd still be a foreigner.

FATHER ZACAYA *(quietly)*. There shall be no quarrels this day. . . .

DOÑA AMPARO *(hastily)*. Oh, no. Please. No quarrels. *(Turning quickly to* LUPITA.) Dear child, how pretty you are. See, I've brought you a present. *(She extends the parcel.)*

LUPITA *(taking it with her fingertips)*. How very nice of you.

ABEL. Don't be a stick, Lupita. Open it.

LUPITA *(without interest)*. Oh. Oh, yes, of course. *(While she opens the package, the others watch her expectantly, as, baffled, she holds up a crocheted nightgown top.)*

ESTER *(clapping her hands)*. Ay, doña Amparo, what elegance. Did you get the design from that fine magazine of yours? (*To* LUPITA.) She has a magnificent magazine with the most beautiful crochet designs.

DOÑA AMPARO (*smuggly*). I've treasured it since 1910. There has never been another like it.

LUPITA. 1910? But this is 1935.

DOÑA AMPARO. Precisely. The years have turned it into a very rare design. Do you like it?

LUPITA. What is it?

DOÑA AMPARO (*crestfallen*). It's a nightgown top. I thought you could sew it to one of your own gowns. (ABEL *turns a burst of laughter into a false cough.* LUPITA *stares impatiently at him, then looks again at* DOÑA AMPARO.)

LUPITA. I'm sorry. I don't sew.

DOÑA AMPARO (*shocked*). You don't sew? (*To* DOÑA BECA.) She doesn't sew.

DOÑA BECA. Poof! I'll teach her myself. (*To* LUPITA.) You'll learn much in our valley, my girl.

LUPITA (*coldly*). I doubt it.

DON ANTONIO (*frowning*). As you say, Beca, she'll learn.

LUPITA *shrugs and turns away toward the window where she drops the crocheting on the seat and gazes off across the valley. There is an awkward pause, and then the priest says, too loudly:*

FATHER ZACAYA. Suppose we show you the house, don Antonio. (*Instantly everyone is animated again.*)

DOÑA BECA. It is in a terrible condition, I can tell you. If you had only let us know last week that you were coming. . . .

DON ANTONIO. I didn't know myself until three days ago. The rebel government has laid a hard exile on all of us who were faithful to the old traditions. But good friends persuaded the new men in power that I am harmless. . . . (*Laughing bitterly.*) Harmless! Well, that is the past. As soon as I got the message that the exile was lifted, I needed only two hours to pack up my children and start for home. Is the house much changed?

DOÑA BECA. It is the same as when you left it.

ESTER (*moving forward*). I'm sorry the tiles don't sparkle.

DOÑA BECA. Into the house with you, girl. Your arm, Antonio. (*To the others.*) Inside, inside, inside. (CARLOS *steps out of their way, and they all enter with the exception of* CARLOS *and* LUPITA.)

CARLOS. You have no wish to see your new home, señorita?

LUPITA (*still gazing across the valley*). I'll see it soon enough.

CARLOS *(crossing to her).* And the valley fascinates you?

LUPITA. All that sand and cactus? Nonsense.

CARLOS. Later in the spring there will be yellow flowers on the cactus, and yellow blooms, sweet as honey, on the thorn bushes. The desert always buys its spring with gold . . . a rarer gold than your father's fortune.

LUPITA *(looking at him for the first time).* That's a strange thought for a candy vendor.

CARLOS. Making candy leaves a man free to listen to tales the wind tells.

LUPITA. I don't imagine the wind in this valley has much to say.

CARLOS. But, señorita, the wind has visited that cloud, that sky, those purple mountains . . . all have much gossip for the wind . . . and the wind tells it to me.

LUPITA. What could the wind in this valley tell you?

CARLOS. It told me a lonely girl was coming . . . a very beautiful girl . . . but very lonely.

LUPITA. You're being impertinent.

CARLOS. All candy vendors are impertinent, señorita. It is a mark of our trade.

LUPITA. Then I suggest you be impertinent to my father. He likes impertinence. I don't. *(They stare at each other, summing each other up.* ABEL *comes out.)*

ABEL. Father wants you, Lupita. *(Realizing he interrupted something.)* Oh, sorry. I didn't know you were having a private chat.

LUPITA. We're not. This candy vendor is just leaving.

CARLOS *(laughs. As he crosses toward the house he sings softly).*
    Shadow of our Lord, St. Peter,
    The river lures me . . . the river lures me.
(At the door.) Some day, señorita, I might finish that song for you.

LUPITA. I won't hold my breath. (CARLOS *laughs again and goes into the house.)*

ABEL. That was a beautiful tune. I'd like to hear the end of it.

LUPITA. Abel, how can you endure it! All these ghastly people!

ABEL. I thought they were very nice. And the girls are certainly pretty.

LUPITA. They're common village chits. There was no need for you to flirt with them!

ABEL. At least they didn't give me a nightgown top! *(Laughing.)* You should have seen your face!

LUPITA. I have an idea. I'll send it to Nancy Moreno. She'll simply die.

ABEL. Dying might improve her.

LUPITA. You were crazy enough about her in New York.

ABEL. She doesn't have an honest bone in her body. But these people are different. They seem so . . . so genuine.

LUPITA. So you're still hurt because Nancy wouldn't marry you when you proposed.

ABEL. She had the right to refuse me. But she didn't have the right to make fun of me to all her friends. What a bunch of half-baked clams!

LUPITA *(angrily).* They are not half-baked clams. They're big people, important people. They could do a lot for us. Why, a smile from Pierre Dumarque would make a singer.

ABEL *(raising his brows).* Make him?

LUPITA. Don't be vulgar! Dumarque is our greatest living music critic. . . .

ABEL. According to Dumarque. Listen, Lupita, all those arty friends of yours are exactly the same. They haven't an honest feeling amongst them. All they cared about was your money. . . .

LUPITA. That's not true! Nancy Moreno said I had real talent as a poet. . . .

ABEL. And she'd teach you for a fee how to write pretty little verses . . . a very substantial fee.

LUPITA. It was only right to pay her. After all, it meant she was taking time away from her own creative effort. . . .

ABEL *(snorting).* Creative! She's about as creative as a limp strand of spaghetti. . . .

LUPITA. I won't have you talk about her that way. You have no right. Abel, don't you understand? Father wants to smother us with this valley . . . cut us off from all the important things in life for . . .for . . . a bunch of goats!

ABEL *(at the gate, looking out).* I like it. The air is so clear, and those distant mountains . . . they look close enough to touch them with my hand. At this moment I could build a bridge to span all the valley. . . .

LUPITA *(screaming).* Stop it! *(Getting control of herself.)* You're not an engineer, Abel.

ABEL. I have a degree to prove it.

LUPITA. Anyone can get a degree in engineering! But God gave us great gifts, Abel. He gave poetry to me, and music to you. To deny those gifts is sacrilegious.

ABEL *(paying her no attention)*. The air shimmers like an opal . . . and all that cactus scattered about . . . and those trees that look like bent pencils . . . I wonder what they are.

LUPITA. Who cares!

ABEL. Come and look at it.

LUPITA. No, I won't. I can't come and look at it.

ABEL *(looking at her)*. Are you afraid of this valley, Lupita?

LUPITA. Yes, I am. It's already trying to cast a spell on you. But I won't let it cast one on me. I won't. I won't.

ABEL *(crossing to her and putting his arm around her)*. Lupita, you're trembling.

LUPITA. I'm afraid, Abel. Really afraid. If father has his way, he'll bury us here. And the wonderful world, where people speak our language . . . where they love beauty the way we do . . . they're going on, into their wonderful future, forgetting all about us. . . .

ABEL. Poor Lupita. All you have to do is open your eyes. There's real beauty here. . . .

LUPITA *(grabbing up the nightgown top and shaking it at him)*. Do you call this . . . this absurdity . . . beautiful? Twenty-five years out of date! That's what's going to happen to us! We're going to be out of date, unless we get out of here now . . . tonight!

ABEL. And leave father? He's counting on us.

LUPITA. He's lived his life. This is his world, not ours.

ABEL. Anyway, I promised to build the powerhouse for him.

LUPITA. He can get a real engineer to build it for him. You've got to admit you don't know much about powerhouses.

ABEL. Perhaps you're right.

LUPITA. You know I'm right. *(They do not see* ESTER *enter from the house.)* Promise me you'll speak to father this very afternoon. Promise me.

ABEL. Why don't you speak to him? You handle him better than I do.

LUPITA. I want him to know it's your wish. I've begged him so often to let me live my own life he won't pay any attention to me.

ABEL. I'll ask him next week, after he's settled, and. . . .

LUPITA. No! You must do it as soon as possible. I know you, Abel. You'll just keep putting it off, and I'll be trapped here. Please, Abel! Today! Promise me!

ABEL *(sullenly)*. I'll try.

LUPITA. Thank God.

ABEL. Let's go into the house. We don't want him to have to send for us. . . . *(He turns and sees* ESTER.*)* Well, hello. Where did you come from?

LUPITA *(sharply)*. How long have you been standing there?

ESTER. Just one little moment. *(Smiling shyly.)* It isn't right for you to be out here alone when you've just returned.

LUPITA. Not returned. We've never been here before.

ESTER. But don Antonio is from here. And he is your father.

ABEL *(amused)*. What's your name?

ESTER. Ester Solás, your servant. Doña Beca is my aunt.

ABEL. Do you live in the village?

ESTER. I used to . . . with my aunt, doña Beca . . . but now I live up here.

ABEL *(surprised)*. In this house?

ESTER. I'm going to work for you. Didn't you know?

LUPITA *(coldly)*. No, I didn't know. *(Abruptly she turns and goes to examine the niche, more to conquer her anger than from curiosity.)*

ABEL. It will be fun having you up here.

ESTER *(startled, her voice runs up the scale)*. Ay. . . .

LUPITA *(indicating the niche)*. What is this thing for?

ESTER. That's for Our Blessed Lady. She's a miracle virgin.

ABEL. Does she cure people?

ESTER. Oh, no. She saved the valley from the French. That was in your great-grandmother's time.

LUPITA. In my . . . ? That's strange. I never thought about my great-grandmother living here.

ESTER. The world says she was a very fine lady.

LUPITA. The world?

ESTER *(with confusion)*. The village. It was for her this house was built. Your great-grandfather built it to welcome her here as a bride. *(Pointing toward the patio gate.)* She came from beyond the mountains. But you will hear all about it tonight. There's going to be a banquet with many speeches . . . all about your family, and how glad we are to have don Antonio home again.

LUPITA *(already bored)*. It sounds enchanting.

ABEL *(frowning at her)*. What do you do here in the valley? To entertain yourselves, I mean?

ESTER. We go to church . . . and sit on the plaza and exchange news. . . .

ABEL. I mean young people?

ESTER. Oh, lots of things. We have picnics, and dances, and on Sunday nights we walk around the plaza.

LUPITA. You must be worn out from the excitement.

ESTER. We had a wedding last year. I was in it. *(With awe.)* The bride had *wax* orange blossoms.

ABEL. Couldn't she get real ones?

ESTER. Poof! Any beggar could have real ones. And the guests gave enough money for the couple to travel all the way to Saltillo. That is eighty kilometers from here!

LUPITA *(to* ABEL*)*. How far is eighty kilometers?

ABEL. About fifty miles.

LUPITA. Do you only go to Saltillo? . . . I presume Saltillo is a city.

ESTER. A magnificent city, of twenty thousand Christian souls.

LUPITA. Do you only go there for honeymoons?

ESTER. But what need is there to go, señorita? The same sun rises over our valley, . . . and, also, we would rather see a friendly face on every corner . . . not all strangers as in a great city. Of course, if you're a traveler like don Rufino. . . .

LUPITA. Who?

ESTER. The mayor of Abasolo. *(With the secretive air of imparting great news.)* He says he has been as far as Mexico City, but this is difficult to believe. Don Rufino is a great liar because he is the Devil's own stepson.

LUPITA. Nonsense! Surely you don't believe that!

ESTER *(proving her point)*. Does he not own many goats? And all the world knows that before the sun shone on the first-day, God herded the sheep and Grandfather Devil the goats. That's why goatherders must be very pious, and be buried with their heads toward the east . . . or the Devil will get them surely.

ABEL. Then why does a man become a goatherd?

ESTER. There is no danger if he says a prayer every morning, lights a candle to St. Anthony every month, and washes his ears every Friday.

LUPITA. Perhaps don Rufino forgot to wash his ears.

ESTER. That's what my aunt, doña Beca, says. He and his goats. He can't think of anything else. He's always talking about them.

Voices sound from inside the house, DON ANTONIO'S *topping them all.*

DON ANTONIO. But what would I do with a flock of goats?

ESTER. You see! What did I tell you? That don Rufino! Already he wants to sell goats to your father and make a fine profit.

The group flows into the patio, DON ANTONIO *and* DON RUFINO *in the lead.*

DON RUFINO. But this is goat country! Farms aren't any good here. There isn't enough water. Join with me in buying some fine merinos in Torreón. Their wool is much sought for blankets. We'll make money . . . lots of money.

DON ANTONIO. I have lots of money.

DON RUFINO. No matter how fat the rooster, he can always eat more corn.

DON ANTONIO *(amused)*. Do I have the look of a goatherd?

DON RUFINO. Pah! Not as a herder . . . as an owner. All the young men in the village are herders. . . .

LUPITA (*to* CARLOS BALDERAS). Are you a goatherd? *(Carlos smiles and shakes his head.)*

DON RUFINO. That candy vendor! He is a worthless good-for-nothing. . . .

DOÑA BECA. You mean he does not depend on you for his living!

DON RUFINO. Would you have him as a son-in-law, doña Beca?

DOÑA BECA. My daughter is marrying the son of don Pablo and doña Amparo, as you well know. . . .

DON RUFINO. And I well know that Julio herds goats for me! I am a generous man. I might even give him a goat for a wedding present, and then he can sell the milk, he can sell the cheese, he can sell the meat, he can even sell the skin to the shoe factory in Monterrey. . . .

DON ANTONIO. After which he'll have no goat left, and he'll be back where he was . . . still herding goats for you.

DON RUFINO. Why not? It is a good life. And there is much money in goats!

DON ANTONIO. There is even more money . . . down there. *(Looking through patio gate at the valley far below.)*

DON PABLO. Money? In our valley?

DON ANTONIO. My valley. When I first left here it was my courage, my hope, the one thing that gave me strength. For over twenty years I've remembered standing here at this gate, and looking down there . . . with the valley spreading wide to the mountains, and in the middle of it, that little village. It has burned in my memory like fire. But now . . . it's not memory. I'm really standing here. And out there is the magic of my valley. . . .

DOÑA AMPARO *(timidly)*. But it's the same as any other valley, Antonio.

DON ANTONIO. Not to me. Never to me. What do you see down there, Beca?

DOÑA BECA *(puzzled)*. What I always see. . . .

DON ANTONIO. And you, my good friend priest?

FATHER ZACAYA. I see a sandy waste studded with cactus and yuccas and flowering thorn. . . .

DON RUFINO. I see goat country . . . a country that is good for nothing but goats. . . .

DON ANTONIO. And I see a rose blooming. For the desert shall bloom like a rose.

DON RUFINO *(laughing sarcastically).* All the world knows that roses need water, and there is no water in the valley . . . only a little river that men need to keep from dying of thirst. . . .

DON ANTONIO. A powerhouse can turn that stream into a real river. . . .

FATHER ZACAYA. A powerhouse!

DON PABLO. Did you say a powerhouse?

DON ANTONIO. Precisely. I am going to put a powerhouse at the bend of that river, pump water into a spider's web of irrigation ditches, plant fields of barley, and, above all, orange and lemon trees. Why, in two years, this could become the finest fruit region in the North! And when I stand here, I'll be looking down on gold . . . real gold . . . God's gold.

FATHER ZACAYA *(slowly).* This valley would become a miniature California.

DON ANTONIO. The ground is richer than California's. The climate is even better for fruit. All we need is water . . . and the power plant will give us more water than we can use.

DON RUFINO. That's all very fine, but what about my goats?

DON ANTONIO *(shrugging).* I'm sorry. There'll be no room for goats.

DON RUFINO. Zas! Don Antonio Lozano speaks and a man's life is ended. . . .

DON ANTONIO. You can always take your goats to the other side of the mountains. . . .

DON RUFINO *(screaming).* But this is the finest goat pasture in the north! *(Suddenly remembering.)* The young men who work for me won't like your dream, I can tell you.

DON ANTONIO. The young men can learn how to be farmers. . . .

DON RUFINO. Some of them own goats in my flocks. *(Turning to* DON PABLO.) Your son Julio owns goats. Will he exchange his fine goats for an orange tree?

DON PABLO *(drawing a deep breath of courage).* He'd exchange anything to get free of you.

DON RUFINO. Would he now? He'd speak differently if he were here.

DOÑA BECA. I doubt it. He loves you no more than the rest of us.

DON RUFINO. Love is not necessary for the bouncing of good money.

FATHER ZACAYA. But love is necessary to lead a decent life. This village has depended on your harsh ways too long.

DON RUFINO. My ways are practical ways. If you put your faith in this dreamer, he will lead you to destruction. Take a look at that river down there! Do you think it has water enough to supply a whole valley? Pah, there are times when it is only a small trickle, and the mud is caked and dry around it. . . .

DON ANTONIO. Not if we made a lake . . . if we store up in the rainy season for the dry. . . .

DON RUFINO. You sound like Brother Joseph in the Bible, he and his fat kine and his lean kine. . . .

DON ANTONIO. He saved Egypt.

DON RUFINO. But you'll never save this valley.

DON ANTONIO. Why do you think I came back here? To sit in the sun and dream idle dreams? Do you think that all I want is to plant an orange tree where cactus grew before? No, my friend. I want something greater, much greater. (*To all of them.*) I have money now, but I know what is to be poor . . . to have even the clothes that cover your naked body gifts of charity. Charity is dry crust that sticks in the throat. I do not give charity. I give only the water. But every family in the valley has land, and savings to buy seeds, young trees, to build their own future. . . .

DON RUFINO. And conquer their own ignorance? Any man can plant an orange seed, true. But there is more to a fine crop of oranges than just the planting. There must be knowledge. . . .

DON ANTONIO. I'll import teachers for them . . . men of experience. . . .

DON RUFINO. And how will they live while they are learning? On hope? Make no mistake, don Antonio. The future of this valley is with my goat flocks. It will always be with my goat flocks. I am a much traveled man, me. . . .

DOÑA BECA. As you've told us a thousand times!

DON RUFINO. This is man's business, woman! (*To* DON ANTONIO.) I've seen the world . . . at least the Mexican world. And I've seen dreamers like you come in to try and change things, but they always failed!

ABEL. Not always.

DON RUFINO. Always! The dreamer's dreams are paper dreams . . . one touch of reality and the dreams go up in smoke. But I am a practical man . . . I know the worth of reality . . . and while I am in this valley there will be no power plant, and no pretty man-made lake! (*At the patio gate.*) I, Rufino Gonzalez tell you this, and you know my word is good. Forget this dreamer. This is my valley, and I intend to keep it. *(He stalks out.)*

DON PABLO. He is a cunning man, and a bad enemy. You will have to fight him, Antonio.

DON ANTONIO. To fight me, he will need money. And he doesn't have enough.

FATHER ZACAYA. You will need more than money, Antonio. The people here have depended upon him for many years . . . and you've been gone too long. Many of the young men don't remember you at all.

DON ANTONIO. Are you saying they prefer the devil they know to the one they don't know?

FATHER ZACAYA. I am saying that what you propose seems too fantastic . . . this valley a great grove of oranges! Even I find it hard to believe when I look down at its dry earth.

DON ANTONIO. But I have a secret dagger up my sleeve. *(He slings his arm around Abel's shoulders.)* My son Abel. He is a graduate engineer. I may be the dreamer, but he is the man of mathematics. He can tell you if the scheme is practical. Eh, Abel?

ABEL *(looking worriedly at* LUPITA*).* Well, Father. . . .

DON ANTONIO. Speak up, boy. Don't be bashful. These are my good friends, and soon they will be yours. Is a power plant in this valley practical?

ABEL *(blurts it out).* Yes! I'll have to study the terrain more. . . .

DON ANTONIO. Time enough for that. Here at last there is time enough!

LUPITA *(facing him almost defiantly).* Father, Abel has something to say to you.

ABEL *(nervously).* Not now, Lupita.

LUPITA. Yes, now. Father, it's important.

DON ANTONIO *(frowning).* Are you forgetting that we have guests, Lupita?

FATHER ZACAYA *(quickly).* It is we who are forgetting. We longed to be with you so much that we forgot you would naturally want some time in your old house alone with your family.

DOÑA BECA. Blessed saints! The banquet!

DON ANTONIO. What banquet?

DOÑA BECA. The village wants to welcome you . . . with food.

DON PABLO. Such a banquet hasn't been held in this village since you left us, Antonio. Tables have been set up on the plaza. . . .

DON ANTONIO. And fried beans?

DOÑA AMPARO. All you can eat. Ice cream, too, sent out from Monterrey. Pablo and Father Zacaya are going to make speeches.

DOÑA BECA. With enough beer there will be many speeches. It will be a fine occasion, Antonio.

ESTER. Even Carlos Balderas has promised to be there . . . to sing for us.

DON ANTONIO. The beautiful old songs. *(Looking around him.)* Whenever I remembered this house, I remembered my mother, early in the morning, singing the song of morning faith.

LUPITA *(bursting out)*. Not now, Father! Not that song!

DON ANTONIO *(paying her no attention as he crosses to the empty niche)*. She's gone now . . . they're both gone: my mother and the guardian lady of this house. What did you do with the Blessed Virgin, friend priest?

FATHER ZACAYA. I've kept her safe in the church.

DON ANTONIO. Soon she will be back here. And the old grace of the new day-hymn will sound again. *(Turning with delight.)* Abel, sing it now.

LUPITA. Oh, Father! *(She is too proud to show her tears, and turns quickly toward the barred window.)*

DON ANTONIO. Sing it, Abel. And you, too, my friends. That will be my real welcome home.

FATHER ZACAYA. Abel, stand here at this gate looking out over our valley. The rest of us will kneel.

As though with a reflex action, LUPITA *sits in the window. All the rest, except* ABEL, *kneel.*

ABEL *(looks around pleadingly at* LUPITA, *but her back is turned rigidly toward him. He shrugs and sings).*

My Lord Jesus, smile on me. . . .

ALL *(except* LUPITA*).*

And on the house where I was born. Amen.

All, save LUPITA, *cross themselves and rise.*

DON ANTONIO. I thought I could see my mother standing there for a moment. Lupita is like her.

DOÑA BECA *(softly)*. True words, Antonio. Very like her.

LUPITA *(harshly)*. Father, will you please listen to Abel?

DON ANTONIO. What is it, boy?

ABEL *(looking around at the others)*. It's just that . . . well . . . that . . .

DON ANTONIO *(jovially)*. That you're hungry. *(Looking at the others and laughing.)* This boy is like an alarm clock. Every two hours, on the hour, he has to eat or faint from hunger.

DOÑA AMPARO. My son Julio is exactly the same!

LUPITA *(insisting).* Abel!

ABEL. What we . . . I mean Lupita and I were thinking, now that you've come home. . . .

DON ANTONIO. Home. I don't know whether I am sleeping or awake. It doesn't seem possible that I am here at last, and with my two children. *(He puts his arm around* ABEL'S *shoulders and holds out his other hand to* LUPITA. *She hesitates a moment, and then slowly takes it.* ANTONIO *smiles at her.)* I went away poor and without hope into the long exile. But now I am home again, with my son and daughter beside me. We three are . . . home. *(There is a pause and he draws a long breath. Then releasing his children he turns to the others.)* Shall we go down to the village? We mustn't keep that fine banquet waiting. Your arm, Beca.

DOÑA BECA. There isn't room in don Pablo's carriage for all of us. The young ones will have to walk. *(Turning to* ESTER *and* CONCHA.) And don't play along the road. Remember, you have to serve the food.

CONCHA. We won't, Mamá.

CARLOS. I'll turn the coach around. *(He goes into the house.)*

FATHER ZACAYA. It is nearly sunset. *(To* LUPITA *and* ABEL.) We do not have a grand church, but seeing it from the plaza, silhouetted against the sunset sky . . . it's a fine sight. Remember, Antonio?

DON ANTONIO *(with* DOÑA BECA *holding his arm, speaking as he goes into the house).* I have never forgotten one little detail.

FATHER ZACAYA *(as he goes into the house).* Come, children.

ESTER *and* CONCHA *giggle together, watching the other two.* ABEL *ostentatiously offers each of them his arm, and they giggle harder than ever as they take it.*

ABEL *(looking at* LUPITA*).* I'm sorry. I know I promised, but. . . . *(Bursting forth.)* What else could I do, Lupita? What could I do? (LUPITA *turns her back on him.)*

ESTER *(timidly).* Aren't you coming, Lupita?

ABEL *(hastily).* She's an independent soul. She'll come when she's ready. *(To* LUPITA.) But don't wait too long. I don't want to have to come all the way back here after you.

When she still doesn't answer, he shrugs and, with the two girls, goes into the house. The patio has grown darker with approaching evening, and LUPITA *goes to the window seat and stares off, with her back to the gate.*

THE CURTAINS CLOSE

ACT TWO

The time is three months later . . . 5:30 of an afternoon in June. The patio has changed considerably. There is a new gate in the patio wall, and a table at the right with two chairs on either side. The bench is near the center and the stool is by the house wall. Flowers in pots have appeared. They stand along the right and rear walls, and there is a basket of cut flowers hanging from a long rain trough projecting from the wall at the left. When the curtains part, we find ABEL *sitting astride one of the chairs, his arms resting on its back. He is talking to* ESTER, *who is sitting on the bench, a pan in her lap, peeling potatoes, and to* CONCHA *who is in the window seat crocheting.*

ABEL. But why won't you teach me the words to that song? (ESTER *and* CONCHA *look at each other and laugh.*) All right. You needn't. I'll learn it from some other girl.

CONCHA *(triumphantly).* No other girl would teach it to you.

ESTER. It's only used for singing the rooster.

ABEL. And perhaps you think I can't sing the rooster?

ESTER *(pointing her finger at him).* La! What girl would listen to you?

ABEL. Carmen, or Rosa, or Lola. . . . *(The girls laugh.)*

CONCHA *(gaily).* Lola, indeed! Alfonso Tóma walked three times around the plaza with Lola. He'd put a knife in your back.

ABEL. I'll walk three times around the plaza with her myself.

ESTER *(shocked).* Ooh, you couldn't do that!

ABEL. If he could, I could. *(The girls shriek with merriment.)* And what's so funny about that?

CONCHA. Don't you know that walking three times around the plaza with Lola means she and Alfonso are engaged?

ABEL. Very well, we'll mark Lola off. But that still leaves Carmen and Rosa. I can sing it to them.

CONCHA *(laughing).* Not that song!

ABEL. What's the matter with that song? I think it's beautiful. (He hums the tune of "Shadow of our Lord, St. Peter. . . .") It sounds like the most weird and mournful air the mind of man could invent.

ESTER. Because that song means you're going to walk three times around the plaza with a girl!

ABEL. Ah . . . you have too many rules and regulations in this valley.

ESTER. We'll teach you another one. Carlos Balderas used to sing this one to Concha all the time.

CONCHA. Until I sent him about his business.

ESTER. Until Lupita came, you mean.

ABEL *(with amused interest).* Has Carlos fallen in love with Lupita?

CONCHA. All the world knows that.

ESTER. And many a broken heart there is in the village. Many a girl has tried to roll the eye at Carlos. (ABEL *laughs.*) Carlos is a fine match for any girl.

CONCHA. Even Lupita.

ABEL *(rising).* Now don't say anything about Lupita. Just give her time. She'll learn.

ESTER. Why should we speak against Lupita? We like her, don't we, Concha?

CONCHA. Of course we do, but she doesn't like us.

ABEL. If you *could* just make her like you. . . .

CONCHA. If we're in the same room with her, she doesn't even see us.

ABEL. It's because she misses her old friends, her old way of living. This new life is hard to get used to. It's even hard on me.

ESTER. You don't seem to be suffering very much.

ABEL. I'd feel much better if you'd teach me the words to that song.

CARLOS *is heard as he comes singing up the path.*

ESTER. Shall I, Concha?

CONCHA. No! *(Looking out the window.)* Here comes Carlos, ask him to teach you. *(Waving her hand.)* O-la, Carlos.

CARLOS *(off left).* O-la.

ABEL. I will learn it from him, and just to punish you, I'll sing it under both your windows. *(The girls giggle.)*

CONCHA. And how angry Mamá would be then!

CARLOS *has entered in time to hear this. He has a small box under one arm, and in his hand a bunch of letters, one long brown envelope among them.*

CARLOS. At what would she be angry?

ESTER. Abel wants to sing "The Shadow of our Lord St. Peter" to us . . . to both of us.

CARLOS *(shaking his head).* Why, Abel, only one wife to a man is allowed in this valley.

ABEL *(taking the letters)*. And perhaps you think I couldn't manage two wives!

CARLOS *(laughing)*. Oh, before I forget, a reporter came out from Monterrey to see don Antonio.

ESTER *(blankly)*. A reporter? *(She looks at CONCHA who shrugs her shoulders.)*

CARLOS *(explaining)*. He writes things for a newspaper. Don Antonio told me to tell you that he is bringing him to supper tonight.

ABEL *(beginning to look through the letters)*. For Lupita, for Lupita . . . hum . . . I wonder why she's getting a letter from Nancy Moreno. *(He smells the envelope and lifts his brows.)* She's using a new perfume. Very nice . . . very nice. *(He holds up the envelope.)* Do you girls want to smell it?

ESTER *(sniffing it)*. It smells wicked.

ABEL. It belongs to a wicked lady. She is . . . *(He looks away from them a moment, then shrugs his shoulders.)* Oh, well, she'd never fit into this valley.

CONCHA *(with eager interest)*. Is she someone you were in love with?

ESTER *(not looking at them)*. I had better go inside and finish cooking supper. *(She turns at the door.)* Perhaps you had better learn the words to that song so you can sing them to her.

ABEL. I'm afraid Nancy wouldn't appreciate it. It wouldn't be modern enough for her.

ESTER. How sad. *(She goes into the house.)*

CONCHA *and* CARLOS *exchange glances, and* CONCHA *shrugs, at which* CARLOS *shakes his head in pity. This is lost on* ABEL, *who is again looking through the letters. He holds up the long brown envelope.*

ABEL. Why would some lawyer in Monterrey be writing to Father?

CARLOS. A trick of don Rufino's, I'll lay you a wager. He's a clever one, and full of clever schemes. You know what he did to don Pablo, Concha.

CONCHA. I remember. That was a terrible time, Abel.

ABEL. What did he do?

CARLOS. About five years ago, don Pablo decided that the village wasn't paying the goatherders enough, so he threatened to take the case to the courts in Monterrey.

CONCHA. The day before don Pablo was to leave, his son, Julio, disappeared.

CARLOS. Of course, don Pablo couldn't leave then; and he and doña Amparo nearly went crazy trying to find Julio.

CONCHA. All the world knew it was don Rufino's doing, but who could prove it?

ABEL. What happened?

CARLOS. Don Pablo finally went to don Rufino and told him that he'd drop the case in the courts, and the next day Julio came home.

ABEL. Julio could have done something. . . .

CONCHA *(hotly)*. Don't blame my Julio! All his money is tied up in goats, and if don Rufino killed his goats, eh? Why, Julio and I could never marry. . . .

ABEL. But surely there are laws. . . .

CARLOS. In this valley only don Rufino's law counts. Personally, I want no dealings with him. That's why I'm a candy vendor.

CONCHA. Have you candy in that box now, Carlos?

CARLOS. That I have, but it's not for you.

CONCHA *(she bursts into a laugh, runs over to the kitchen door and calls)*. Ester! Ester! Carlos has brought you a fine present!

CARLOS *(upset)*. Will you stay out of my affairs, daughter of doña Beca?

ESTER *(entering from the house)*. Why would you bring me a present, Carlos Balderas?

CARLOS *(flustered)*. I'm sorry, Ester. It's not for you. I mean . . . I . . . well, I brought it for . . . for someone else.

CONCHA *(delighted)*. Carlos is blushing! He means Lupita. He means Lupita!

CARLOS *(putting the box on the table)*. I just bring a little present, and all the world has me rolling the eye at her. I'll leave it here where she can find it, and a good afternoon to you!

ABEL *(stopping him)*. Not so fast, friend. How would Lupita feel to get a present second-hand?

CARLOS. Let go of me, Abel. I have work to do in the village.

ABEL. First, Lupita. Ester, go and get her, but not one word about the candy.

ESTER. I swear by the petticoat of our Blessed Virgin! *(She runs into the house.)*

CARLOS. You're children, all of you, playing games.

ABEL *(dreamily)*. I can see it now. Lupita will come out. Then Concha will guard the house door and I the mountain pass . . . and you'll be alone with Lupita. . . .

CARLOS *(yelling)*. No! *(Then with more self-possession.)* You still don't know our customs. A man and girl can only be alone together *after* they're engaged. Concha, you explain to him. . . .

CONCHA *(with solemn mischief).* You're the man. You tell him.

CARLOS. Listen to me, Abel. I'm no fool. I'm just a candy vendor. What have I to offer your sister? I can't even afford an orchestra to serenade her. . . .

ABEL. I'll serenade her for you . . . if you teach me the words to the great song. . . .

CONCHA. He means "Shadow of our Lord, St. Peter". . . .

CARLOS *(shocked).* Certainly not! Serenades start with simple songs . . . I mean, that's a very important song. . . .

ABEL. The words to that song is my price. If you won't teach it to me . . . well . . . your arm, Concha. We'll join Ester in the kitchen and leave Carlos alone here. . . .

CONCHA. I think I hear Lupita coming!

ABEL *bows and offers* CONCHA *his arm. They make a great ceremony of strolling toward the door.*

CARLOS. Wait! *(He draws a deep breath and speaks the lyrics.)* "Shadow of our Lord St. Peter, the river lures me, the river lures me. And thus your love would my poor love allure . . . my love allure. . . ."

ABEL *(surprised).* Do you mean that's all there is to it?

CARLOS. And enough it is, when you sing it at night. . . .

CONCHA. When even the roosters are quiet and there are no dogs barking. . . .

CARLOS. A girl will feel so sorry for you she can't help marrying you. Eh, Concha?

Before she can answer, LUPITA *enters from the house, followed by a giggling* ESTER.

LUPITA. What is all this mystery? Ester looks as though she had swallowed a pound of butter.

ABEL. Carlos has something for you, Lupita.

LUPITA. Really? Good afternoon, Carlos.

CARLOS. Good afternoon, Lupita. I . . . I brought up a . . . a box of candy.

LUPITA. That was nice of you. It's a long climb up the mountain side. *(Opens the box.)* Why this looks delicious. Did you make it yourself?

CARLOS *(straightening and beaming on the others).* All of it. That's burnt milk, and that's made from pumpkin . . . and that from sweet potatoes. Those little round ones are almond paste.

ESTER. Ooh . . . that's feast day candy . . . the almonds.

CARLOS. Do you like it, Lupita?

LUPITA. I'll have to eat it to see. How much is it? Ester, fetch me my purse.

The girls and ABEL *are embarrassed into silence.* CARLOS *grows very stiff and dignified.*

CARLOS. Nothing, señorita. I brought it as a gift. I also brought the mail. Good afternoon. *(He gives her a sweeping bow and leaves by way of the gate.)*

LUPITA *(biting her lip).* You, Ester, what are you doing out here? Don't you realize that it's almost time for supper? Don Antonio will be hungry. Into the house with you.

ESTER *(subdued).* Yes, señorita. *(She runs into the house.)*

LUPITA *(turning to Concha).* I know you're fond of your cousin, but after all she has work to do. You mustn't waste her time.

CONCHA. You needn't worry. I'm not staying. I just came to tell you that Mamá is going to pay you a visit this afternoon. *(She turns before she vanishes.)* Good-by, Abel.

ABEL. Good-by, Concha. *(He watches her go into the house, and then turns furiously on* LUPITA.*)* You're a fine one!

LUPITA *(defensively).* How was I to know that he was bringing it as a gift?

ABEL. If you weren't always so wrapped up in yourself you would have realized it.

LUPITA. Certainly nobody else is ever concerned about me. You go off down to the plaza with all your friends, with never a thought as to how lonely I might be.

ABEL. You wouldn't be lonely if you tried to make a few friends for yourself.

LUPITA. With Concha, Ester, doña Amparo, doña Beca? You expect me to talk to them?

ABEL. Why not? They try hard enough to talk to you. And don't get the idea you're too good for them, either. "He who was born to be a gourd will never become a painted vase."

LUPITA. You're as bad as father, quoting your village proverbs.

ABEL. I like them better than the bright speeches of your fine friends, that have to cut and hurt other people before they're considered witty.

LUPITA *(catching his shoulders).* Abel, you're not growing to . . . *(She lets go of him and steps back.)* . . . love this valley are you?

ABEL. I'm finding something here . . . something that I've wanted all my life.

LUPITA *(almost beyond speech)*. Are you being serious?

ABEL. Certainly. You want art. Look at the stone carvings on the outside of the church. It took a great master to change stone into frozen lace.

LUPITA. That isn't art . . . that's design. Art carries the message of a new freedom.

ABEL. I know. Like the statue that bright little friend of yours made . . . what was his name . . . the Russian?

LUPITA. Boris?

ABEL. That's the one. He made a curved line like that . . . *(Gesturing in the air.)* called it "Flight of a Bird" and expected the world to stand back and gasp. He's still waiting.

LUPITA. The world doesn't always recognize genius. And it does take genius to carve in stone something that is only a flash of light in the air.

ABEL. What kind of genius does it take to carve a man's belief in God so powerfully that he makes others believe, too? And then there's music. The people here don't have to crowd into concert halls to hear a man sing. They open their throats and let the music pour out of their own hearts.

LUPITA. If you can call it music.

ABEL. Of course it hasn't all of the technical tricks of Nancy Moreno's fine compositions. What was her latest effort? That one where she used the factory whistle to show the boy's love for the girl?

LUPITA. Even Pierre Dumarque considered that a masterpiece. And you're just showing up your own ignorance. It wasn't a boy and a girl. It was two robots. She was showing the pulse of the future in sound. The music around here just. . . .

ABEL. Shows the pulse of a human heart, and people aren't as important as robots.

LUPITA. I suppose you'll be telling me that they have a great literature here, too.

ABEL. Last month when I was camping out with the surveyors, we'd sit around the campfire at night and listen to some of the traveling goatherders telling stories. I'd always get a thrill when one of them recited his little opening verse: "The drunkard drinks wine and the boy eats bread. If this tale's a lie it's not out of my head." We'd sit there all wrapped up in our blankets with the stars bending close down above our heads, and the fire protecting us with its warm red glow, and listen to stories of the strongest man in the world who had a bear for a father; of the woman who must weep every night because she betrayed her people to Cortez.

LUPITA. What you're really trying to say is that you want me to release you from your promise.

ABEL *(turning away, slowly).* Yes.

LUPITA. That's the valley speaking, Abel, not you yourself. I'm holding you to your promise.

ABEL. Then I'll break it.

LUPITA. Not you. You're too much like father. You won't break it. You said you'd leave just as soon as the powerhouse was finished.

ABEL. Unless something extraordinary happened.

LUPITA. Nothing extraordinary will happen. And then, Abel, we'll go away. You'll forget this valley.

ABEL. I won't live any place near Pierre Dumarque and Nancy Moreno and that crowd. I might put up with her earrings, but not with red polish on his finger nails.

LUPITA. We don't have to live in New York. We can live in London . . . or Paris. *(She sits on the bench, dreaming.)* Think of dressing for dinner again, sitting down to a perfectly appointed table . . . having deft waiters serve you while an orchestra plays softly, and people chatter and laugh all about you. That's living, Abel. Cultured living. That's what we really want . . . not this barbaric place!

ABEL. But if you'd just give it a chance! It's not barbaric. . . .

LUPITA. Abel, you promised. Father has always taught us to hold a promise as sacred. . . .

ABEL. When I made that promise I didn't know what this valley would mean to me. But now I do. . . .

LUPITA. You're talking like a child! Have I ever guided you wrong, Abel? Have I?

ABEL *(reluctantly).* No.

LUPITA. Dear Abel, this valley is a new toy to you . . . something to play with for a little while. But in time you'll grow bored with it, and then you'll know that the world out there is the only world for both of us.

ABEL *(weakening).* I never could fight you. . . .

LUPITA. My dear brother, my dear baby brother . . . it isn't what we want in this world that's important . . . it's the things we need, to survive as true individuals.

They stare at each other. ABEL *despondently turns away to gaze out over the valley.* ESTER *enters from kitchen.*

ESTER. Your pardon, Lupita, but would the reporter like the bananas fried or served with rice?

LUPITA. What reporter?

ABEL *(sulkily).* He drove out from Monterrey to get a story about the powerhouse. Father invited him to dinner.

LUPITA *(excitedly).* A reporter? A man who can talk about something besides goats coming here? Why didn't you tell me?

ABEL. I forgot.

LUPITA *(piteously).* You forgot! For the first time in three months somebody comes I can talk to . . . and you forgot!

ABEL *(embarrassed).* I'm sorry, Lupita.

LUPITA *(brushing his comment aside).* No matter. He's here. He's really here. Ester, set the table exactly the way I taught you. . . . Oh, I wish I had some decent silver and plates. We'll have candles instead of a lamp and . . . *(Turning to* ABEL.) You can sing for us afterwards. Do you remember anything of Nancy Moreno's?

ABEL. No!

LUPITA. Then you'll have to sing Dumarque's "Song Without Melody."

ABEL. I can't remember songs that don't have tunes to them.

LUPITA *(horrified).* That's the most important song that's been written in the last twenty-five years. Dumarque says so himself. How could you have forgotten it? (ABEL *does not answer.*) Oh, very well. Sing anything you like . . . but not one of the village songs! I won't have this evening spoiled by a single reference to this valley. Ester, when will he be here?

ESTER. Carlos Balderas is bringing him from the boardinghouse. . . .

LUPITA. The boardinghouse! He can't stay in that . . . that flea dump! He'll stay here. How is that room down the hall from father's? Is it ready for a visitor . . . a very important visitor?

ABEL. A reporter important? When we left New York you wouldn't even speak to a reporter.

LUPITA. When we left New York I didn't know what it was to be so lonely for companionship I'd even talk to myself. *(To* ESTER). Do try to remember to set the table correctly.

ESTER. I'll try. Do I wait to set it until after doña Beca leaves?

LUPITA *(blankly).* Doña Beca? What has she to do with this dinner?

ESTER. She's coming to call this afternoon.

LUPITA. Oh, dear. Why should she. . . .

ABEL *(sharply interrupting).* Don't forget, she's a good friend to this family. I'd even say she is more important than this reporter.

LUPITA *(coldly).* That is a matter of opinion. Ester, see that the guest room is prepared, and wait to set the table until after doña Beca leaves. *(She looks down into the valley.)* It seems like a dream. I was terrified loneliness would drive me down there to the village. But now I have someone to talk to . . . someone to understand me. . . . Ay, it will be wonderful just to be able to talk again! *(She goes into the house.)*

ESTER *(looking after her)*. I don't understand her. She can talk. Why, sometimes the words pour out of her like water in the new powerhouse. Of course, they don't seem to mean anything. *(She shrugs and starts into the house.)*

ABEL. Ester! Don't go in. I want to ask you something.

ESTER *(nervously)*. What is it?

ABEL. Why do you run away everytime I try to speak to you?

ESTER. Was I not speaking to you earlier this afternoon?

ABEL. But Concha was here then.

ESTER *(nervously)*. She should be here now.

ABEL. Please, Ester, don't you like me just a little?

ESTER. Faces we see . . . hearts no.

ABEL. I'm wearing my heart right up here on my face for you to look at.

ESTER *(not looking at him)*. Then you should wear your hat on the back of your head to show it more plainly.

ABEL *(bending toward her and singing softly)*.

> Oh, moon, can you hear me sing to you?
> If I should be so bold?
> Will love find me at last, at last,
> Before I grow too old, too old?

ESTER *(retreating toward the house)*. Doña Beca will soon be here. She will hear you.

ABEL *(continues his song, and taking her hand)*.

> The moon would say, "Are you afraid, my pretty maid, are you afraid?
> Love's a snare. Love will welcome you if you dare, pretty maid, if you dare."

ESTER *(pulling her hand away from him in some confusion)*. Big pumpkins grow from little ones, and you are a very large pumpkin.

ABEL. Why? Because I . . . like you?

ESTER. You must not say such things. After all, you are the wealthy young Lozano and I am just a village girl. You should keep your songs for your sweetheart in the States.

ABEL. What sweetheart?

ESTER. The one from whom the letter came today. My hair does not hide my face. I know that you are only rolling the eye at me.

ABEL *(laughing)*. Nancy Moreno does not mean as much to me as the mosquito that sang in your ear last night.

ESTER. Those are easy words to tumble out of your mouth. I have heard other boys speak them as easily. But the fruit that has been pecked is the one that knows best about birds.

ABEL. You must believe me. Don't you realize, Ester, that. . . . (DOÑA BECA *calls from the house.)*

DOÑA BECA *(off left)*. Niece! Niece! Where are you?

ESTER. Doña Beca is here. *(He holds her hand tightly. She pulls free, runs up on the stoop, where she turns and looks back at him).* When the black sky is dyed red, then perhaps I will believe you. *(She runs in, calling.)* I'm coming, Aunt Beca . . . I'm coming.

ABEL *stands still a moment, then deliberately kicks the bench just as* DOÑA BECA *appears in the doorway.*

DOÑA BECA. Eh, the temper grows violent, and on such a hot day. (ABEL *shakes her hand.)* What are you doing? Loafing as usual?

ABEL *(shrugging and flinging out his hand)*. Now, doña Beca, I worked this morning. It's too nice a day to waste in work.

DOÑA BECA *(looking up at the sky)*. For you it is always too nice a day or too bad a day. Work and hour never seem to meet. *(Suddenly pointing her arm at him.)* And what were you singing awhile ago?

ABEL *(innocently)*. I was trying to learn a new song.

DOÑA BECA. I doubt if you need any more lessons on it. (LUPITA *enters from the house. She has obviously put on her company manners.)*

LUPITA. A good afternoon to you, doña Beca.

DOÑA BECA. Um! Lupita, this brother of yours is more worthless than I thought.

ABEL. I am sorry you think that, doña Beca. Your servant. *(He makes her a little bow and starts into the house.)*

LUPITA. Abel, you're not going down to the village, are you?

ABEL. No. I am going up to my room to. . . .

DOÑA BECA. Study singing?

ABEL. To write a letter to Nancy Moreno.

LUPITA *(very pleased)*. Are you, Abel? Really?

ABEL *(looking toward the house)*. I want to get her opinion of me in writing. *(He nods his head to both of them and goes inside.)*

LUPITA *(staring after him, puzzled)*. I wonder what he meant by that?

DOÑA BECA. This Nancy Moreno. She is a friend of yours?

LUPITA. She is my dearest friend.

DOÑA BECA *(puzzled, in her turn).* Then why do you object to his writing her?

LUPITA. I don't object . . . I'm glad he is, but . . . I feel he's up to some mischief. We had quite a talk this afternoon. He frightened me. He's beginning to like this valley.

DOÑA BECA. And you still hate it. But if you gave yourself a chance you could come to love it. . . .

LUPITA. Never! I hate if for stripping me of everything I ever wanted. And worst of all, for what it's doing to Abel. It's actually turning him into a vegetable, without ambition or any memory of our old friends . . . our important friends. . . . *(She pauses and looks wonderingly at the door.)* And yet he said he was going to write to Nancy Moreno. Is he reaching out toward her again. . . . Could he be thinking of going back, and taking me with him?

DOÑA BECA. You're more American than Mexican. An American girl would go by herself. . . .

LUPITA. Father would never let me go . . . and I have no money. . . . Oh, if I only had some money of my own! I'd leave on the first train . . . be free of this prison. . . .

DOÑA BECA. And free of Carlos Balderas?

LUPITA. Carlos Balderas? What has he to do with me?

DOÑA BECA. That was why I climbed your hill this afternoon . . . to talk to you about Carlos. *(Picking up the candy box.)* I see that he has already been here. *(She tries a piece of candy, and nods.)* Umm . . . Carlos is improving. But don't tell him I said so.

LUPITA. Doña Beca, just what is on your mind?

DOÑA BECA. Many things . . . most of them no concern of yours. But I have watched you, Lupita. You like frankness . . . so do I.

LUPITA. Well?

DOÑA BECA. Carlos is really an extraordinary fellow. He followed Pancho Villa during the Revolution. He is quite a hero. Did you know that? (LUPITA *mutely shakes her head.*) And he has also traveled . . . all the way to Mexico City. Someday he may even become mayor of Abasolo. But that is for the future! I am concerned with the present. Has Carlos sung the rooster to you yet?

LUPITA *(amused at* DOÑA BECA'S *naïvete).* Certainly not!

DOÑA BECA. He walks slowly, that young man. I must have a talk with him. It is really time that this affair is settled between you.

LUPITA *(beginning to grow angry).* Just what affair are you talking about, doña Beca?

DOÑA BECA. Your marriage to Carlos Balderas.

LUPITA. My marriage to . . . to that candy vendor! *(She bursts into laughter.)*

DOÑA BECA *(watching her with a frown).* The future mayor of Abasolo.

LUPITA. If he were the future mayor of Monterrey it would still be preposterous!

DOÑA BECA. Why? Because you have lived in the great world? Well, let me tell you something, my girl. Great world or small village, the best cure for your stupidity is an honest husband and a houseful of children.

LUPITA *(really angry).* And let me tell you something, doña Beca. This conversation has gone far enough. My life is mine . . . mine! It is none of your affair.

DOÑA BECA *(thoughtfully).* Hmm. I could say you are impertinent. . . .

LUPITA *(coldly).* If I have offended my father's old friend, I'm sorry. But I won't have everyone in this valley trying to run my life.

DOÑA BECA *(crossing to the patio gate).* Come here, Lupita.

LUPITA. Don't try it, doña Beca. My father is always pointing out the beauty of the valley. But it is not beautiful to me. It will never be beautiful.

DOÑA BECA. So . . . you are afraid to look at it.

LUPITA. I am not!

DOÑA BECA. Then come here. *(After a moment,* LUPITA *slowly moves toward her.)*

LUPITA *(on a long breath).* Well, I've looked at it.

DOÑA BECA. Notice especially the village . . . that little village of Abasolo that you despise so much. When the first Spaniards came to the north in 1590, they built the church you see down there, with its square tower and its rock walls. That church has seen so much. It has seen gentlemen in plumed hats and ladies in satin with lace veils hiding their dark eyes. It has seen soldiers in steel armor. It has seen swords flashing in the moonlight, and dead men rotting in the sun. It has seen golden dreams, and broken hearts, and much . . . too much . . . ambition.

LUPITA. That's all very romantic, doña Beca. But I see more than the church. I see the tumbled-down houses, the narrow streets filled with mud and filth, the scrawny chickens and the bony dogs. . . .

DOÑA BECA. But you can't see the hearts of the people!

LUPITA. Can I not! The people are worst of all. They keep their eyes fixed on the ground, their hands always curved as though fastened on the plow. They're worse than the chickens and the dogs! They're weeds growing out of the earth.

DOÑA BECA. From the earth comes all life, Lupita . . . and the souls of men.

LUPITA. From the earth comes everything that I hate most in life: stolid peasants, dirt, labor that twists the bones.

DOÑA BECA. And in New York people are not like that? There is no dirt, no misery? Only a great white city shining in the sun?

LUPITA. In New York there are my friends . . . people who understand me. . . .

DOÑA BECA. Abel tells me they are people who can be bought with money . . . who love you for your money. . . .

LUPITA. That's not true!

DOÑA BECA. Abel says they were always borrowing money from you . . . or trying to sell you their statues and their songs. . . .

LUPITA (*almost in tears*). Abel doesn't understand! Artists can't be bothered with cheap things like . . . like making money. They are put on the earth to create . . . to be supported by less talented people like me. You can't put a value on beauty!

DOÑA BECA. How much does a song cost?

LUPITA. This is a childish argument!

DOÑA BECA. You mean you can't answer my question. But Carlos Balderas could answer it. He knows a song is one of God's gifts . . . like the wind and the flowers and the line of black mountains against the flame of sunset. Beauty that does not come from the heart is worth nothing, Lupita. But beauty from the heart . . . that is what Abasolo has. And until you understand that, Lupita, there is no place for you in this valley. (*She goes quietly into the house.*)

LUPITA *remains quiet for a moment, then, abruptly, she reaches out and swings the gate shut as* DON ANTONIO, *followed by* FERNANDO PEREZ, *enters from the house.* PEREZ *is a pompous man filled with the importance of* FERNANDO PEREZ. DON ANTONIO *has a worried expression which brightens as he sees* LUPITA.

DON ANTONIO. Ay, Lupita, I've brought a guest home with me. He's going to put my picture in the paper. Fernando Perez, my daughter, Lupita.

FERNANDO (*shaking hands with* LUPITA). Your servant, señorita.

LUPITA (*still rather subdued, but brightening with pleasure at seeing him*). Your visit gives me pleasure, señor.

DON ANTONIO. We met doña Beca in front of the house. What mischief has she been up to now? She looked like a mouse that has stolen the cheese from a trap.

LUPITA. Did she, indeed? Perhaps doña Beca has overreached herself. But no matter. You look tired, Father. Have you been working hard today?

DON ANTONIO. I've been showing the valley to Señor Perez.

LUPITA *(surprised)*. Are you interested in valleys, Señor Perez?

PEREZ. A little, a little, as I am interested in all things. I am a man with very . . . shall I say . . . very wide interests? For example the work of my good friend . . . I trust that you are my good friend, don Antonio? *(With his hand spread out on his breast and a brief bow toward the older man.)*

DON ANTONIO *(with a smile)*. All the world is my good friend, señor.

PEREZ. You are a lucky man, a very lucky man. As I was saying, the work you are doing here . . . *(He turns to LUPITA.)* but it is magnificent, señorita . . . without parallel. I felt that together we were making history as I watched your father plant the first orange tree today.

DON ANTONIO *(enthusiastically)*. It is the beginning at last, Lupita. With my own hands I broke the soil and started the wealth of this valley.

LUPITA *(anxiously)*. Father, you shouldn't do things like that. It tires you out too much.

DON ANTONIO. Tired? I? *(He laughs, but sinks rather wearily on the bench.)* Yes, I am a little tired, but it's a good tired that comes from good work well done. Sit down, sit down, señor.

LUPITA. Perhaps the señor Perez would care to rest before dinner. *(Looking up at the sky.)* It is nearly time to serve it.

DON ANTONIO *(laughing)*. You see, señor, my little Lupita is learning to tell time by the sun. Soon she will be as clever as any girl in the village. *(LUPITA steps back and raises her hand to her face as though she had felt him strike her.)*

PEREZ. Me, I learned to read the sun on a boat in the Mediterranean. You see, I have traveled to every place of importance: Paris, London, Naples . . . even Sydney, Australia.

LUPITA *(sincerely)*. Ay, señor, it will be fascinating to hear stories of your travels. . . .

DON ANTONIO *(sharply)*. Not now, Lupita. The señor Perez is tired. See if the water is hot enough for his bath.

LUPITA. I have already attended to it. *(To PEREZ.)* If you'll follow me . . . naturally you'll stay here as our guest . . . *(She and PEREZ go into the house. Inside, we can hear her calling:)* Ester! You can set the table now.

ESTER *(inside the house)*. Very good, Lupita.

In the meantime, DON ANTONIO *nervously paces up and down, then sits with folded arms, his face worried. He glances up as* ESTER, *a folded tablecloth over her arm, comes out.*

DON ANTONIO. Ester, has don Rufino been up here this afternoon?

ESTER *(busy at the patio table, clearing it).* I haven't seen him, don Antonio. *(Finding a letter on the table, she hands it to him. He opens and reads it.)*

DON ANTONIO. Where is Abel?

ESTER. I think he's asleep.

DON ANTONIO. Bah! He's so lazy, a dead moth has more life than he!

He is again immersed in the letter. She holds a knife in her hand and looks down at the table puzzled. She looks at him, then back at the table.

ESTER. Don Antonio.

DON ANTONIO. Umm.

ESTER. Where does the knife go?

DON ANTONIO. On the table.

ESTER *(persisting).* But where on the table?

DON ANTONIO. Next to the plate. Don't bother me.

ESTER. Yes, Don Antonio.

She picks up the fork, and holds the two of them together. This doesn't suit her, so she changes the fork to her left hand. Again she doesn't like this, so she reverses them, putting the knife in her right hand. Even this doesn't work. Then she has a bright idea. She puts the knife at the top of the plate, the fork at the bottom, then stands off and admires her handiwork. She is interrupted by DON RUFINO'S *voice calling from the house.*

DON RUFINO *(off left).* Is there no one in this house?

ESTER *(tapping the old man on the shoulder).* Don Antonio, I hear don Rufino outside.

DON ANTONIO. So he came, eh? Send him in here. And don't you listen at the door.

ESTER. Why, don Antonio, I wouldn't. . .

DON ANTONIO. Hurry up! Hurry up with you.

ESTER. Before you can say "Mamá."

She runs into the house. DON ANTONIO *takes off his glasses, puts them away in their case in his pocket, and standing, faces the door as* DON RUFINO *enters. The two men look at each other.*

DON ANTONIO *(jerking his head).* You wanted to see me?

DON RUFINO. Just a little talk.

DON ANTONIO. With what face do you look at me?

DON RUFINO. A friendly one.

DON ANTONIO. Sit down. (DON RUFINO *sits on the bench.* DON ANTONIO *stands by the table.*) I received a letter today. Do you know anything about it?

DON RUFINO *(shrugging).* You receive so many letters, don Antonio.

DON ANTONIO. Not from lawyers' offices in Monterrey.

DON RUFINO. Perhaps if you told me a little about it. . . .

DON ANTONIO. It says that the people who own the land in this valley are not going to allow me to dig irrigation ditches on their property.

DON RUFINO. Ay, that is very sad. Without the ditches you can have no farms. And of what use is the powerhouse? All that good money thrown away. You would have done better had you bought goat flocks.

DON ANTONIO. Every dog to his own kingdom. I prefer to buy land.

DON RUFINO *(quickly).* Land in this valley is not for sale.

DON ANTONIO. Anything is for sale.

DON RUFINO. Don Antonio, I will speak plainly, with my hat on the back of my head to show I hide nothing.

DON ANTONIO. Remember the blind are not always naked. I will listen to you.

DON RUFINO. The shoe factory in Monterrey is very powerful.

DON ANTONIO. Then I shall buy the shoe factory.

DON RUFINO. Ah, but that factory is not a single company. It is owned by men who have other interests, too . . . such as building materials.

DON ANTONIO. Are you threatening to hold up the construction of the new flour mill?

DON RUFINO. Now, don Antonio, there is no need for anger. I am merely asking you to be sensible.

DON ANTONIO. You mean you want me to leave you alone to rule this valley to suit yourself.

DON RUFINO. Precisely. We've done without you for thirty years. We don't need you now.

DON ANTONIO. For thirty years I've been making plans . . . that never included you.

DON RUFINO *(shrugging).* That was where you made your mistake. They should have included me. The fish that sleeps is swept away by the current.

DON ANTONIO. So you are beginning to realize that. I thought you imagined only goatherders lived here.

DON RUFINO. That's all they are . . . all they are fit for. You've dazzled them with this money of yours. They don't know what it's going to do to them, but I do. The young men won't be content to stay here any longer. They'll take the money you pay them and go away to the States . . . to the beet fields and to the factories. The girls will leave for the cities. Soon none will be left here but the old and infirm. The roofs of the houses will tumble in. The church will be empty . . . and all of your fine farms will change back to what has always been here: yuccas, flowering thorn, cactus.

DON ANTONIO (with a wry smile). So you're trying to save the valley from my evil influence?

DON RUFINO. You see, you have all misjudged me, don Antonio. I am really a very humane man. I think only of my people's good.

DON ANTONIO. And goats, incidentally! How do you pay your goatherders?

DON RUFINO. In goats. Property means more to these people than money.

DON ANTONIO. But they need money to buy food and clothes, eh?

DON RUFINO. When they need those things they come and sell me back the goats.

DON ANTONIO. How much do you pay them for their . . . property?

DON RUFINO (virtuously). I pay according to the demands of the shoe factory in Monterrey.

DON ANTONIO. You mean you pay as little as possible. You were right, don Rufino. You are a very humane man, and as cunning as an eagle with its shoes off!

DON RUFINO. After all, I must look out for my own interests. I have to live.

DON ANTONIO (standing). I think I've been very patient with you. I've listened to everything you have to say.

DON RUFINO (his voice rising). It isn't a question of. . . .

DON ANTONIO. Silence! (With the tone of a strong man who knows his mind.) I will build that powerhouse. I will build those irrigation ditches, and neither you, nor the shoe factory, nor all of Monterrey is going to stop me.

LUPITA enters in a formal evening gown. She pauses in the door of the house to fasten her bracelet, and looks up startled at the two men.

DON RUFINO (rising angrily). Do not step on thorns with your eyes open, don Antonio. This is your last chance.

DON ANTONIO. Little man, don't think that you can hinder me! (He shakes the letter at him.) Tie up building materials. I'll go elsewhere for them.

DON RUFINO. The railroads won't bring them in.

DON ANTONIO. Then I'll build that flour mill from the rocks in the river bed. Make no mistake, I'll build it.

DON RUFINO. It will never be finished.

DON ANTONIO. It will be finished, if I have to lay every stone with my own two hands. Take your lawyers and your goats and your shoe factories and keep them where they belong, outside of this valley.

DON RUFINO *(frightened)*. You can't frighten me. There's more than one way of whipping you down.

DON ANTONIO *(moving toward him)*. You'll never find that way. *(With cold fury.)* Now get out! Get out of my house!

DON RUFINO *(retreating)*. You will weep over this moment!

DON ANTONIO. I wear shoes against your thorns.

DON RUFINO *(grunting)*. We'll see.

He stalks past LUPITA, *who has stepped out of the doorway to let him pass. She gazes after him, then looks in amazement at her father, who is rubbing his hand across his forehead.*

LUPITA. Father! What . . . what has happened?

DON ANTONIO *(straightening)*. He thinks he can whip me down. Nothing can whip me. I can't fail. I've planned too long. *(He walks to the gate.)* Trees growing in the desert. Trees bearing fruit. Trees bearing life. Trees pushing up through the soil, their roots drinking the water, their leaves eating the sunlight. And he thinks he can stop it. *(Patting her on the shoulder.)* Don't let it frighten you, Lupita. Nothing can defeat my valley.

LUPITA *(catching hold of him)*. You're trembling, father.

DON ANTONIO. It is only a little storm. But see . . . *(He points out above the wall.)* the moon is rising. Soon the stars will be out. Stars that are the eyes of young virgins who died in love. Stars never shine before rain. No more tempests here. (ABEL, *dressed in a white linen suit, enters from the house.)* My son, is your sleep ended? Why is it that small things can tire a man, when he can work all day in the fields and be strong at evening? Perhaps it is because he has been working in the rich brown earth. *(After a moment.)* The earth is a strong, kind mother, I can't turn away from her now. She put this valley in my trust, and I shan't fail her, no matter what comes. I shan't fail her! *(He sinks down on the chair.* ABEL *looks curiously at* LUPITA, *who shakes her head and puts her hand on her father's shoulder.)*

LUPITA. You should rest for awhile.

DON ANTONIO (*patting her hand*). No, no, I must speak to Abel first. (*He pulls her hand down and looks at it.*) You have such pretty hands, Lupita. They are so warm and firm and strong. Good hands. Hands made for working. You don't have long thin fingers and soft white palms like that newspaper fellow. (*He pats her hand against his cheek as* ESTER *comes to the door.*)

ESTER (*almost in tears*). Lupita! The most terrible thing has happened. (*She begins to weep.*)

ABEL (*anxiously*). What's the matter, Ester? Did you burn yourself? (*She shakes her head, but does not answer.* LUPITA *goes to her.*)

LUPITA. Nothing is that much of a tragedy. What is it?

ESTER (*trying her best to get it out*). Instead of soaking the celery in salt water. . . .

LUPITA. Well?

ESTER. I soaked the bananas.

ABEL (*amused but sympathetic*). Poor Ester.

LUPITA (*angrily*). And what of my poor supper? What shall we serve with the rice, eh? (*Catching* ESTER *by the arm and jerking her inside.*) You, Ester!

DON ANTONIO. Abel, have you noticed how much Lupita is like doña Beca?

ABEL. I believe I told her that this afternoon, Father.

DON ANTONIO. Eh! And where were you this afternoon?

ABEL. Here at the house.

DON ANTONIO. Doing what?

ABEL (*easily*). I did a good many things. I learned a new song, and wrote a letter, and went to sleep.

DON ANTONIO. Didn't you do any work on the plans for the flour mill?

ABEL. But I just finished building the powerhouse. Surely I deserve one day's vacation.

DON ANTONIO. With the nearest flour mill two hundred kilometers away? Vacations are for the baby.

ABEL (*sulkily*). I had an important letter to write.

DON ANTONIO. And who is more important than a flour mill?

ABEL. Right now . . . Nancy Moreno.

DON ANTONIO. May the saints have patience!

ABEL. I wanted her to say on paper that she wouldn't marry me. I need it to show somebody.

DON ANTONIO. And all that is more important than flour mill plans!

ABEL. To me it is.

DON ANTONIO. Sometimes I wonder if you are my own son. Does this valley mean so little to you that you can neglect it for something of no value?

ABEL. My happiness has value!

DON ANTONIO. The valley is your happiness.

ABEL. Father, do you realize what you are saying? I don't think you can, or you wouldn't say it.

DON ANTONIO. Am I to be constantly torn at by these little things? Why must I go on fighting when I thought my days of fighting were finished?

ABEL. I knew you loved this valley, but I didn't think you'd put it before . . . me.

DON ANTONIO. Abel, can't you understand? Helping these people has been my religion for thirty years. Now that I can help them, do you help me? No. You sit at home and write letters.

ABEL. I'm beginning to think Lupita is right.

DON ANTONIO. Lupita? What has she to do with it?

ABEL. She said this valley was a poison that seeped into a man's blood. *(He sits.)* It's in yours. I'd never realized it before. And it's beginning to get in mine.

DON ANTONIO. Lupita has fancies. They mean nothing.

ABEL. So I thought. But I'm seeing a little clearer now. What right have you to keep her here when every nerve in her body cries out against staying?

DON ANTONIO. What right has she to want to go?

ABEL. The right of every person to carve out his own life.

DON ANTONIO. You told her you couldn't go, didn't you?

ABEL. I told her I didn't want to go.

DON ANTONIO *(smiling with relief).* There spoke my son.

ABEL *(with an abrupt change of tone).* But I've changed my mind. I'm going to take her just as soon as I can.

DON ANTONIO *(unable to comprehend this).* You mean you would leave me . . . leave the valley?

ABEL. That's exactly what I mean.

DON ANTONIO. You can't do it. I forbid it. (ABEL *gets to his feet.*)

ABEL *(feeling as though he were trying to batter down a wall).* We don't want to stay!

DON ANTONIO. Your desires are childish.

ABEL *(still not believing it).* You'd keep us here against our will?

DON ANTONIO. Yes. *(As* ABEL *draws back, he tries to justify his answer.)* I've worked hard during my life, sacrificed much. I haven't very long to live. And when I die I want to know that you and Lupita are finishing what I can only begin. For centuries my people have been whipped down to the earth, first by the Spaniards and then by men like this Rufino. Protecting them is your duty. I place it upon you.

ABEL. Leaving us in bondage to set them free?

DON ANTONIO. What is your bondage compared to theirs?

ABEL. Are they goats that we must herd them to see they don't nibble on cactus and get thorns in their noses?

DON ANTONIO. They have been crushed down too long. They don't know how to help themselves.

ABEL. Let them learn. Lupita and I need to go back to the States and drink a little freedom of our own. *(He starts toward the house calling.)* Lupita!

LUPITA *(inside the house).* Yes, Abel?

ABEL. Start packing your things. We leave for the States tomorrow.

LUPITA *(inside the house, crying out ecstatically).* Abel. *(She appears in the door, an apron tied around her waist, and wiping her face with the back of her hand.)* Do you mean that?

ABEL. Ask father. *(LUPITA looks at DON ANTONIO who is sitting in the chair, his head bowed, his eyes closed. Then she looks back at ABEL.)*

LUPITA. I can't believe it!

ABEL. It's true enough. I'm going down town. Don't expect me home to dinner. *(He goes past her into the house.)*

LUPITA *(calling after him).* Where are you going?

ABEL *(from inside the house).* Down to the saloon to get drunk!

LUPITA *stretches out her hand and half starts toward the house when a moan from* DON ANTONIO *stops her.*

DON ANTONIO. Abel!

LUPITA *(going over to him, and kneeling down beside him).* Father. What happened?

DON ANTONIO *(pushes her away and standing up).* Go back to the States with him. The two of you aren't fit to stay in my valley. Go back to the long exile. Until dust covers my eyes I shall weep because I am childless, and my tears shall make the ground fertile. *(His voice almost choked with his emotion.)* But I shall be at home, at home, while you will be homeless and far away. Because when you leave you shall never return.

LUPITA *(appealingly).* Father, this never could be our home.

DON ANTONIO. When the days crawl into other days, you will listen for voices laughing with the wisdom and joy of the earth. No air perfumed with orange blossoms and flowering thorn and night-blooming jasmine will be in your nostrils. No friendly heart will open to your smile. You will know then what it is to desperately long for something of home. *(She looks up at him a moment, then buries her face in her hands and begins to cry. He looks down at her for a moment.)* Weep all you can now. Afterwards there will be no tears. That is the last great tragedy. *(He turns and goes slowly into the house, no longer a fine straight figure, but bent and old. Inside the house* PEREZ *speaks heartily.)*

PEREZ. Your house is magnificent, Don Antonio . . . but magnificent. *(As he speaks,* LUPITA *hastily wipes her eyes. He comes into the patio looking back, puzzled, over his shoulder.)* Is your father ill, señorita?

LUPITA *(trying to smile).* No . . . no, he's not ill. He's just . . . tired.

PEREZ. I see. Myself, I never tire. I am as strong as John the Bear.

LUPITA *(trying to be polite).* Who was John the Bear?

PEREZ. A legendary figure of these mountains. He had a bear for a father. In a small way I am interested in the folklore of these simple people, just as you interest yourself in . . . *(He gestures towards her apron.)* in cooking.

LUPITA *(blankly).* Cooking? *(Realizing she is still wearing the apron, she hastily takes it off.)* It's just an amusement. Servants are so difficult to find in this remote valley . . . good servants, I mean.

PEREZ *(having examined the patio, he now wanders over to the patio gate).* I know what you mean. Personally, I like perfection in all things, even the merest details. Strange. There seems to be smoke down by the river.

LUPITA. Fog, probably.

PEREZ. From your tone, señorita, I gather you have no interest in the valley.

LUPITA. Interest? I hate it. *(Suddenly bursting out.)* But now I shall be free . . . free! I can't believe that I'm going away . . . I'm going away . . . I'm going away tomorrow!

PEREZ *(frowning).* You are leaving all this?

LUPITA. Back to New York . . . it's like a dream.

PEREZ *(thoughtfully).* But I understood, señorita, that your father owned vast tracks of land here . . . that he is quite . . . ah . . . wealthy. Surely he wouldn't care to exchange this pleasant country living for the smoke and gray skies of New York.

LUPITA. Not my father! Abel . . . my brother . . . and I. We're going back to our old friends, our good friends, our talented friends.

PEREZ. Talented?

LUPITA. Oh, yes. One is Pierre Dumarque, the composer. He wrote "Song Without Melody," a composition that will change all future music. He says so himself.

PEREZ. "Song Without Melody." *(Obviously lying.)* I believe I have heard of it. Magnificent, really magnificent. Tell me, señorita. This Dumarque, is he a truly free spirit? I mean must he labor at some grubby little job and then compose in his pitifully few free hours?

LUPITA. Oh, no. He says that artists should be supported by the State. People like me, with very little talent, find it a real privilege to help Dumarque expand his . . . his great creativity.

PEREZ *(coming toward her, with real interest).* Indeed? I . . . ah . . . entirely agree with Dumarque, but unfortunately Mexico has no soul for artists.

LUPITA. No wonder, with every candy vendor spouting silly folk songs.

PEREZ. You say you have a little talent. May I ask in which of the arts?

LUPITA. I write a little. I've even had a poem published! Under another name, of course.

PEREZ. But I adore poetry. Perhaps I know your creation.

LUPITA. You probably know the magazine. It's very small, very select, edited by my good friend Nancy Moreno. It's called *Nothing*.

PEREZ *(baffled).* It's called what?

LUPITA. *Nothing.* Nancy calls it that because the writing she publishes is like nothing else in the world.

ESTER *appears in the doorway twisting her apron into knots.*

PEREZ. I can imagine. Tell me, señorita, is it so exclusive that contributors pay for their poems to be published?

LUPITA. Why, yes. How did you know?

PEREZ. I'm thinking of starting that type of magazine myself. May I ask what you paid this . . . this *Nothing?*

ESTER *(from the doorway of the house, in a loud whisper).* Lupita! Ssst, Lupita!

LUPITA *(unaware of ESTER).* It was just fifty dollars. But the poem was only worth that.

PEREZ. Fifty dollars. That would be . . . *(Suddenly smiling)* four hundred pesos. Yes, I must start such a magazine.

ESTER *(louder).* Please, Lupita!

LUPITA. Be quiet, Ester. *(To PEREZ.)* Why, that would be fascinating, Señor Perez. What are your plans for it?

ESTER *(nervously)*. Where is don Antonio?

LUPITA. How do I know where he is? Go find him yourself. *(To* PEREZ.) Do tell me about it.

PEREZ. I think I shall call it *Tomorrow*. A simple title, but it embraces the entire future.

LUPITA. Oh, yes, yes it does.

PEREZ. As I visualize it, I see sections in Spanish, naturally, but also English, French, perhaps even Russian. Señorita! I have just had a magnificent idea. How would you like to be the English editor?

LUPITA. Me?

ESTER. It's important, Lupita.

LUPITA. Be quiet, Ester! *(Then.)* Me, an editor?

PEREZ. Naturally you realize that an editorship in my *Tomorrow* will be much coveted by all artists. Ordinarily I would have to charge quite a large sum for the privilege. But since you are really my inspiration in creating the idea . . . for you it would be a mere bagatelle . . . a mere two thousand pesos. *(He looks royally off to allow her to admire him.)*

LUPITA *(thrilled beyond speech)*. Oh . . . oh, Señor Perez. Such an opportunity!

ESTER *(desperately)*. Lupita! The powerhouse is on fire! *(Both* PEREZ *and* LUPITA *look at her blankly. Then, coming to, they rush to the patio gate.)*

PEREZ. That smoke I saw!

LUPITA. If that powerhouse burns down, it will break my father's heart! Ester! Try the back garden. You know he often sits there in the sun! *(*ESTER *hurries into the house.)*

PEREZ. I think I can see men rushing around.

LUPITA. I hope they save it. Oh, I hope so.

PEREZ. It must have cost a great deal of money.

LUPITA. What does the money matter? It's my father's whole life!

PEREZ. I do hate to see money burn. *(*DON ANTONIO *runs in from the house.)*

LUPITA. Father! How do you think it started?

DON ANTONIO. It was Rufino. *(He hurries past them to the patio gate.)* I should never have let him stay in the valley.

LUPITA *(trying to stop him)*. You mustn't go down there!

DON ANTONIO *(hurrying out)*. This is my work, and no one will stop it!

LUPITA. Father! Come back! *(She starts after him, but* PEREZ *catches her arm.)*

PEREZ. If you go down there, you might be injured. I wouldn't like anything to happen to you . . . not now!

LUPITA. Poor father. I should hate to leave him with the powerhouse burned.

As she sinks down, crying, the lights dim. Darkness holds for a moment, and then the lights come up again. LUPITA *and* PEREZ *are seated at the table. He is intent on lighting a cigarette but her interest is fixed on the patio gate.*

PEREZ. I am sorry that you are leaving tomorrow. I should have liked to have known you longer. You have a mind that would be very easy to mold.

LUPITA *(absently)*. So Pierre Dumarque used to say.

PEREZ *(stiffly)*. My dear girl, once in a while I say something altogether original.

LUPITA. I'm sorry, I didn't mean to. . . . *(Voices can be heard laughing and shouting off left.)* Listen! What's that? *(She runs to the gate.)* There's a mass of people coming up the road, and . . . father . . . and Abel!

PEREZ *(frowning)*. A crowd? I was hoping that we could plan my magazine together this evening.

LUPITA *(ignoring him)*. Abel! What have you done to yourself?

FATHER ZACAYA *(off left)*. He is a true hero, Lupita.

ABEL *comes through the gate followed by* DON ANTONIO *and a gay crowd of villagers including the priest,* DON PABLO, DOÑA BECA, CARLOS BALDERAS *and* CONCHA.

DON ANTONIO *(proudly)*. He saved the powerhouse.

LUPITA. Look at your clothes!

ABEL *(glancing down at himself and laughing. His trousers are dirty and torn, he has lost his coat and tie. He catches her by the arms and swings her around in a circle)*. What do clothes matter? Don't you understand? The powerhouse is saved!

CROWD. Viva! Viva!

FATHER ZACAYA. Luckily he passed the powerhouse just as the blaze started.

CARLOS. He put it out all alone.

ABEL. You pulled me out from under that blazing timber. *(He stops laughing, goes over and shakes* CARLOS *by the hand.)* Thank you for saving my life.

CARLOS *(embarrassed)*. You would have done the same for me.

VOICES *(off stage)*. Viva! Viva! *(More people pour into the patio from the house, bringing* ESTER *and* DON PABLO'S *son,* JULIO ROMERO.*)*

NEW CROWD. Long life to this house, don Antonio!

FULL CROWD. Viva!

DON PABLO *(excitedly quieting the crowd)*. My son, Julio, was also a hero! Tell them what you did, Julio!

JULIO *(strutting a little)*. Personally I took Rufino to jail!

VOICE FROM CROWD. He should dance with a rope around his neck!

ANOTHER VOICE. Rufino has lighted his last cigarette! *(The crowd laughs.)*

DON PABLO *(trying to quiet them)*. Did you lock him up safely, my son?

JULIO. If he can escape now, then my name is not Julio Romero.

CONCHA. Julio is so brave.

JULIO. And I left him a bottle of tequila to remember me by.

A VOICE FROM THE CROWD *(laughing loudly)*. Let the tequila make him forget he was ever in this valley.

ANOTHER VOICE. We want no more long-eared goats among us. . . .

CARLOS *(yelling)*. Who fed us tallow instead of good yellow wax?

CROWD. Don Rufino!

CARLOS. Who tripped over his own tail?

CROWD. Don Rufino!

JULIO. But who saved the powerhouse?

CROWD. Abel!

ESTER *(excitedly)*. Oh Abel . . . *(Then, shyly.)* . . . I'm so glad.

ABEL *(standing in front of* ESTER*)*. Are you, Ester?

ESTER *(fleeing to the safety of* DOÑA BECA.*)* I . . . I . . . *(The crowd laughs loudly.)*

FATHER ZACAYA *(holding up his hands)*. Let there be peace on this house! *(The crowd is silenced. The men remove their hats, the women draw their veils over their heads.)* Let the Lord bless us and keep us. . . . *(He points to* CARLOS.*)* And fill our hearts with the beauty of music. *(The crowd relaxes with laughter.)*

CARLOS *(jumping up on the table.)* Songs should come from heroes. And today our hero is Abel!

DON PABLO. Abel shall sing for us!

JULIO. A good song, Abel.

CROWD. The best song, Abel.

ABEL. I have a song for you. How do you like this one, Ester? *(He swings her up on the bench and sings triumphantly.)*

Shadow of our Lord St. Peter,
The river lures me,
The river lures me.
And thus your love would my poor love allure,
My love allure.

ESTER. Saints in Heaven!

VOICES FROM THE CROWD. He sings the rooster before he even walks around the plaza! And what a rooster! Be careful, Ester, that he doesn't bring you to the altar before he proposes!

ABEL. Does it not wring your heart with sadness? Have you no sorrow for my lonely state?

DOÑA BECA. You shameless one! What does this mean, Abel?

ABEL. What can it mean, doña Beca? Will you speak for me, Carlos . . . Julio?

CARLOS and JULIO *(stepping forward)*. We will indeed. *(They turn to* DOÑA BECA *and make her a low bow, much to the delight of the crowd.)*

CARLOS. Doña Beca, our friend begs the honor of your niece's hand.

JULIO. He brings money and land to the marriage.

CARLOS. A house.

JULIO. A trousseau for the bride.

ABEL. And she can have a thousand orange blossoms made out of wax, if she wants them.

CARLOS *(frowning)*. Silence, Abel. It is not your place to speak. *(He turns to* DOÑA BECA.) He waits for your answer with a humble heart.

DOÑA BECA. And what do you say to this, Antonio?

DON ANTONIO. I have nothing to say. Abel leaves the valley tomorrow.

LUPITA *(going to Abel)*. Abel, we can't take Ester. What would we do with her?

ABEL. I'm sorry, Lupita, but I didn't think about having to leave Ester when I told you I'd go.

ESTER *(looking down at Abel)*. If you want to go, I won't hold you. Lupita is right. There is no place for me outside of the valley.

ABEL *(to* ESTER). But I'm not going to leave you. *(He turns to* DON ANTONIO.) When I saw smoke from the windows of the powerhouse, I realized what you were trying to tell me this afternoon. I helped to build it, to create it out of nothing, and no one can destroy it. You were right. My place is here, guarding this valley. Can you forgive me . . . for what I said? *(They look at each other a moment, and then give each other the abrazo, while the crowd claps loudly.)*

CROWD *(turning to each other occasionally)*. Viva don Antonio! Viva Abel! Viva! Viva!

DON ANTONIO *(fairly glowing)*. We shall hold a wedding here on New Year's day!

CROWD. A great wedding . . . a fine wedding.

LUPITA *(bitterly, to ABEL)*. I hope you'll be very happy in a little stone house down by the river bank, with children in the front yard and orange trees in the back.

ABEL. I know how bitter you must feel, Lupita, but after awhile you'll come to love this valley, too, just as I love it.

LUPITA. I won't. I'll never love it, because I won't be here.

DON ANTONIO. What's that?

LUPITA. I'm going away . . . alone.

DOÑA BECA. And what will you use for money?

DON ANTONIO. You'll not get a cent of my money for such foolishness . . . that I promise you.

LUPITA. I don't need your money. Señor Perez has offered to make me the New York editor of his magazine. He'll help me.

PEREZ. Just a moment, señorita . . . one little moment! After all, the magazine is still just a dream!

LUPITA. Then I'll write to Nancy Moreno.

ABEL. Do you think Nancy would send you money? She squeezes every dollar until the juice runs out!

LUPITA. She believes in helping creative artists. Before today, I had nothing to offer. But now . . . (*She turns to* PEREZ.) When she finds out you trust me enough to make me an editor, she'll help me. You'll see. You'll all see.

ABEL. She won't waste a stamp on an answer.

LUPITA. I know Nancy Moreno. She'll answer by return mail. And when her letter comes, I'm leaving. I won't stay in this valley a moment longer than I have to.

DOÑA BECA. And once you're gone, the valley will call you back . . . you'll return to us.

LUPITA. Never! I'll be free of this valley forever. And I'll thank God for it with every breath I draw. *(Turning on the crowd.)* Have your party. Have your fun in your silly, stupid little way! I don't want any part of it! All I want is to get away from here, and to stay away . . . forever!

As she runs into the house,
THE CURTAINS CLOSE

ACT THREE

It is three-thirty in the afternoon on the 12th of December. There is very little change in the patio, and the light is very brilliant. ESTER *is sitting at the table sewing, and* CONCHA *is seated on the stool at the left, her arms fastened about her knees.* DOÑA BECA *is standing in the gate looking down the path, her hand shading her eyes.*

ESTER (*to* CONCHA). Next we went to the store of the Three Brothers. They had the most beautiful wedding dresses, Concha. One of them had a veil of lace that went down to the floor.

CONCHA (*sighing*). It must be wonderful in Monterrey.

ESTER. It is . . . but the streets are so hard they hurt my feet. Lupita took me into the great market. It was on Saturday and a band was playing on a little platform right in the center of it. A man sang, but (*Proudly.*) he couldn't sing like Abel. There was pink netting on the grapes to protect them from the flies, and an old woman was making mats out of straw.

DOÑA BECA. Why doesn't Julio come with the sugar? He's doubtless sitting at the mill munching cane.

CONCHA. He will be here in a moment, Mamá.

ESTER (*looking at* DOÑA BECA, *then leaning forward confidentially*). I did something very wicked.

CONCHA. What?

ESTER. Lupita had given me a little money, and she left me by a pottery stall while she went to buy wool for her embroidery. Just across the way from me was a public letter writer.

CONCHA. You didn't. . . .

ESTER (*giggling*). Yes, I did. He wrote a letter from me to Abel. It looked beautiful. He drew a dove at the top of the page with a heart in a net of roses dangling from its beak. And you should have seen the writing. All curves. (*She demonstrates in the air.*) The A in Abel was beautiful. It took up most of the page.

DOÑA BECA (*coming into the patio*). Stop your mumbling, Ester, and get to work. You'll never have those things finished by New Year's. You promised me you'd be done with them if I let you come this afternoon.

CONCHA (*sitting down on the bench*). Do you think Lupita will be pleased with the surprise?

DOÑA BECA. There won't be a surprise unless Julio returns with the sugar. People must be fed. Sometimes I think Rufino put a black magic spell on him.

CONCHA. I heard don Pablo say that he was going to let don Rufino out of jail today. He's been in it a long time. June . . . *(She counts the other months rapidly on her fingers but silently moving her mouth.)* December. Seven months. Don Pablo said he ate more than any prisoner we've ever had.

DOÑA BECA. You shouldn't be listening to gossip. (LUPITA *comes into the patio, a subdued* LUPITA *with sad eyes and a listless manner. She wears a very modish silk dress.)*

LUPITA *(pausing for a moment at seeing them, then coming forward).* Good afternoon. I didn't know you were here.

DOÑA BECA *(going to her and kissing her on either cheek).* A happy Saint's Day to you, Lupita.

CONCHA. May Heaven smile on you, Lupita.

ESTER. And bring you joy.

LUPITA *(without interest).* Saint's day?

DOÑA BECA. Have you forgotten that this is the twelfth of December?

CONCHA. All the Republic worships Our Blessed Lady of Guadalupe today.

ESTER. It must be wonderful at the miracle shrine near Mexico City, with all the people climbing the long stairs on their knees and holding candles in their hands.

DOÑA BECA. Don't turn your eyes astray, girl. We have a miracle Virgin in this very patio. May she bless us all. *(They all cross themselves.)*

CONCHA *(standing).* If you give me permission to leave a moment, Mamá.

DOÑA BECA. Go away, go away. *(As* CONCHA *starts into the house.)* And if you see that Julio Romero, tell him to hurry.

CONCHA. On the back of a swallow. *(She runs into the house.)*

LUPITA *(to* ESTER). Has Carlos brought the mail yet?

ESTER. I've not seen his face since yesterday.

DOÑA BECA *(sniffing).* So you've had no answer yet to all your letters to your fine friends.

LUPITA *(quickly).* They will write just as soon as they have time . . . I know they will. There is so much to do in New York. It is hard to settle down to writing a letter.

ESTER. Why don't they go to a public letter writer? He could do it so quickly.

LUPITA. They don't have them in New York.

ESTER *(shaking her head).* What a sad thing, because not everyone can write with flourishes.

DOÑA BECA. How do you know so much about them, miss?

ESTER *(bending over her work).* I've heard tales of them. (CONCHA *enters with a bouquet of flowers hidden behind her back.)*

CONCHA *(to* LUPITA). Guess which hand.

LUPITA *(wearily).* I don't feel like playing games, Concha.

CONCHA *(teasing).* Just this once, Lupita.

LUPITA. The right. (CONCHA *grins and shakes her head.)* The left. (CONCHA *giggles and shakes her head.)* Both of them, then. (CONCHA *draws forward the flowers and hands them to her.)* Are these for me?

CONCHA. For your Saint's day.

LUPITA *(smiling a little).* That was very sweet of you, Concha. Will you put them in water, Ester? Oh, no, you're busy. I'll do it. *(She moves slowly toward the house.* CARLOS *is heard singing faintly off stage.)*

DOÑA BECA. Did you see the worthless Julio, Concha?

CONCHA. No, Mamá. Just Carlos Balderas riding up the trail on his old long-eared donkey. (CARLOS' *voice constantly gets stronger.)*

LUPITA *(with more animation).* Carlos! Perhaps he has . . . *(She gives almost a sob and starts running toward the patio gate.)*

DOÑA BECA *(reaching out and catching her by the back of the dress).* Not so fast, miss.

LUPITA *(trying to pull away).* But I want to go and meet him.

DOÑA BECA. What conduct for a decent girl. He will come in here and meet you where others are present. That is only decent. (LUPITA *drops her hand and comes back.* CONCHA *takes the flowers from her.)*

CONCHA. I'll put them in water for you. . . . (CARLOS *can be heard singing from far off left.)*

CARLOS *(off stage).*
> The four cornstalks are left all alone
> On the ranch that was my own, ay-yay.
> The house that's so tiny,
> So white and so shiny,
> Is left very sad.

DOÑA BECA *and the others continue to speak against the background of his song, which comes closer and closer.*

> There're no deer on the mountainside gray,
> Everything is withered today, Ay-yay.
> For no birds are flying,
> The roses are dying,
> Since I've been away.

DOÑA BECA. There comes Carlos, singing as usual.

CONCHA. Has he sung the rooster to you yet, Lupita?

LUPITA *(laughing quickly and turning away, shaking her head)*. No.

ESTER *(wisely)*. Have no fear. He will. He's shy.

DOÑA BECA. Which no one can say about Abel . . . the more pity to him.

CONCHA. I'll see if Julio is coming, too. *(She runs into the house.)*

DOÑA BECA. Ay, it takes young eyes to see the tortoise move.

LUPITA *(calling through the patio gate)*. Carlos! Carlos, did you bring me a letter?

CARLOS *(calling off)*. O-la! O-la!

LUPITA. He knows how much I want it. Surely he'd call out if he had it.

DOÑA BECA. Ester, run down to meet Carlos.

ESTER. But, Aunt Beca, he'll be here in a just a moment.

DOÑA BECA. Do as you're told, girl. *(She waits until ESTER runs through the gate, then turns on LUPITA.)*

DOÑA BECA. A fine one you are . . . making a good man like Carlos wait and wait. . . .

LUPITA. I've told you a thousand times, doña Beca . . . I've no intention of marrying Carlos.

DOÑA BECA. Oh, no! You'll spend your smiles on someone like that newspaper reporter. . . .

LUPITA. I don't want to think about Perez and his promises. . . .

DOÑA BECA. Ha! Sense at last! I've seen hundreds like that one. All he wanted was your money . . . and when he found out your father wouldn't give you any, he dropped you quickly enough. Personally, I think your friends in New York are exactly like him!

LUPITA. Stop it! You have no right to. . . .

DOÑA BECA *(sharply)*. I intend to see you happy if I have to slap you into good sense!

LUPITA. Don't you see? They're all I've got! They're all I've got! *(She bursts into tears. DOÑA BECA looks at her a moment, then puts motherly arms about her.)*

DOÑA BECA. There, there, child. Once I had dreams, too. I think every woman, at one time in her life, must love the flying birds. *(She strokes LUPITA's hair.)* In this valley there was a man with a dream . . . a great dream . . . so great that it pushed him out into the world. I was a fool, and fell in love with him. I thought he could love me, but . . . he flew away on the wings of his dream. I could have shut myself off from life, just as you are doing. *(She turns LUPITA's face up to meet hers.)* But I didn't. I married a good man . . . and if the wild abandon was not there, it didn't matter. I've had a fine life, and now that I am old . . . too old for dreaming . . . I have no regrets. Marriage to that wild dreamer would have destroyed me. My dreamer had his dreams . . . that was all he wanted. But a woman has to have more. She has to be needed . . . to fill a place in a man's life no other woman could fill. And Carlos Balderas really needs you.

LUPITA. Carlos needs a girl like Ester . . . sweet, simple, in love with a home.

DOÑA BECA. Carlos needs ambition! He needs a woman behind him to push him. He has great talent . . . he has courage, he's dependable, he's honest . . . every man in this valley would follow him if he chose to lead them. But he prefers to stand in his candy kitchen and watch the world pass by . . . when the world, his world, this valley, needs him. You could give him that push, Lupita. A girl like Ester would destroy him . . . make him even worse than he is now.

LUPITA. Doña Beca, you don't understand . . . you've never understood. I wouldn't be content with this valley. It isn't big enough for me. But it is big enough for Carlos . . . and that is the difference between us.

DOÑA BECA. There's a circle of mountains around this valley, but Carlos has climbed their peaks many times. He left them behind him when he went to fight with Pancho Villa. When Villa captured Mexico City, did you know he put Carlos in charge of the whole Republic?

LUPITA *(startled).* Carlos? Carlos Balderas?

DOÑA BECA. Yes. Who knows? He might have been president, if Villa hadn't been driven out of the City . . . his army broken up. An ambitious man would have stayed and fought for his rights, but Carlos was sick of fighting, sick of political squabbles. He wanted to come home . . . to peace. But married to you, Lupita, he can always climb those mountains again.

CARLOS *(calling off).* Who wants a present for a Saint's Day?

DOÑA BECA. Think about it. *(Then calling to* CARLOS.) Put your candy under your arm and walk through the gate. (CARLOS, *followed by* ESTER, *comes laughing through the gate. Under one arm is a box of candy.)*

CARLOS *(shaking hands).* A good afternoon to you, doña Beca.

DOÑA BECA. Um. If it doesn't rain.

CARLOS. As God wills.

ESTER. Did you bring almond paste?

CARLOS *(grinning).* Perhaps. *(He goes to* LUPITA, *and shakes hands with her.)* A happy Saint's Day.

LUPITA *(rising).* Thank you, Carlos. *(Anxiously.)* No letters?

CARLOS *(shrugging).* Nothing of importance. *(Extending the box.)* This is for you.

LUPITA *(her sadness returned).* Thank you. *(She manages a smile.)* I won't offer to pay for it this time.

CARLOS *(laughing).* Do not mind. We forget easily in the valley.

DOÑA BECA. Room enough for one friend, there's room enough for two.

LUPITA. You are all so friendly, and I . . . you must hate me.

ESTER *(shocked).* No. Lupita.

DOÑA BECA. A fool is known by the nose he wears.

CARLOS *(gently).* We couldn't hate you, Lupita. *(He jerks his head.)* Aren't you going to see what kind of candy it is?

ESTER. It couldn't be better than almond paste.

DOÑA BECA. Unless it were cheese of pecans.

CARLOS. Open it. (LUPITA *looks up at him, then lifts the lid from the box. Her expression changes to surprise as she looks into it, and then to pleasure and then pure happiness.)*

LUPITA. Carlos!

DOÑA BECA. What is it?

ESTER *(excitedly).* I'm sure it's almond paste.

LUPITA. Oh, Carlos. *(She suddenly puts her hand to her face and begins to cry.)*

CARLOS *(anxiously).* But what is there to cry about, Lupita?

DOÑA BECA *(pushing him away).* You fool, what did you put in the box?

ESTER. Almond paste never made me cry like that.

LUPITA. It isn't almond paste. It's. . . .

DOÑA BECA. The letter!

LUPITA. Yes! The letter! *(She flings her arms about* DOÑA BECA.*)* Oh, I'm so happy!

ESTER. The letter? *(Accusingly.)* Carlos! And you with your face behind a barn door.

CARLOS *(concerned).* I didn't mean to make you cry, Lupita.

LUPITA *(wiping her eyes).* I'm not crying, Carlos. I'm just . . . happy.

DOÑA BECA. Well, well, what does it say?

LUPITA. Oh . . . oh, yes. I ought to read it, shouldn't I?

DOÑA BECA. She waits seven months, and then forgets to read it!

CARLOS *(taking the box, lifting out the letter, and handing it to* LUPITA). You open it.

DOÑA BECA. And why shouldn't she? Isn't it her letter? (LUPITA *looks at all of them, then turns the envelope over in her hands.)*

LUPITA. It's from Nancy Moreno.

DOÑA BECA. Do you think to read it through the envelope?

LUPITA. No, I . . . *(She rubs her hand over the envelope, looks at them again, then tears open the envelope and takes out the sheet of paper. They are all watching this intently.)*

ESTER. I had a letter once. My grandmother sent it to me.

LUPITA (*suddenly pushing the letter into* DOÑA BECA's *hands*). Read it to me. I . . . I can't see the words.

DOÑA BECA (*with a disgusted glance at* LUPITA, *she opens the sheet, shakes it, looks down at it, then frowns*). Am I a magician that I can read English?

LUPITA (*puzzled*). I wonder why she wrote in English? She's as Mexican as we are.

ESTER. That comes of living away from the valley.

DOÑA BECA. Call Abel, Carlos. He reads English. (CARLOS *goes quickly into the house.*)

ESTER. Let me see it. (LUPITA *hands her the letter and she looks eagerly at it, then she makes a little face of disappointment.*) It has no doves drawn on it.

DOÑA BECA (*slowly*). Ester!

ESTER (*hastily handing the letter back to* LUPITA, *her voice showing her guilty conscience*). Yes, Aunt?

DOÑA BECA. When were you at a public letter writer's?

ESTER. Why, Aunt, I. . . .

DOÑA BECA. When were you?

ESTER (*shamefully*). In Monterrey.

DOÑA BECA. And to whom did you send it?

ESTER. To Abel.

DOÑA BECA. So! This is why I reared you! I took you, an orphan child, and reared you . . . so that you could write letters to a man!

ESTER (*all in one breath*). But I'd been in Monterrey two weeks, and Abel was out here, and I hadn't seen him, and I thought. . . .

DOÑA BECA. You think too much for a decently brought-up girl!

LUPITA. Please! Don't scold her. Not today. I'm too happy today.

ABEL *enters from the house with* CARLOS. *He waves mischeviously to* ESTER.

DOÑA BECA. I thank you to remember your manners, Abel Lozano.

ABEL (*in mock repentance*). I'm sorry, doña Beca.

LUPITA. The letter came from Nancy. But she wrote in English, and I haven't spoken English in so long, I'm all confused. I can't . . . I can't understand what she's saying.

ABEL (*taking the letter and, as he reads it, frowning*). There's no need to understand it. (*He slowly folds it into the original creases.*)

LUPITA. What does she say?

ABEL *(bursting forth).* What do you care about Nancy Moreno and her worthless crowd!

LUPITA *(frozen).* She doesn't want me to come. *(Fiercely.)* I want you to tell me exactly what she says.

ABEL *(on a deep breath).* All right. She says that she can't afford to support you . . . your talent isn't worth her time. Without your money, they don't want you.

LUPITA. Even Pierre Dumarque? He said he loved me!

ABEL. She wrote for all of them.

DOÑA BECA. Just like Fernando Perez! No money . . . no friendship.

LUPITA *(bursting forth).* I don't believe it! Not a single word! It's a trick . . . a trick from all of you!

ABEL. Lupita! Be sensible!

LUPITA. You're trying to hold me here. That's it! You're trying to make me stay in this valley. But I won't stay! I won't!

CARLOS. Do you think we're that cruel, Lupita?

ABEL *(extending the letter).* Translate it word for word for yourself! (LUPITA *turns her back on him.)*

CARLOS. Stay with us, Lupita, where you're safe.

LUPITA. Take your music to another house! *(She suddenly realizes what she has said.)* Oh, now I'm even speaking proverbs! This valley is destroying me! But I won't let it. I don't need Nancy . . . I don't need Pierre . . . I can depend on myself! I'll get away somehow! I'm not beaten yet!

CARLOS *(stretching out a hand toward her).* Please, Lupita. . . .

LUPITA. Don't touch me! *(She runs into the house.)*

ABEL. I'd like to wring the necks of everyone of those New York devils. Why did they have to do this to her?

DOÑA BECA. The surgeon's knife is cruel but kind. It was better to take away all her hope than lead her on.

CARLOS. They didn't have to be that cruel! *(He turns, suddenly, and goes out through the patio gate.)*

ESTER *(looking after him).* Poor Carlos. He sings to chase away sorrow these days.

ABEL. If he had the sense of a three-day-old crocodile, he'd hit Lupe over the head and make her listen to him. (CONCHA *enters from the house.)*

CONCHA. Mamá. Julio and I. . . .

DOÑA BECA. Ay, so Julio has returned, has he? Did he forget that he was supposed to go for sugar? Or did he just take himself to the village and escort himself back?

CONCHA. He brought the sugar but. . . .

DOÑA BECA. But what?

CONCHA. Well, we were trying to put planks on sawhorses to make tables in front of the house and. . . .

DOÑA BECA. And Julio fell over the side of the mountain?

CONCHA. No, not Julio. One of the sawhorses!

DOÑA BECA. Into the house with you! What daughter of mine is this that rolls the eye so much that a man throws sawhorses down a mountainside? Am I a good mother, or am I the victim of Grandfather Devil? Into the house! *(She swoops down on* CONCHA, *who gives a shriek and dashes ahead of her. They both go inside.* ABEL, *who has been laughing at* DOÑA BECA'S *anger, now turns and looks at* ESTER. *She hastily goes over and starts to gather up her sewing.)*

ABEL. There was a postscript on that letter of Lupita's.

ESTER. Abel! You didn't. . . .

ABEL. What?

ESTER. It really said for her not to come, didn't it?

ABEL. Oh, yes, it said that all right. The postscript was for me. I wrote Nancy Moreno, too, you know.

ESTER *(slowly)*. I remember. *(She looks down at her sewing.)* You still love her, don't you?

ABEL. How can you think that, Ester?

ESTER. Don't make the bad promises, Abel. If you do love her. . . .

ABEL. Let me read it to you. *(He opens the letter and glances at the end of it.)* "Abel, why should I marry a man whose money is spent on a valley? I wasn't born to be a fool."

ESTER. Eh, but she is a woman and you are a man, and it is well known that rabbits are born for the fox to eat.

ABEL. Are you calling yourself a fox?

ESTER *(protesting)*. I don't write letters.

ABEL. No? Not even with the drawings of doves decorating the page?

ESTER. I don't know what made me do that. You must think me a very wicked, forward girl. Now you will go to New York and marry her. *(She nods toward the letter in* ABEL'S *hand.)*

ABEL. And who taught you such lies? I will make you pay for each one. *(He darts toward her, but she gives a startled shriek and runs around the table from him.* CARLOS *comes to the gate, but neither notices him as* ABEL *catches* ESTER.)*

ESTER. I will call Aunt Beca!

ABEL *(lifting her up and swinging her around)*. Call her. And get a lecture for your pains. *(He sees* CARLOS *and puts* ESTER *down on the floor.)* But the rooster must not frighten the dove.

ESTER. Or else the dove will peck out both his eyes . . . so. *(She tosses him a kiss and runs into the house.)*

ABEL *(turning to* CARLOS). I'm sorry, Carlos. I don't think Lupita wants to see anyone now.

CARLOS. I think she'll see me. I have a plan.

ABEL. Carlos, I like you. I think . . . I hope . . . we're good friends. You even saved my life. But Lupita is not the girl for you.

CARLOS *(stiffly)*. Good friends do not interfere in important matters. Please ask her to see me. (ABEL *shrugs and goes into the house.* CARLOS *stands at the gate looking out over the valley, and at first does not notice* RUFINO *peering in through the window. Then he turns and sees him.)*

CARLOS. You, Rufino, what are you doing here?

DON RUFINO *(sullenly)*. I didn't come to see you. *(He pushes* CARLOS *aside and comes into the patio.)* My quarrel is with don Antonio. He stole my goats. I have come to revenge myself.

CARLOS *(following him)*. He stole nothing from you. It was your own stupidity that put you in jail.

DON RUFINO *(pulling out his knife)*. Do not try my patience, Carlos Balderas. I am not a squealer of words like you. I'm a man of action, me. Behold, a knife from Oaxaca, where they know how to make real knives, even to the motto. And mine has a great motto. *(He reads from the knife.)* It says, "Old hide, I need you to make my drum."

CARLOS *(pulling out his own knife)*. And mine is from the hand of Pancho Villa. This, too, has a motto.

DON RUFINO. Better than mine?

CARLOS. It says, "Scatter, chickens, here comes your hawk."

DON RUFINO *(laughing sarcastically)*. A fine, brave motto for a candy vendor.

CARLOS. Mottoes have no value. But days have value. And this is the Day of Guadalupe . . . the Saint's Day of Lupita. You're not going to spoil it.

DON RUFINO. And you think to stop me, candy vendor?

CARLOS. If I have to. You're drunk, Rufino.

DON RUFINO. Not too drunk to knock you down! *(He takes a sudden lunge at* CARLOS. *The next moment they are fighting, with* RUFINO, *at first, getting the best of it with his wild lunges. Then* CARLOS *settles down to real fighting, and in a moment he has* RUFINO *down on his knees with one arm pulled up behind him.)*

CARLOS. I've put up with your nonsense in my valley long enough.

DON RUFINO *(screaming)*. Your valley. It's mine! Mine!

CARLOS. And a fine mess you've made of it! And the village let you do it . . . all the men were mush! And I have no more use for mush than for you! But upsetting Lupita is a very different thing! She *is* my business. *(He gives* RUFINO *a sudden push that sends the man sprawling.)* Now get out of this house and stay out of it.

DON RUFINO *(struggling to sit up)*. I'll get my revenge on this house. Never fear.

CARLOS. If you try it, you'll deal with me! Remember that! (RUFINO *stares sullenly at him as he rises.* LUPITA *enters from the house.)*

LUPITA. Abel said you wanted to speak to me Carlos. I . . . *(She suddenly notices* RUFINO *and is silent.)*

CARLOS. Don Rufino is just leaving, Lupita. He came to give you his regrets that he can't stay for your saint's day party. A good day to you, don Rufino. (RUFINO *glares at both of them, then tries to swagger out.)*

LUPITA *(going up to* CARLOS). What happened? You look as though you'd been fighting!

CARLOS. Oh that. It was nothing. *(He takes a small bag from his pocket and puts it on the table.)* Here, Lupita. This is for you. (LUPITA, *puzzled, opens the sack and pours some coins into her hand.)*

LUPITA. Why it's . . . it's gold!

CARLOS. I saved it over the years. But for what? A candy vendor needs very little. There's enough there to take you to the States, and keep you until you find a job.

LUPITA *(putting the money back into the sack)*. You'd give me your life's savings?

CARLOS. I'm going to speak to you with my hat on the back of my head. When I first saw you, I knew you were my woman. And the more I've seen you, the more I've wanted you.

LUPITA. Carlos, please. . . .

CARLOS *(fiercely)*. Don't say anything! I must finish this now. I hoped, in time, you'd come to love the valley. But you belong out there . . . beyond the mountains. To you they are a prison wall. To me they are protection and peace. Those who love the mountains never leave them . . . while you must voyage on strange seas.

LUPITA. Carlos, I don't know what to say. I . . . *(Clutching the gold to her, she runs into the house, nearly colliding with* DOÑA BECA.)

DOÑA BECA. That was a fine bit of politeness. What has happened between you two?

CARLOS. Forgive me, doña Beca. This is a great feast day, and I have many orders for candy. *(He goes quickly out through the gate.* DOÑA BECA *follows him.)*

DOÑA BECA *(calling off)*. I don't like secrets, Carlos Balderas! It won't take me long to find out what happened!

CONCHA, *pursued by* JULIO *runs in from the house.* JULIO *is carrying a pulley and rope. Not seeing* DOÑA BECA, *he catches* CONCHA *and aims a kiss at her cheek, which* CONCHA, *with a dainty shriek, manages to evade.*

DOÑA BECA. I'll thank the two of you to behave with dignity! *(They both swing around, embarrassed.)*

JULIO. We didn't see you, doña Beca.

DOÑA BECA *(dryly).* That was quite obvious.

CONCHA. Oh, Mamá, such a scandal! We passed Lupita's room and we could hear her crying.

DOÑA BECA. Lupita's tears are private to Lupita.

JULIO. But she cries all the time. No one can escape noticing.

CONCHA. She needs friends, Julio. She's very lonely.

JULIO *(winking at her).* So am I. Of course, if we were to get married tomorrow. . . .

DOÑA BECA. You'll get married when I set the date. *(She goes into the house.)*

CONCHA. Mamá is right, Julio. Now put that pulley up there on the rain trough, and quickly! Everyone will arrive before we're through.

JULIO *(standing on the bench, and attaching the pulley to the rain trough).* What is to be the *piñata?*

CONCHA. A beautiful crepe paper watermelon. I made it myself.

JULIO *(bending toward her).* Then it should be in the church, for it was made by an angel.

CONCHA *(laughing).* Ay, Julio. Put your hat on the back of your head.

JULIO. Why should I lie? To me you are a true angel. *(Yanking on the pulley.)* Will it have candy inside?

CONCHA. Carlos Balderas has been making it these two days.

JULIO. Now there's one who will be singing the rooster up here in the nights to come.

CONCHA. Ay, and "The Shadow of our Lord Saint Peter" will be one of his songs, I can tell you.

JULIO. I like Lupita. I don't know why I do . . . but I do.

CONCHA. We all like Lupita. Perhaps, someday, she'll like us.

JULIO *(stepping down from the bench).* How does that look?

CONCHA *(examining it).* It will do. I wonder who will break the *piñata?*

JULIO. If I run the rope up and down, you can break it.

CONCHA. You will run no rope. Are you don Antonio that you are filled with your own importance?

DOÑA BECA *now enters the patio with* FATHER ZACAYA, DON PABLO, DOÑA AMPARO, *and a crowd of men and women.*

DOÑA BECA *(to* FATHER ZACAYA, *as they enter).* Did you meet Carlos Balderas as you came up the trail?

FATHER ZACAYA. No.

DOÑA BECA. That stupid fool!

FATHER ZACAYA. Is there something wrong?

DOÑA BECA. For the first time in my life, good priest, I have no answer! *(She suddenly bears down on* JULIO.) Did you fix the pulley?

JULIO *(pointing).* There it is.

CROWD. This will be a fine *piñata* . . . Lupita should like this. . . . Hush, I hear her coming.

THE CROWD *opens to leave a free path for* LUPITA *to enter.* ESTER, *however, comes in. She looks as though she had seen a ghost.*

ESTER. She is coming, and . . . wait until you see her!

DOÑA BECA *(anxiously).* What is it?

ESTER *(flinging out her arm).* Look!

LUPITA *comes slowly into the patio. She has changed her clothes, and now wears the colored skirts and the gay blouse of a village girl. She really is pretty now. She stops in surprise at seeing all of the people.*

LUPITA. Why . . . what. . . .

DOÑA AMPARO *(bearing down on her).* A happy Saint's Day, Lupita. We have bought you a *piñata.*

LUPITA. You have bought me . . . what?

DOÑA BECA. A *piñata.* You will find out what it is soon enough. But here is Father Zacaya.

LUPITA *(going up to him and kissing his hand).* A good afternoon to you, Father. To all of you. This house is yours. (*To* DOÑA BECA.) Isn't Carlos . . . ? I . . . I mean. . . .

CONCHA. He's busy as usual, making candy.

LUPITA. Oh . . . yes, of course.

DOÑA BECA *(sharply, to* CONCHA). Silence, miss. (*To* LUPITA.) This *piñata* is a surprise for you. Are you surprised?

LUPITA. I . . . I don't know what to say.

DOÑA BECA. Silence is the best speaker.

FATHER ZACAYA. Shall we wait for don Antonio?

DOÑA BECA *(sarcastically).* He's probably with Abel, gazing with delight on the new flour mill.

FATHER ZACAYA *(holding up his hands).* No matter. We can proceed without them. Will you please kneel? *(Everyone kneels except the priest.* LUPITA *hesitates just a moment before she goes down on her knees. The*

men remove their hats and the women cover their heads with their veils.)
This house stands in the shadow of Our Blessed Lady who has worked miracles.

CROWD. Amen.

FATHER ZACAYA. She wears many names, Our Lady of Sorrows, but her most beautiful name is Guadalupe.

CROWD. Blessed is her name.

FATHER ZACAYA *(turning and facing the niche).* May peace dwell in this house forever . . . we, your servants ask it.

CROWD. Amen. *(He kneels down, and* DOÑA AMPARO, *rising, comes up to* LUPITA *and puts both hands on the girl's head.)*

DOÑA AMPARO. I, who have borne children and walked in the land of death, I bless this girl who wears the name of Our Sacred Lady.

CROWD. Amen.

DOÑA AMPARO. On her I put the ancient prayer.

CROWD. Amen.

DOÑA AMPARO. With the blue mantle of Our Lady of Guadalupe and with the white robe of Her Beautiful Son may you and all of yours be enveloped. May no storm, nor fire, nor heathen enemy, whether Moor or Comanche or those who are privileged to ride with spurs, ever touch you. May you never thirst in the desert, suffer from drought, feel the trembling of the earth, or be struck by lightning. May you be delivered from dangerous roads and swollen rivers and from Grandfather Devil and all small devils. May you never fall into mortal sin. May your enemies have no eyes to see you, nor feet to overtake you, nor hands to lay hold of you, nor tongues to bear false witness against you. May you be secure from poisonous serpents, from the guile of traitors, and from sudden death. Mary and Joseph accompany you at all hours. May you be hidden in the wounds of the Holy Ribs. May you marry with joy and bear many sons and two daughters. Jesus, the sweet name. Amen!

CROWD. Amen. *(They all rise quietly to their feet, crossing themselves.)*

FATHER ZACAYA *(beginning to sing and the others taking it up).*
    My Lord Jesus smiles on me,
    And on the house where I was born. Amen.

The women remove the shawls from their heads.

CONCHA *(suddenly breaking the spell).* And now the *piñata!*

CROWD. The *piñata!* The *piñata!*

CONCHA. Ester! *(They run into the house together to get it.)*

LUPITA *has stood all this time as though dazed. Now she abruptly turns to* DOÑA AMPARO *and kisses her on the cheek.*

LUPITA. You are too good to me.

DOÑA BECA *(patting* LUPITA'S *shoulder).* You have been in exile, Lupe. Will you come home to us?

LUPITA *(turning away).* I wish . . . oh, I wish . . . *(She breaks off as* DON ANTONIO *and* ABEL *enter, each of them with a firm grasp on the arms of* CARLOS BALDERAS.)

ABEL. We found this fool sitting on top of the powerhouse gazing down into the river.

DON ANTONIO *(jovially).* He tried to make excuses . . . but no excuses for Lupita's Saint's Day, eh? (CARLOS *and* LUPITA *are careful not to look at each other.* DOÑA BECA *stares thoughtfully at both of them, then waves her hand to* DON ANTONIO.)

DOÑA BECA. Lupita has had her blessing. Now it's time for the *piñata.*

ESTER *and* CONCHA *enter, bearing the watermelon* piñata *between them.*

CROWD *(yelling).* Viva! Viva!

CONCHA *(excitedly, to* LUPITA). The first to break it will be married first!

ABEL. Then that will be me. Eh, Ester?

ESTER. Abel, have you no shame?

JULIO. I'll be the first. And to hasten the wedding . . . *(He bows in front of* DON ANTONIO.) Don Antonio, may I offer my services to help hang the *piñata?*

DON ANTONIO *(jovially).* I am honored, friend Julio. *(They both take the* piñata *from the girls and fasten it to the pulley.* ESTER *and* CONCHA *link their arms around* LUPITA'S *waist.)*

CARLOS *(suddenly).* Lupita should be the first. It's her Saint's Day.

LUPITA *(quickly).* Ay, no! *(She looks quickly away from him.)* You be first. I know nothing of this game.

ESTER *(excitedly).* Yes, Carlos! You try!

CARLOS. I resign the honor to Don Antonio.

DON ANTONIO *(taking the stick from* JULIO, *he bends over so that* CONCHA *can blindfold him).* I warn you, I'm very good at breaking *piñatas.* Remember, Beca? (DOÑA BECA *takes up the rope.)*

DOÑA BECA. That was when my father was pulling the rope. I have a better technique! (DON ANTONIO *laughs and swings the stick, but the* piñata *whirls up out of his reach. The* CROWD *laughs.)*

DON ANTONIO *(laughing also, and pulling off the blindfold).* Here,

Carlos. This game needs a steadier hand than mine. You try it. *(While* CONCHA *blindfolds an unwilling* CARLOS, DON ANTONIO *takes hold of the rope.)*

DON ANTONIO. I'll do this now.

DOÑA BECA *(firmly).* You've been away too long. You don't know how to do it.

DON ANTONIO *(grinning).* The swallow may leave the nest, Beca. But it always can find its way home. *(He takes the rope while she moves reluctantly out of the way.* CARLOS *comes up and takes a swing, but again the* piñata *flies out of reach.)*

VOICES FROM CROWD. Show your strong muscles, Carlos. . . . Beat the air, Carlos. . . . Be a man and break it, Carlos! *(*CARLOS *tries again and misses again. He laughs and pulls off the blindfold.)*

DOÑA BECA *(disgusted).* Sometimes the swallow gets in the wrong nest!

DON ANTONIO *(laughing).* Well, Lupita, do you think you can break it now?

CROWD. Yes, yes! Let Lupita try. . . . Break it, Lupe. . . . Remember it's your Saint's Day! *(*CARLOS *comes up to* LUPITA *with the handkerchief. They are both embarrassed. He ties it around her eyes, and presses the stick into her hands, then suddenly whirls her around three times.)*

LUPITA *(crying out).* That's not fair!

CARLOS *(as the crowd laughs).* It's your Saint's Day. You'll have to find the *piñata* alone.

LUPITA. I'll find it. *(She swishes the air, entirely the wrong direction.)*

DON ANTONIO *(laughing with the crowd).* You'll never find it that way, Lupita.

LUPITA *(sharply).* Ester. Is it true that the one who breaks the *piñata* first will be married first?

ESTER *(laughing).* That's the promise, Lupita.

LUPITA. Very well! *(Suddenly she pulls off the blindfold and, before they realize what she's doing, she stalks over and breaks the* piñata, *candy cascading all around her.)* There! *(She turns to face* CARLOS, *and stares straight at him. He stares at her in complete surprise.)*

ABEL. That wasn't fair, Lupita!

LUPITA. I'm a woman. I don't have to play fair! Do I, doña Beca?

DON ANTONIO *(disturbed).* What's wrong with you, my daughter?

DOÑA BECA. I think she's just come to her senses.

LUPITA. I want to hear singing. I want to hear the songs of this valley. Will you sing for me, Carlos Balderas?

CROWD. Yes, Carlos, a song . . . a good song. . . .

CARLOS. What kind of a song do you want, Lupita?

ABEL. Why don't you try "Shadow of Our Lord, St. Peter"?

DOÑA BECA. Keep your mouth shut, Abel, on the outside of your teeth!

DON ANTONIO. Lupita . . . my little daughter. . . .

LUPITA. I want this house . . . and this valley . . . and . . . and . . . *(She suddenly breaks off and turns away.)*

DON ANTONIO *(putting his arms around her)*. Oh, welcome home, my daughter . . . my dear, dear child.

DOÑA BECA. And what is the third thing you want, Lupita?

ESTER *(walking up to* CARLOS*)*. I would say it's something for Lupita to want, and . . . and . . . *(Shyness suddenly overcomes her, and she hastens back to* ABEL.*)*

CONCHA *(convulsed with laughter)*. And someone else to guess!

Someone in the crowd suddenly laughs. In a few moments everyone, looking at CARLOS, *also laughs.*

CARLOS *(suddenly laughing at himself, jumping up on the table)*. You want a song, Lupita? I'll give you a song, if you promise to walk three times around the plaza with me Sunday night.

DOÑA BECA. Carlos Balderas! You have no more shame than Abel!

CARLOS *(ignoring her)*. Well, Lupita?

LUPITA *(tossing her head)*. And who says I'll even be on the plaza Sunday night?

ESTER. How wonderful, Lupita!

CONCHA *(delighted)*. You've learned to talk like a real valley girl!

LUPITA, *head lowered, moves away from them and, at the patio gate, gazes out over the valley.*

FATHER ZACAYA *(holding up his hands)*. There's only one song for this moment.

ABEL. You're right, good priest. *(He takes* DON ANTONIO'S *hand, and the two go up to join* LUPITA *with* DON ANTONIO *in the center. He puts his arms about both of his children.)*

CARLOS *(singing)*.
"My lord Jesus, smile on me. . . ."

CROWD *(joining in)*.
And on the house where I was born. Amen."

While they are singing:
THE CURTAINS CLOSE

My Lord Jesus

The River Lures Me

O Moon, Can You Hear Me

SPRING FOR SURE

Book by Catherine McDonald

Music by Wilton Mason

A scene from *Spring for Sure,* by Catherine McDonald and Wilton Mason. Originally produced by The Carolina Playmakers in 1950.

THE AUTHOR: *Catherine McDonald*

A Tennessean, Catherine McDonald graduated from the University of Tennessee in 1931 and became a woman's page reporter on the *Chattanooga News-Free Press,* a family enterprise. Later she was to be associated with the American Red Cross as a recreation worker in a Navy hospital in Aukland, New Zealand.

Having been active from time to time in several educational and community theaters, mostly as an actress, Miss McDonald decided to try her hand at writing plays. So, she packed her typewriter and came to Chapel Hill, where she enrolled in some playwriting and related courses at The University of North Carolina. To earn a higher academic degree was of secondary importance to this talented young lady (writing plays always came first), but this, too, she accomplished with credit during her stay here.

At first, playwriting was a slow business. She had many disappointments. Her plays were not selected for production. Then, one day as she was flying over the Smoky Mountains on a short visit home to Chattanooga, she happened to read a news story in a Knoxville paper about a forced landing in that very area by a Park Avenue girl who was piloting her own plane. Kitty looked down at the scattered cabins below and thought what a sensation that flying machine must have caused when it came to an abrupt stop in some mountaineer's cow pasture. An idea for a play was born. Upon her return to Chapel Hill, she quickly roughed out the book and some lyrics for a "mountain musical."

Spring for Sure, with musical collaboration by Wilton Mason, is a warm, but comic treatment of a group of Tennessee hill people and their unsophisticated manner of living—based on a prior and inherited English folk culture. The principal characters are clearly defined, and the story is advanced not only through dialogue, but by song and dance—showing strong influence of the *Oklahoma!* technique in musical playwriting. It preceded by several years the slicker version of the American folk musical, *Lil' Abner,* and the farcical television serial, *Beverly Hillbillies.*

The original production was staged entirely by students as a studio production of The Carolina Playmakers in their campus theater. The announced purpose was to increase the Frederick H. Koch Memorial Fund. (Proff Koch had died several years previously, and the organization he had founded was eager to complete its outdoor theater and dedicate it to his memory.) The venture was a success, financially as well as artistically. Every performance was a sellout, and the run was brought to an end only because another show was scheduled to begin its rehearsal period.

By popular demand, *Spring for Sure* was revived two years later as a major season ticket attraction, this time still for a limited run, but in a larger campus auditorium. This was followed by two two-week tours (24 performances) in cities in North Carolina, South Carolina, Georgia, Alabama, Tennessee and Kentucky. In 1963, the Playmakers revived the play once more—this time being staged by The Junior Carolina Playmakers, in summer residence here; and over the past eighteen years, it has been produced by scores of educational and community theater groups over the country by direct permission of the authors. This is the first time, however, that the play, with its music, has appeared in print.

Catherine McDonald had one other play which came to life during her student career as a playwright at Chapel Hill. It was a one-acter, *Close Quarters,* staged on a New Plays bill by the Playmakers in 1948, and later presented by NBC for the "Chevrolet on Broadway" television series, out of New York.

At the present time, Miss McDonald is back in Chattanooga, writing a weekly feature column for the *Chattanooga News-Free Press,* gardening, and directing plays for the Senior Neighbor organization there.

THE COMPOSER: *Wilton Mason*

In the summer of 1948, a young teacher in the Music Department at The University of North Carolina in Chapel Hill, Wilton Mason, from Greenville, South Carolina, was laboring on his Ph.D. dissertation: the transcription of some eighteenth-century lute suites for harpsichord and piano. When he was asked by fellow-student Catherine McDonald, in the Department of Dramatic Art, to collaborate with her in writing a folk musical, he saw an opportunity to vary his work pattern in the hot months ahead. He read an early draft of the script, liked it, and almost immediately came up with the tune for some lyrics which contained the phrase "How can I get to be a slicker quicker?" From then on, he pleasurably divided his time between fulfilling the requirements of the doctoral program and readying *Spring for Sure* for its first production.

Working in the living theater was not a new experience for this multi-talented artist. During his undergraduate days here, and while he was earning his Master's degree, Willie had been very active with The Carolina Playmakers. He had played a role in Paul Green's *The House of Connelly* and had composed a musical score for the Forest Theatre production of *Macbeth*. Later he was to create the leading role of Abraham Lincoln in *Goodbye, Proud Earth,* and to be musical director for a number of Playmakers' Broadway-musicals in Memorial Hall.

From time to time, he has interrupted his distinguished career at The University of North Carolina by earning a diploma at the Juillard School in New York, by studying in Italy for a year on a Ford Foundation grant, and for work in the symphonic form, made possible by the Benjamin Composition Commission. One of the longest interruptions came during World War II, when for five years he served as an officer in the Army Medical Administrative Corps, ending up as adjutant of the Ninety-seventh General Hospital.

Among his various compositions are many songs ("Journey's End" was made popular by Helen Jepson in concerts throughout the country), a number of choral arrangements, and an opera, *Kingdom Come*. As a performing artist, he has appeared as piano soloist with the North Carolina Symphony Orchestra and given concerts in England, France, and Germany. Currently he takes time off from his academic commitments to serve as accompanying artist to about half the roster of the Metropolitan Opera.

In a department of the University long noted for its excellence in musicology, Professor Mason has always striven to build up an equal reputation in the creative and performing fields. He founded the Opera Workshop as a producing organization for the Department of Music, and for a number of years he has personally directed, staged, and conducted at least one standard operatic work each season.

Dr. Wilton Mason is now chairman of the Music Department at The University of North Carolina at Chapel Hill.

PREMIÈRE PLAYBILL CREDITS

Spring for Sure, by Catherine McDonald, with music by Wilton Mason, was originally produced by The Carolina Playmakers on May 4, 5, 6, and 7, 1950, in the Playmakers Theatre, Chapel Hill, North Carolina, under the direction of David Walter Morris. The lighting was by Richard Verigan, the settings by Hal Shadwell, the costumes by Jean Brown, and the choreography by John and Charlotte Lehman. Benjy Haywood was at the piano, and Frank Matthews at the organ.

THE CAST

CINDY HIGGINS	Doris Fowler
MAW HIGGINS	Lillian Prince
ZEKE	Bob Thomas
ZEB	Milton Bliss
ZACK	Jack Clinard
ZO	Richard Smith
REUBEN	Sam Greene
JOSH	John Lehman
LEE TOMPKINS	Richard Lewis
SETH	Donald Treat
IVADIE	Elizabeth Stoney
LURANIE	Barbara Young
MOSSY BELLE	Wilma Jones
VI'LET	Charlotte Lehman
JEREMIAH JONES	Lanier Davis
PAW HIGGINS	Nat White
MRS. CORNELIUS VAN DEVERE	Catherine Covington
MILLICENT, *her niece,*	Mary Jo McLean
PROFESSOR PERCY SHELLY BROWN	William Hardy
MATT	Gerald Honaker
CORETTA NORTON	Florabel Wolff
PERLAMINA	Virginia Young
PRIMROSE	Lee Noll
GENEVA	Elizabeth Kearney

COLUMBINE...................... Patricia Hole
NATH.......................... Brad Arrington
HUNTSMAN..................... Gerald Honaker
AIRLINES PILOT.................. Donald Treat

SCENE AND TIME

ACT ONE: Slippery Creek, Tennessee. An afternoon in May.
ACT TWO: The same. Dawn, the next day.

ACT ONE

The scene is a cove in the remotest part of the Tennessee-Carolina mountains. Partly visible, at upstage right, is a mountain cabin, weathered for a century and beautiful because of its age. Adjoining the raised front porch is a split-rail fence. Contrasting with this, is a half-completed cabin, downstage left, built of fresh, new logs. Clustered around each of the cabins is a mass of rhododendron, and accenting the waxy green leaves, now and then are branches of white dogwood, indicating that it is Maytime, when dogwood is in bloom. At upstage center left is a gray stone bluff. The stone is only two or three feet in height, as the audience sees it. But a backdrop of wide open sky, bordered by distant peaks of misty blue, indicates that back of that stone bluff is a sheer drop of hundreds of feet to the valley below.

It is mid-afternoon on a day in May, and on the porch of her old log cabin, MAW HIGGINS *is seated at a spinning wheel, really spinning. She is dressed in the calico Basque-waisted style of the pioneers, and in her mouth is a corncob pipe. On the fence, a-settin' and a-whittlin' are her four teen-age sons,* ZEKE, ZEB, ZACK, *and* ZO, *who are stair-stepped in size. Throughout the play, the boys "follow the leader," their motions being done in sequence.* CINDY, *a pretty mountain girl who is barefoot and wears an old-fashioned dress of yellow cotton and a sunbonnet tied loosely around her shoulders, is on her knees in front of the half-completed cabin, filling a flower pot with geraniums to put in the window.* JEREMIAH, *who makes a belated entrance during the first song, is* CINDY'S *beau. He is a handsome, broad-shouldered mountaineer, a "beautiful hunk of man" and the catch of the countryside. As the curtain opens,* CINDY *and her family are singing.*

CINDY.

Springtime looks so purty,
Here in Tennessee,
Every year the spring
Looks purtier to me;

This version of *Spring for Sure* follows very closely the script used for the second (tour) version, as produced by The Carolina Playmakers in 1952. Several characters listed on the première playbill and the "folk ballet," which came in the second act, have been eliminated.

ZEKE.
> Now that the dogwood trees are bustin' into bloom,

CINDY.
> Now that I want to be the blushin' bride of a handsome
>   groom;

ZACK.
> Things are lookin' purty
> Here among the hills

CINDY.
> All the woods are full
> Of yaller daffodils;'
> If there's a heav'n on earth, I reckon it would be

ALL.
> When it's springtime in Tennessee.

MAW.
> Giss it's time we's takin' spring tonic,
> Some quinine and sassafrass tea;

ZEB.
> When Maw gits to mixin' that quinine, boys,
> Hit's time for us to go and climb a tree.

CINDY.
> I don't need a tonic,
> Anyone can see,
> I'm glad to be alive,
> I'm happy as can be;
> Tonic is wasted on a girl who feels like me,
> When it's springtime in Tennessee.

The music continues as four MOUNTAINEERS *bring in a log and put it
on the log pile.*

A MOUNTAINEER *(speaking over the music).* Cindy, we brought you
another log fer your house-raisin'.

CINDY *(speaking).* That's mighty nice of you boys. Whar's
Jeremiah?

MOUNTAINEER *(speaking).* Jeremiah's been doin' the sawin'. He's on
the way.

Entering just after the boys are three mountain girls, IVADIE, CORETTA,
and GENEVA.

IVADIE *(speaking over the music).* And Cindy, we each baked a pie
fer tonight.

MAW *(taking the basket)*. What kind be they?

IVADIE. Dried apple.

MAW *(taking the basket to the porch)*. That makes fourteen apple. We'll jest stack 'em and slice 'em at the same time.

A MOUNTAINEER *(singing)*.
> [Bar 18 of music]
> This sunshine's mighty nice and warming,
> It's sure a spring day today;

GIRLS *(singing)*.
> [Bar 22 of music]
> That ground hog couldn't cast a shadder,
> With a spring like this upon the way.

The MOUNTAINEERS *encircle the girls, each taking a partner, and they do a dos-à-dos.*

MAW *(speaking over the music)*. Land sakes, don't start dancin' now. You'll be plumb wore out afore tonight.

The GIRLS *giggle. The* BOYS *lead them off, swinging hands.*

MAW. Wall, I see it's hand-holdin' time.

CINDY. Maw, ain't it nice of the folks hereabouts to come to our house-raisin' tonight? I betcha in about two more house-raisin's they'll have it ready fer me and Jeremiah.

MAW. Effen they do more house-raisin' than hell-raisin'.

(JEREMIAH'S *voice is heard singing offstage.*)

JEREMIAH.
> [Bar 3 of music]
> Spring is lookin' purty
> Here in Tennessee,
> Every year the spring looks purtier to me. . . .

He whistles with the music during the following dialogue and until his entrance.

CINDY *(speaking over the music)*. Thar's Jeremiah!

MAW. Zeke! Zeb! Zack! Zo! Git in the house. Git to hustlin'. Ever time Jeremiah sees thirteen kids in Cindy's family, he gits plumb outta the notion to pop the question.

ZEKE *(nodding to the boys)*. Follow the leader! *(The* FOUR BOYS *dance to* JEREMIAH'S *whistling, following the leader, up one step, down one step, up and into the house.)*

JEREMIAH *(entering singing).*
[Bar 18 of music]
All the woods are full of flowers,
Makes a feller feel mighty fancy-free;
I saw some baby-birds a-tryin' flyin',
And a-braggin' when they make the other tree.
CINDY *(singing).*
All the birds are singin',
JEREMIAH.
What are they singin' of?
CINDY.
Could be they're a-singin'
Because they're all in love,
JEREMIAH.
Maybe the singin's here, inside of you and me,
BOTH.
When it's springtime in Tennessee.

CINDY *gets a home-made broom from inside the half-completed cabin, and starts sweeping the log step.* JEREMIAH *goes over to the fence, starts whittling, then sees her sweeping.*

JEREMIAH *(watching* CINDY *sweep).* Cindy, what in tarnation air ye a-doin'?
CINDY. Oh, I come over here once a day and sweep off the step—it's sorta like playin' house, I reckon.
JEREMIAH. You're the fool-headedest gal in the hull Smoky Mountains.
CINDY *(sitting on the step and patting the place beside her).* Jeremiah, put up your whittlin' and come over here.

JEREMIAH *gets up, folds his knife and drops it.*

CINDY *(gasping).* Oh, Jeremiah, you dropped your knife!
JEREMIAH *(picking it up).* Well?
CINDY. That means a womern is a-comin'!
JEREMIAH. Oh, yeah?
CINDY *(admiring the cottage).* I think the cabin's lookin' extry good, don't you? I jest cayn't wait 'til they've got it done.
JEREMIAH *(walking on past her to upstage center, so he can look over the bluff).* And what heve we got when we got it done? Just a passel o' no'count mountain land.
CINDY. Jeremiah, you know somep'n? Tomorry, I'll be sixteen year old!

JEREMIAH. You're about *growed*.

CINDY. 'Bout growed! A'risin' sixteen! And not married yit! I'm an old maid!

JEREMIAH *(coming over to her)*. Cindy, I ben studyin' 'bout somep'n all day.

CINDY *(hopefully)*. Yes, Jeremiah, what?

JEREMIAH. Stayin' up hyar on this mountain is not my idy of livin'. These infernal hills of Judea, whar folks jest set around with fifty-leben kids, livin' on nuthin'! Wall, hyar's one that ain't gonna settle until he's got somep'n shore-nuff to settle on. I want a rich farm down thar in the river-bottom.

CINDY. Oh, Jeremiah, why don'tcha jest fergit that river-bottom farm. You'll niver git it.

JEREMIAH *(coming back)*. Yes, I will too. *(Pulling out an old worn purse.)* I got twenty-six dollars saved up. All I need is nine hundred and seventy-four.

CINDY. That's like sayin' all I need is the moon and stars. Why don't you jest put that twenty-six dollars in a few apple trees and be carntent?

JEREMIAH. A lot you know about farmin'! Twenty-six dollars wouldn't even begin. Besides, I want to do things BIG! And what I got in mind is a river-bottom farm!

CINDY. That river-bottom farm sounds fine, but a mountain cabin— jest like this one, with laurel blossoms 'round it—would be fine fer any couple that's thinkin' about gittin'—(JEREMIAH *is still absorbed.*) Jeremiah! You ain't ben hearin' a word I said.

They sing.

CINDY.
> Did you ever stop to think about the reason why a passel of
>   honeybees start to swarm?

JEREMIAH.
> No, marm.

CINDY.
> When you're walking through the clover and the harvest
>   moon is over you, whaddya think about?

JEREMIAH.
> My river-bottom farm.

CINDY.
> Did you ever think how nice 'twould be if you and me could
>   allus go everywhere arm in arm?

JEREMIAH.
> No, marm.

CINDY.

> When you see me dressed fer Sunday and a-dreamin' of
> that one day, what do you think about?

JEREMIAH.

> My river-bottom farm.

JEREMIAH.

> Now the only thing some folks think about, is a wedding ring
> for their hand.

CINDY.

> Well, they're not as bad as a stubborn man, who thinks of
> nuthin' but land.

CINDY.

> When you're freezin' in your feather bed on winter nights,
> you know instead that you could be warm,

JEREMIAH.

> Please, *marm!*

CINDY.

> When you drive me to distraction by your lack of any action,
> what are you thinkin' of—as if I didn't know?

BOTH.

> That river-bottom farm!

CINDY *(walking away and speaking)*. Wonder who that womern is?

JEREMIAH. What womern?

CINDY. The one that's a-comin'! You dropped your knife, didn't you?

Suddenly there is the SOUND OF AN AIRPLANE, swooping down, and a BIG CRASH.

CINDY *(going into* JEREMIAH'S *arms)*. Jeremiah! What wuz that?

JEREMIAH. I don't know. Don't see nuthin'. Musta ben a clap of thunder. *(The proximity of* CINDY *in his arms gets him. He continues to hold her.)* Cindy, if—I—uh—would you—

CINDY *(hopefully)*. Yes, Jeremiah?

JEREMIAH *(looking at her tenderly)*. If I only had nine hundred and seventy-four dollars, do you know what I would do with it?

CINDY *(softly, eagerly)*. No, Jeremiah, what?

JEREMIAH *(standing and smacking his fist into his hand)*. I'd—I'd buy a river-bottom farm!

MAW *(coming out on front porch with a wooden waterbucket in her hand)*. Jeremiah, would you mind goin' to the spring afore you leave? I heerd a crash of thunder. Hit must be goin' ter rain.

JEREMIAH. Why, yessum. I'll be back. *(He goes off whistling "River-bottom Farm.")*

MAW. Has he named it to you yit?

CINDY. Naw. Here the folks got the cabin fer me and Jeremiah half-done, thinkin' he wuz all ready to name the day, and he ain't named nothin'!

MAW. Wall, your Paw'll be back from the clearin' afore long. Mabbe he'll name it to him.

CINDY *(singing to* JEREMIAH, *who is offstage).*
> When you're freezin' in your feather bed on winter nights, you know instead that you could be warm,
> So warm,
> When you drive me to distraction by your lack of any action, what are you thinkin' of—
> As if I didn't know!

CINDY, *and* JEREMIAH *echoing offstage.*
> That river-bottom farm!

Entering with PAW HIGGINS are three travelers, MRS. VAN DEVERE, *her niece,* MILLICENT, *and the* PROFESSOR. *The two ladies are fashionably dressed for a luncheon, with smart frocks, wraps of mink and sable, and hats that are both awful and awfully expensive. The* PROFESSOR *is dressed in dapper attire, including a waistcoat; and as a final touch to his sartorial splendor, there is a red carnation in the buttonhole of his sports coat.*

PAW. Cindy, whar's yer Maw? *(Calling.)* Maw! Hyar's furriners!

MAW *(coming out on the porch).* Whar?

PAW. Hyar! (CINDY *and* MAW *stare at the foreigners.)* Mabbe you kin make head or tail outa whut they're a-sayin'. I cayn't.

MRS. VAN DEVERE. I'm Mrs. Van Devere, the third, of New York City—*(Gasping for breath.)*—Oh, dear, I'm so out of breath from that steep climb—my niece, Millicent—Professor Percy Shelly Brown. Our aeroplane just crashed nearby. Fortunately, no one was injured— the gin *(Taking a bottle from her bag, and holding it up.)* for the Martinis didn't even break!—but it *was* a forced landing, and we need help.

CINDY, MAW, *and* PAW *make no comment. They only stare, and stare hard.* MILLICENT *begins straightening her hat, and brushing herself off.*

PROFESSOR. Let me try. How do you do? Our plane crashed. We were en route to Natchez, Mississippi, where I was to give a lecture before the Garden Club. This young lady, in piloting the plane, got off the course, became lost over these mountain peaks. In circling around, we quite depleted our fuel supply.

There is no comment; only stares.

MRS. VAN DEVERE. Perhaps they didn't hear. I say, I'm Mrs. Van Devere and this is my niece—

MILLICENT *(impatiently)*. Oh, Aunt Phyllis! Let me handle this. *(To* PAW, *speaking rapidly.)* Will you phone the nearest available airport to send four experienced mechanics to repair the splintered propeller of an airplane. No, on second thought, just phone Mr. Cornelius Van Devere, Park Avenue, New York City, and tell him to send another plane for us. Hurry, and while you're phoning, I'd like a clothes brush, please. *(She begins brushing herself off. There is complete silence, only stares. After a pause, she looks up, surprised.)* Oh, I give up. *(To* CINDY.*)* Will *you* telephone Mr. Cornelius Van Devere, Park Avenue—

PAW *(pantomiming the ringing of an old phone)*. Did you say somethin' 'bout a telephone? One of them things you ring?

MILLICENT *(pantomiming the dialing of a modern phone)*. Yes. Telephone, telephone. Hurry, please. I'm late for a dinner date. *(She gets out a lipstick and starts applying it.)*

PAW. Ain't no telephone hyar-abouts.

MILLICENT. No telephone? What's the name of this place?

PAW. This yere's Slippery Creek.

PROFESSOR *(looking around)*. A beautiful spot! Somewhere in the Southern Appalachians, I surmise. A remote spot.

MILLICENT. Remote! It isn't even on the map.

PROFESSOR. Beautifully remote. Away from cities, crowds, confusion!

MILLICENT. And telephones!

PROFESSOR. How far is it to Asheville or Knoxville?

PAW. Dunno. Ain't niver been thar.

MRS. VAN DEVERE *(gasping)*. Look, Professor! Look at that spinning wheel! It's actually being used!

PROFESSOR *(dashing around and looking over the cabin)*. This spot is amazing. Closed in by these mountain peaks, they're livin in the past, like the pioneer families of old. A hundred years in the past! It's as if Daniel Boone—

MILLICENT *(impatiently)*. My date is not with Daniel Boone! *(To* PAW.*)* Where is the nearest telephone?

PAW. I saw one wunst down in the valley at New Hope.

MILLICENT. And how far is New Hope?

PAW. Oh—a whoop and a holler away.

MRS. VAN DEVERE. How far is that?

PAW. 'Bout sixty mile.

MILLICENT. Sixty miles!

MRS. VAN DEVERE *(timidly)*. Is there any place just a *whoop* away?

PAW *(reflecting)*. Giss not.

MRS. VAN DEVERE *(to PAW)*. Would you go to New Hope for us?

PAW *(reflecting)*. Don't rightly know as I kin.

MRS. VAN DEVERE. Why not?

PAW. Don't want to. *(There is a silent pause for the New Yorkers to recover from the shock.)* You kin have my mule and wagon.

MILLICENT. Then let's start. Harness the mule, Professor!

PAW *gives harness to the* PROFESSOR.

PROFESSOR *(harness in hand)*. Ah! Be quiet! *(He whistles, and there is a whistled answer.)* There's the woodthrush, the Hylocichla mustelina, singing to his mate. She differs from other species in that her underparts are white, and she's rather olive on the rump.

MAW. She is?

MRS. VAN DEVERE *(explaining)*. Our dear Professor Brown gives lantern slide lectures on bird calls. He was to have appeared today at my Garden Club luncheon in Natchez.

PROFESSOR *(listening)*. Be quiet! Be quiet! This is indeed the mating season. *(Again listening.)* There's our friend, the Southern robin, the Turdus migratorius. *(He whistles a wolf call and gets a louder wolf call answer.* CORETTA *enters, as he turns to explain to* MAW.*)* Her tail is somewhat larger.

MAW *(incredulous)*. It is for a fact, 'cause that ain't no robin. That's Coretta Norton!

CORETTA *(crossing the downstage "road" from left to right, but staring over her shoulder the entire time until she is out of sight)*. Howdy.

MAW. Howdy.

CORETTA, *a buxom blonde, is simple, with beautiful curves, and the* PROFESSOR, *in a trance, starts down the road, following her and holding out the harness.*

PROFESSOR. Ah! The simple beauties of nature!

MILLICENT *(watching him start toward* CORETTA*)*. I said to harness the *mule*, Professor!

PROFESSOR *(doing a double-take)*. Oh, yes. *(He starts in the direction of* PAW, *but gives a longing backward look toward* CORETTA.) Why not spend the night here?

MAW. Wall, now, we'd be mighty proud to hev you. Got plenty of chicken and country ham.

The FOUR BOYS *come out of the back of the house, staring. Soon there is a crowd of mountaineers standing in a straight row and staring. They turn their heads from one conversation to another, like spectators watching a tennis match, throughout the scene.*

MRS. VAN DEVERE. We should hate to impose. Your cabin seems rather small—and there are three of us.

MAW. Three? Shecks, as many as we got here, that ain't a spit in the bucket. Paw and I will sleep in the loft with the kids. *(With an expansive gesture.)* The place is yourn! Cindy, go in and tidy up. (CINDY *goes in the house, staring back over her shoulder.)* And 'sides, you'll be here for the house-raisin' tonight!

MRS. VAN DEVERE. House-raisin'? What is that?

MAW. Wall, 'round hyar—*(She sees* CORETTA *coming back with a cup in her hand.)* Whut *you* want, Coretta?

CORETTA. Want to borry sody.

MAW. Sody! I happen to know you got plenty—you don't hev to borry sody to look at them folks, jest stand there and stare! *(After a pause.)* 'Round hyar, when you want a cabin built, like thatten fer Cindy and Jeremiah *(Pointing to the half-completed cabin.)*—you jest git the logs ready, and then you *in*vite the neighbor-folks to help raise it.

MRS. VAN DEVERE. How quaint! I should like to see one.

PROFESSOR. So should I!

MILLICENT. Well, I wouldn't! I have a dinner date! *(She starts lighting a cigarette and the crowd presses in closer and closer in order to see her.* MILLICENT *becomes uncomfortable as they look her up and down.)* Do you want to speak to someone? *(The mountaineers say nothing. They stare.)* Can I help you?

A MOUNTAINEER. Jest lookin'.

MILLICENT *(pleading).* Professor, where is the mule?

PAW. You gotta git him ketched.

PROFESSOR *(turning to go, suddenly stops).* That word, ketched. That's Anglo-Saxon! I've been fascinated by the dialect I've heard. Do you realize, my dear Mrs. Van Devere, that these people are of the purest old English blood and speak seventeenth century—

MILLICENT. For heaven's sake, Professor!

PROFESSOR. Oh, yes, I'm leaving. *(Looking at the harness.)*—as soon as I can figure out this harness. *(He starts trying to figure it out.)*

MRS. VAN DEVERE *(to* PAW*).* How long will it take to go to New Hope by—*(Wincing.)*—by wagon?

PAW. 'Bout three day.

MILLICENT. Three days! *(Walking to the bluff, upstage.)* But the valley is just down there, isn't it?

PAW. Yep, and New Hope's just below us. But that thar's a bluff called Devil's Drop—

MILLICENT *looks over and leaps back.*

MILLICENT. Oh!

PAW. —And halfway down it is Slippery Creek Falls. In a wagon, you gotta go back and beyanst the mountain and come up the valley.

PROFESSOR *(hanging the harness around his neck and taking out a pencil and notebook).* In which direction do we go?

PAW. Wall, you drive down the creek bed to Three Pine Point—

PROFESSOR *(writing).* Three Pine Point. That should be easy to locate—three pines.

PAW. Yeah. 'Cept they ben cut down.

PROFESSOR *(jotting notes).* Continue.

PAW. Then you sorta zigzag until you come to Rattlesnake Branch.

MRS. VAN DEVERE *(gasping).* Rattlesnakes!

PAW. Yep. Right snakey thar. Now, effen you push on a spell to Tater Knob—

PROFESSOR *(writing).* Effen you push on a spell to Tater Knob—yes? And then?

PAW. Then, you know you done come the wrong way. Turn back three mile to the fork and go 'round the bluff. That wagon trail's right narrow thar. The wagon sorta leans over, so the three of you better shift all your weight to the high part of the wagon bed, and hold on!

MRS. VAN DEVERE. We'll tumble over the bluff!

PAW. Don't worry 'bout it none ef you do. I ben wantin' to git rid of that mule anyway. And effen you do git around the bluff, that's when you take the trail down the mountain.

MRS. VAN DEVERE. I know we'll get lost!

PAW. Naw, you cayn't git lost there, 'cause you git to goin' so fast downhill, you cayn't turn off. You'll go spang down to the foot of the mountain fer sure, 'cause ain't nuthin' goin' to stop you.

MRS. VAN DEVERE. Oh, dear! Millicent, do you think it's advisable?

MILLICENT. It's better than staying here forever. At least, we'll have some excitement. *(She sinks down on the bench.)* I've never been so bored!

JEREMIAH'S *voice is heard off-stage. He is singing an old English ballad.*

JEREMIAH.
> I found my own true love
> On a summer morning;
> The wind was blowing
> All about her face.

MILLICENT *(raising up suddenly and speaking above the song)*. Who is that?

PAW. That's Jeremiah. He lives over yan in the mill.

PROFESSOR. Listen, listen! That is an old Elizabethan ballad. How exciting!

JEREMIAH *(singing)*.
> And where she set her foot
> On the grassy—

JEREMIAH *appears with a bucket of water. He stops singing when he sees the strangers. He stares, then crosses to* CINDY *who had come out on the porch as soon as she heard his voice.*

JEREMIAH *(handing the bucket of water to* CINDY.*)* Cindy, hyar's the water. *(In whisper.)* Who's they?

CINDY. Furriners. Fur-piece furrin'. New York!

CINDY *takes the bucket of water into the house.* JEREMIAH, *bashful and frightened, starts to leave.*

JEREMIAH. Giss I'll be goin'.

PROFESSOR *(rushing to him)*. My boy, my boy, where did you learn that song!

JEREMIAH. It's an old-timey song. Granny larned it to me.

PROFESSOR. It is old indeed. It's an Elizabethan ballad. To think that these mountains have been so isolated that a ballad of the sixteenth century has been preserved. It's amazing! Sing all of it, would you?

JEREMIAH *(surprised)*. Wall, effen you want me to—

CINDY *has returned to the porch.* JEREMIAH *takes her hand and leads her downstage. He sings the "Old Ballad" to her.*

JEREMIAH.

>I found my own true love
>On a summer morning;
>The wind was blowing
>All about her face.
>And where she set her foot
>On the grassy hillside,
>The blades of grass
>Showed never a trace.
>She wore a yellow dress
>With flowers on it,
>She had a ribbon of silk
>To tie her hair;
>Although I've looked and looked
>The whole world over,
>I've never found her match
>As she stood there.
>I lost my own true love
>On a winter evening;
>The wind blew cold
>All about her face;
>Now when I walk abroad
>On a summer morning,
>I care not if there's sun
>Or cloud above;
>I care not what the day
>Or what the weather,
>Because I walk without
>My own true love.

The PROFESSOR *leads the applause.* JEREMIAH, *bashful, starts to leave.*
I'll be goin'—

MILLICENT. Don't go. Where did you learn to sing like that?

JEREMIAH. I allus sung.

MILLICENT *(to herself, as she looks over his physique).* These mountains may not be so dull after all!

JEREMIAH. Whadja say, marm?

MILLICENT. I was just thinking. We *had* better stay here overnight, Aunt Phyllis. Sixty miles in that wagon, rattlesnakes, and traveling at night, around the bluff—

MRS. VAN DEVERE *(shuddering)*. Oh, that bluff.

MILLICENT. It's really not advisable, is it, Professor?

The PROFESSOR *has worked with the harness until he is now completely entangled in it.*

PROFESSOR *(in despair)*. Indeed, it isn't.

MRS. VAN DEVERE. I'm so glad you've decided to be sensible, Millicent.

MILLICENT *(shrugging)*. It's the only thing to do.

MAW. Wall, now, we're glad to hev you. *(To the boys.)* Zeke, Zeb, Zack, Zo. Git stovewood. Git a chicken. Got company. Paw—go help 'em.

MRS. VAN DEVERE. If we won't be too much trouble—

MAW. Law, no. Think you're doin' the right thing—'cause hit's a-fixin' to rain. I heerd a crash of thunder a while back.

PAW *(leaving)*. Crash of thunder! That wuz them. A flyin' machine!

JEREMIAH. A flyin' machine?

PAW. Yep, hit landed in my new pastur. Hit like to a-landed on *me*.

JEREMIAH. One of them flyin' machines that whiz over here ever day? *(To* MILLICENT.*)* Do you live in it?

MILLICENT *(amused)*. Partly. Most of the time I live in a penthouse on Park Avenue, New York City.

A MOUNTAINEER *(to the* CROWD*)*. Come on, let's go see it.

CORETTA. Naw, might miss somep'n.

The CROWD *rushes off, all but* CORETTA.

JEREMIAH. A flyin' machine! I gotta see that. *(He starts off.)*

MILLICENT *(stopping him and taking him .by the arm)*. Wait—*I'll* show it to you.

JEREMIAH *(surprised)*. Thankee, marm.

MRS. VAN DEVERE. I'm glad we're staying. I want to see that picturesque old mill.

PROFESSOR *(out of the harness by now)*. And I'm going to begin recording native speech. Where are my notebooks? *(He pulls one out of his pocket.)* I've just decided to write a book on Anglo-Saxon. *(He sits down on the bench and starts scribbling in his notebook.)*

MILLICENT *(As she takes* JEREMIAH *off in the direction of the plane)*. What did you say your name is?

JEREMIAH. Jeremiah Jones.

MILLICENT *(seductively)*. Then come along—Jerry! *(They exit.)*

MRS. VAN DEVERE *(pointing off left)*. Whose old mill is that?

MAW. That's Jeremiah's.

MRS. VAN DEVERE. It's charming! How old do you suppose it is?

MAW. I dunno. Hit belonged to Jeremiah's paw afore him, his paw afore him,—and let's see, now—wall, his paw afore him, his paw afore him, his paw—

MRS. VAN DEVERE *(having counted on her fingers)*. But that's five generations. That goes back to Revolutionary days. Do you think he would mind if I went over and looked around?

MAW. Law, no. Hit's the tore-downdest place. I'd go with you, but I got to git ready for the house-raisin' frolic.

MRS. VAN DEVERE. You people have always lived in these mountains, haven't you?

MAW. As fur as I know. My great-grandpaw fit the Tory British at Kings Mountain.

MRS. VAN DEVERE. Then you could be a member of the D.A.R.!

MAW *(taking a puff from her pipe)*. Whut's that?

MRS. VAN DEVERE. Daughters of the American Revolution.

MAW. Daughters, huh? Borned on the right side of the bedkiver?

MRS. VAN DEVERE. I beg your pardon?

MAW. Air they *decent?*

MRS. VAN DEVERE. Oh, yes, yes, it's quite an honor to belong.

MAW *(pleading)*. Now, don't be givin' em my name too hasty. I'll study 'bout it. What do they do?

MRS. VAN DEVERE. They keep tracing their ancestry.

MAW. You mean to find out who daddied *them* and who daddied *him*—

MRS. VAN DEVERE *(as she leaves for the mill)*. Yes. All the way back. *(She exits.)*

MAW *(to herself)*. All the way back. Whew! Purty resky, keepin' tab on that many American men! *(She starts in the house.)* Jest foller that thar path and hit'll take you to the mill.

PROFESSOR. Oh, Mrs.—

MAW. Higgins.

PROFESSOR. Mrs. Higgins, I am beginning my questionnaires. I hope you will be the first to help me. If you'll just begin talking—

MAW *(brushing past him)*. A-law, I'm busy. You'll have to git somebody else. *(She goes in the house.)*

PROFESSOR *(writing in his notebook)*. Anglo-Saxon in the Appalachians. There. Good title, I think. *(He looks about him and sees* CORETTA*).* Ah! My dear little girl! Woud you please come here and help me?

CORETTA *(coming toward him, but cautiously)*. Whatcha want me to do?

PROFESSOR. I wish to record some of your native speech.

CORETTA. Whadja say?

PROFESSOR. Just sit down. *(She does.)* Now, begin talking. *(He has notebook in hand and pencil poised.)* I wish to record your every word. Don't be self-conscious. Just let the conversation flow as it will. Say something.

CORETTA *(wide-eyed)*. Sech as whut?

PROFESSOR. Splendid! *Sech* for *such,* a true Elizabethan expression. Do you know it was used by the queen mother of Henry VII? Splendid, my girl!

CORETTA *(pleased as Punch)*. Twarn't nuthin'.

PROFESSOR. Twarn't. *(Jotting it down.)* We find that in Chaucer. There also is the double negative. It's amazing. Anglo-Saxon preserved. Those are just the expressions I want. Keep talking, don't stop, just let yourself go!

CORETTA *(clutching onto the bench, thoroughly frightened)*. I'm afeared.

PROFESSOR. *Afeared.* Shakespeare. In *Hamlet* are those very same words. I'm afeared you make a wanton of me.

CORETTA. That's jest whut I wuz afeared of.

PROFESSOR. Keep talking. I'm recording it. Remember that scholars throughout the land will read what you say.

CORETTA *starts to speak, but thinks better of it. The* PROFESSOR *motions for her to go ahead, encouraging and expectant.*

PROFESSOR. Go ahead.

CORETTA *starts to speak, but thinks better of it.*

CORETTA *(rising)*. I gotta be a-moseyin'.

PROFESSOR. Can't you say something more?

CORETTA. No. Shore 'nuff, I gotta go on over to the mill.

PROFESSOR. Then I'll come along and complete my questionnaire. *(They start out.)* Now, how can I get you to say something else? I know! Tell me all about yourself, my dear. How did you get here?

CORETTA. I wuz borned.

PROFESSOR. *Borned?* Good, I'm pleased. *(Jotting it down.)* B-O-R-N-*E-D,* borned. Elizabethan, but who? Lord Bacon?

CORETTA. Maw niver said. *(And they hurry out.)*

JEREMIAH *is heard whistling "Springtime in Tennessee" off-stage. He and* MILLICENT *appear very shortly. He is loaded with bags, two suitcases, a hatbox and a cosmetics case.*

CINDY *(hearing* JEREMIAH'S *whistle, flies out of the house).* Thar's Jeremiah! *(She sees* MILLICENT *with him and is taken aback.)* Oh, that city gal's with him.

JEREMIAH *(coming in).* Cindy! You ought to see Miss Park Avenoo's flyin' machine. It's big as a barn! *(He sets the luggage on the steps.)*

MILLICENT. Thanks for carrying those heavy bags, Jerry. You're so sweet.

JEREMIAH *(pleased).* Glad to obleege.

MILLICENT. You handle them so easily. You must be strong. *(She strokes his arm.)*

JEREMIAH *(still more pleased).* Yessum. Right strong. I'll go back for the otherns. *(He exits, whistling "Springtime in Tennessee.")*

CINDY. Are all them suitcases yourn?

MILLICENT. Most of them.

CINDY. All full of clothes that's store-bought?

MILLICENT *(amused).* Yes. Want to try them on?

CINDY. Could I? Oh, no, I giss I'd better not.

MILLICENT *(shrugging).* Go ahead. Choose something for the party tonight.

CINDY. Do you mean it fer true? *(She opens a bag.)* Look*ee!* Taffety and lace! Look how many! And look how fancy! Whur would you wear a fancy dress like thatten?

MILLICENT. I wore it last night. *(She yawns.)* Richard took me to the Stork Club.

CINDY *(to herself).* Stork? They must hev the same trouble we'uns do. *(Then, holding up a black dress to* MILLICENT.) That's too bad. You must hev went to a funeral.

MILLICENT. A funeral? To the opera, with Prince Hubert—same thing.

CINDY. And look at that! Ivoree satin. That's purty. Where did you wear thatten?

MILLICENT. Week-end houseparty with Bill.

CINDY. A party lastin' a hull weekend. That *shore* musta been an affair.

MILLICENT *(looking startled).* Not necessarily.

CINDY. Too bad you broke yer airplane and cayn't git back up there.

MILLICENT. Oh, I'm not too bored. That little Jerry is sweet, isn't he? He's vahstly amusing.

CINDY. Yeah. Right vahstly.

MILLICENT. He's so—so virile. Such a contrast to Tucker.

CINDY. Who's Tucker?

MILLICENT. Tucker Beaumont. Stuffy, bored, and boresome. An old family. Main Line. Tucker is at the end of the line.

CINDY. Sorta—tuckered out? Just think, Prince Hubert, Richard, Bill—and now Tuckered. Why do you want so many fellers?

MILLICENT *sings "It's a Matter of Taste."*

MILLICENT.

> It's a matter of taste,
> And my taste is so changeable,
> If my love is misplaced,
> Then a change is arrangeable.
> Each time I'm sure I've got the real thing,
> I find it's suddenly spring, and I want a last fling,
> And whadda ya know—there I go!
> It's a matter of taste,
> And my heart is a gadabout;
> I can never be sure
> Just which one I am mad about;
> I can't see the fun
> Of concentratin' on one
> And letting all the rest go to waste;
> So where men are concerned,
> It's a matter of taste.

The music continues and MILLICENT *begins dancing, first around, then on the bench, then up the steps.*

CINDY *(watching, entranced).* Where'd you learn to dance like that?

MILLICENT. I've been taking dancing lessons since the age of six.

JEREMIAH *arrives with the other bags and watches her dance, impressed.*

JEREMIAH. Cindy, watch Miss Park Avenue dance!

MILLICENT *finishes her number by dancing along the top log of the fence with all the grace of a ballerina. Then she holds out her arms to* JEREMIAH.

MILLICENT. Help me down. *(She comes down in* JEREMIAH'S *arms, looking most seductive in the process.)*

JEREMIAH *(confused).* You—you're light as a feather.

MILLICENT *(to* JEREMIAH, *pointing off left).* Is that a mountain stream over there?

JEREMIAH. The creek? Yess'um. That goes by my mill.

MILLICENT. I've always wanted to go wading. (*To* CINDY.) Do you know I've never gone wading? I think I shall.

JEREMIAH. Better be keerful, ma'am. That's Slippery Creek. You can slip easy on them mossy stones.

MILLICENT. Why don't you come along—and show me where all those dangerous places are.

JEREMIAH. Well'um. Maybe I'd better.

CINDY *looks after them with a woebegone look.* MAW *comes out on the porch with a pan of potatoes to peel.* CINDY *starts investigating the suitcases.*

MAW *(calling out).* Zeke, Zeb, Zack, Zo!

The FOUR BOYS *come from the upstage side of the house.*

ZEKE. Yes, maw.

MAW. Start totin' buckets of water to the kitchen washtub. Them city folks'll want to warsh up afore the frolic.

ZEKE *(starting to count out, beginning with himself).* O-u-t spells out, you old dirty dishrag—*(It comes out on him.)*—I started wrong—*(Beginning again.)*—O-u

MAW. No use countin' out. They'll want all four buckets!

ZEKE *(getting four buckets from the porch as the boys line up in single file to go to the spring).* Four buckets fer jest three people! Dadburn!

ZACK. Dadblast!

ZEB. Dadblame!

ZO *(in a deep voice).* Damn! *(They march out.)*

MAW. Cindy, whatcha doin' with that city gal's clothes?

CINDY. She said I could pick out a dress for the doin's tonight. *(Holding one up.)* Look, Maw!

MAW. Git away from them fancy frills! Come here and give me a hand with this tater-peelin'.

CINDY *puts down the dress reluctantly and goes up on porch to help with potato-peeling.*

CINDY. Oh, Maw! I gotta uneasy feelin' that Miss Park Avenue has set her cap for Jeremiah.

MAW. Jeremiah? He won't pay her no mind.

CINDY. I dunno, Maw. She's cagy and full of worldly wisement. She knows how to cast her fishin'-line 'round kinda keerless-like, and Jeremiah is a-swallowin' all the bait she puts on the hook, the big ten-toed sucker!

MAW. Don't worry. You know how slow Jeremiah is.

CINDY. Yeah, but she ain't. Right now, she's snaked him into goin' wadin' with her in Slippery Creek. Effen she slips—and she'll see to it that she does—he'll catch her around the waist, and then she'll giggle, and then he'll giggle, and then she'll find a place too deep fer jest lil' ole her, and then he'll reach down and carry her across. The hussy!

MAW. How do you know?

CINDY. I know all right. *(Smiling in remembrance.)* I've allus found that Jeremiah's right handy when it comes to crossin' a creek. *(Hearing* MILLICENT's *feminine laughter ringing out over the hills, followed by the hearty laugh of* JEREMIAH.) Oh! *(She goes over to the clothes with grim determination.)* Wonder how she gets inta them funny clothes when she's a'aimin' to lure a man. *(Looking into the cosmetics case.)* Look, maw! Hyar's some of that red stick she puts on her lips. And look at that face-whitenin'. *(She looks up, sees several of her girlfriends coming up from the road, down right, and calls to them.)* Ivadie! Pearlamina! Mossy Belle! Come yar! And look, maw, she don't even wear her own eyelashes.

MAW. Git away from them contraptions of the devil.

CINDY *picks up a mirror and starts putting on a large blob of lipstick. Five girls arrive—*IVADIE, LURANIE, GENEVA, PEARLAMINA, and MOSSY BELLE.

IVADIE. Lookee!

PEARLAMINA. Lookee yander!

MOSSY BELLE. Lookee thar!

IVADIE. Cindy, whar air you a-doin'?

CINDY. Oh, Ivadie! You ain't niver seen nothin' like these clothes. They's all store-bought. And that Miss Park Avenoo said we could wear 'em to the frolic tonight.

IVADIE. She did?

MAW. Foolish virgins—campin' with the Philistines.

CINDY. I'm gonna try one on.

MAW *(going down to* CINDY). Git away from her stuff, I tell you.

She and CINDY *sing "A Gingham Dress."*

MAW *(singing).*
> A gal could never learn nothin' good
> From a bold piece of trash like her.

CINDY *(looking in the suitcase).*
> You're wrong there, maw, there's plenty to learn
> And that's what I'm here fer.

MAW.
> She's up to no good, that's plain to see,
> And besides all that, she's as brazen as can be.

CINDY *(holding up a dress to her).*
> Well, if she's what you mean by a city slicker,
> How do you get to be slicker quicker?
> A gingham dress is all very well
> As long as you're on the farm.

MAW.
> And button-up shoes and sensible stockin's
> Never done no gal harm.

CINDY.
> But as long as I keep my hair in a braid
> And wear such sensible clothes,
> As long as my lips ain't red like hers
> And my slip occasionally shows,
> I know romance will pass me by.

(CINDY *holds up a slinky black dress to her.)*

MAW.
> Now, it ain't silky drape as much as the shape
> That will turn a feller's head.
> Jest watch a man go after calico
> Ef the figger what's in it ain't bad.
> Now them shined up gals may glitter like brass,
> But all what glitters ain't gold;

CINDY *(dropping the satin and pointing to her calico).*
> And what does it matter as long as they glitter
> While this gold just sets and gets old.
> I know romance will pass me by.

CINDY *(speaking).* I'm gonna git all glitterin'—jest like her.

MAW *(going back to her potato-peeling).* Humph!

As the GIRLS *cluster around the suitcase,* CINDY *gets in back of them and changes her own dress for a black satin dress, one that is caught together at the front for a quick change. It is slinky, with a plunging neckline and a skirt that is slit up the front, looking very strange with* CINDY'S *bare feet.*

PEARLAMINA *(holding up a dress)*. Look, Ivadie. This dress jest has one shoulder. Musta ran outa cloth.

IVADIE *(choosing another dress)*. This dress ain't got *no* shoulders. Wonder how it's helt up?

GENEVA *(displaying another)*. Look at this dress *(She gasps.)* Hits plumb scandlous! I'd be ashamed if I wuz her. Tsk! Tsk! Ain't it sin-ful-l-l! *(Greedily.)* I'll take thissen.

PEARLAMINA. Ivadie, whaddya suppose these little bottles are? *(She holds up a case of perfumes.)* They smell awful purty! *(She sniffs.)*

IVADIE *(taking them and sniffing)*. Must be love potions—betcha them New Yorkers has rigged up all kinds of love potions we ain't even thought of mixin'. Look at the name—*Beau-catcher!*

LURANIE. Lookee thar. *My Love!*

PEARLAMINA. Lookee yander! *My Sin!*

GENEVA *(pointing to a label)*. Look on this nightgown! Sex! Sex-Fifth Avenoo!

CINDY *emerges dressed, with one long black eyelash on her right eye. She swaggers up and down in exact imitation of* MILLICENT.

IVADIE *(gasping)*. Cin-dee Hig-g-ins!

MAW. I niver seed such foolishness.

CINDY *(imitating MILLICENT)*. Prince Hubert, wouldst fetch me my ivory fan? *(She winks three times with the long eyelash, and sings without accompaniment.)*

> It's a matter of taste,
> And my taste is so changeable,
> If my love—

She stops as she sees MILLICENT *and* JEREMIAH. MILLICENT *is being carried by* JEREMIAH, *her bare feet dangling. She is carrying a large bouquet of violets, and there is a large cluster of crab apple blossoms in her hair.*

CINDY. Why, Jeremiah! Look at you!

JEREMIAH *(dumping MILLICENT)*. Cindy! Look at you! Lordamercy, ef you don't look a sight! Go on in the house and take off that riggin'— yeah, and warsh that coal soot off yer eyes!

CINDY *(crushed)*. Yes, Jeremiah. *(She starts in the house.)*

JEREMIAH. I'll be back, Miss Mel'cint.

MILLICENT. All right. And thank you, Jerry, for picking these violets.

CINDY *sees the violets and is even more crushed.*

JEREMIAH *(looking at* CINDY *again).* Lordamercy! *(He exits.)*

GENEVA *(to* MILLICENT*).* Why you got them apple blossoms in your hair?

MILLICENT. In New York, girls often wear flowers in their hair.

GENEVA. Say they do? *(In a stage whisper to* IVADIE.) Ivadie, dija hear that?

The FOUR BOYS *come out on the porch with empty buckets. They put them up and get ready to sit down on the steps.*

ZEKE. Miss Park Avenoo, we brung you some warter to warsh. We toted four hull buckets. We toted it a fur piece.

MILLICENT. Thank you. *(To herself.)* Only four buckets. That won't half-fill a bathtub. Oh, boys! Do you mind an extra trip?

MILLICENT *goes in the house. The* FOUR BOYS *pick up the buckets and march in a single file back in the direction of the spring.*

ZEKE *(muttering).* Eight buckets!

ZEB. And all fer herself!

ZACK. Anybawdy who needs eight buckets of warter to warsh!

ZO. She must be a-aimin' to go 'till Chrestmas!

CORETTA *enters. She is carrying a flat, hand-woven basket, jammed full of stuff.*

IVADIE. Hey, Coretta, you want some store-bought clothes to wear to the frolic? They's new.

CORETTA. No, I don't want nuthin' that's *new. (Holding up her basket.)* I'm collecting *old* stuff. I want somep'n that's *quaint.*

IVADIE. Whatever fer?

CORETTA *(setting her basket on the steps).* I'm gonna set up a—a— what did she say?—a souv'nir stand.

The FOUR BOYS *appear with their buckets and watch her, amazed.*

GENEVA. Whaddya mean, souv'nirs?

CORETTA. I ben talkin' to thet New York lady, Miz Van Devere, over yan at the mill, and *she says* they's a Smoky Mountin' Natio*nill* Park right chere clost by, and *she says* they's people in autymobiles that ride by and look. Jest look! And *she says* them tourists will buy anything—

coffee grinders, old cracked plates, 'cause they's rustic. They is—whad she say?—they's *Americana*. And *she says* I'm Americana.

MAW *(sarcastically)*. Why?

CORETTA. 'Cause I'm simple.

MAW. We ben knowin' that all along.

CORETTA sings *"Thar's Gold in Them Thar Hills."*

CORETTA *(singing)*.
> I'm fresh and unspiled, she said so,
> I'm a relic of a day gone by;
> In my lavendar-blue pokebonnet
> I could catch a passing tourist's eye.
> She says I can sell 'em souv'nirs

(She reaches in the basket and starts displaying wares.)
> So I got me some little brown jugs,
> Then I'll hang out some peacock bedspreads
> And a passel of hand-hooked rugs,
> With that spinnin' wheel in the corner
> And a wash-pot settin' out chere,
> Why, this plain board shack ain't a plain board shack—
> It's got *at*mosphere!
> I'll sell 'em straw brooms that's homemade *(showing broom)*,
> Straw flowers fer their windersills *(showing a limp bouquet)*.
> Little dolls that are made of cornshucks *(showing a doll)*,
> Shucks, thar's gold in them thar hills!
> I'll sell 'em
> Pink flamingoes,
> Cane-bottom chairs,
> Some hand-wove mats,
> And similar wares,
> Some mountain dew,
> From a mountain still,
> But the place won't be
> Complete until
> I have some plaster angels,
> China dogs, too,
> A little cedar bucket
> And a birch canoe,
> Some smoked-up lamps
> And old buggy shafts
> And all sorts of folksy arts and crafts.

(Holding up a fringed pillowtop, painted "Friendship.")
      I'll sell pillows all purty and painted
      And printed with a bee-yoo-tiful pome,
(Holding up a string of fish.)
      I'll sell fish to the men that ain't ben fishin'—fer fish—
      And need a string of fish to take home!
      Oh, I'm fresh and unspiled, she said so;
      In my gingham, purtied up with frills,
      If they can take my picture,
      Thar's gold in them thar hills!

CORETTA *starts putting wares back in her basket. The* FOUR BOYS *leave with their buckets.*

ZEKE *(leaving).* Sech a rumpus!
ZEB *(following).* Whut a disturbamint!
ZACK *(also following).* Them city folks sure caused a commotion!
ZO *(bringing up the rear).* This hull mountain's gone plumb daffy!
IVADIE *(to* CORETTA*).* When you gonna start this souv'nir stand?
CORETTA. Next week. You kin help me, Ivadie. *(As she leaves.)* Bye, y'all!
IVADIE. You know, Coretta's got a smart idy. Maybe that's the way *we* could make some cash money.
MAW. Forget it. A-law, I've heerd of them thar tourists. Thet Smoky Mountin' Nationill Park is *three* mountains over. Coretta Norton! That gal is right well filled-out, but it ain't with brains!

MRS. VAN DEVERE *and the* PROFESSOR *arrive. The* PROFESSOR *waves to* CORETTA *and starts after her.*

PROFESSOR. Oh, Miss Coretta!
MRS. VAN DEVERE *(dragging him back).* Professor!

The music of "Springtime in Tennessee" begins.

MAW *(shaking out a red-checked tablecloth).* Dark's a-settin' in. You folks better go home and git cleaned up fer the frolic. *(Calling.)* Cindy! Come around back and help with the eatin's.
MRS. VAN DEVERE. If it's time for the party, I'll come help you.
GENEVA. Come on, Ivadie! I cayn't wait to get in this here dress.
IVADIE. Glory be, ain't this somep'n! *(Singing.)*
      Things are lookin' fancy
      Here in Tennessee,
(The other girls join in.)

We're glad to be alive,
We're happy as can be,

CINDY *comes out of the house, having changed glamour for homespun.*

IVADIE *(pulling* CINDY *out).*
Now that the dogwood trees are bustin' into bloom,
(Teasing CINDY.)
Now that she wants to be the blushin' bride of a handsome
groom—
(The GIRLS *start dancing to music.)*
PROFESSOR *(speaking over the music).* Sh! Be quiet! *(The music
stops. The* GIRLS *stop dancing.* MAW, MRS. VAN DEVERE, *and* CINDY *stop
dead in their tracks.)* If my ear and memory are to be trusted, that is the
yellow-throated warbler—*(Everyone cocks an ear.)*—I could be deceived,
but I feel safe in saying—*(All look toward him.)*—or am I? *(Everyone
relaxes. The music begins again. The* GIRLS *go on dancing as they leave.)*

A MOUNTAINEER *(entering and going to* IVADIE*).* Ivadie, you goin' to
the frolic with me?

IVADIE. I don't know, Mr. Smarty! (IVADIE *dances off. He runs after
her.)*

MAW *(calling from the house).* Cindy!

CINDY. In a minute. *(She edges toward the* PROFESSOR *as he
bird-listens.)* Professor, whut wuz you a-sayin' this afternoon—about—

PROFESSOR. My book on birds? Ah, yes, I was saying that any female
bird is quite sly about her courting. Haven't you noticed how she flutters
around the male after he has proposed. But only for a moment. She then
flits off to another field.

CINDY. Another field?

PROFESSOR. A far-off field. She feigns complete indifference.

CINDY. In-indiffrunce?

PROFESSOR. Perhaps it's maidenly reserve—but I prefer to call it
tantalizing shyness.

CINDY. She acts like she don't keer?

PROFESSOR. She pecks at him. She tells him she hates him.

CINDY. I know how she feels. But she ain't really mad at him.

PROFESSOR. Of course not. But that makes him go after her, eager in
his pursuit.

CINDY. Air you shore he goes after *her* instidda somebawdy else? You
know, a bird in the hand is worth two, somewhur off in the bush.

PROFESSOR. True, but not in this case. He goes after her, because
he's not sure of her.

CINDY. I hope it works.

PROFESSOR. She may not be his.

CINDY. Oh, yes, she's his'n. She can't help herself. He may not be *hern,* but she's *his'n.*

PROFESSOR *(jotting notes as he goes in the house).* I must write that down. "He may not be *hern,* but she's, she's *his'n.*"

CINDY *(to herself, as she sees the evening star).*

Star light, star bright
First star I see tonight
Wisht I may, wisht I might
Have—JEREMIAH!—*(Gasping as* JEREMIAH *enters.)*—whur'd you come from? (JEREMIAH *is all dressed up, in a stiff collar, striped shirt, store-bought suit, hightop button shoes, all reminiscent of the Gay Nineties.)*—'n look at you! If you ain't a bir-r-d! All spruced up!

JEREMIAH *(carefully casual).* No more'n usual.

CINDY. No more'n usual! Jest look at you! Sunday shoes, Sunday suit,—and you never wear a tie, 'cept on Easter!

JEREMIAH. Hit's gittin' twards Easter.

CINDY. And look at yer hair! Well, I wish I may never! All slicked down with bear grease.

JEREMIAH. Hit ain't bear grease. Hit's store-bought *po*made.

CINDY. Hit's bear grease *(Sniffing.)* No mistakin' that. *(Sniffing again.)* A dead bear at that!

JEREMIAH. Cindy, I come over to tell you, I won't be dancin' the first set with you tonight.

CINDY. Land sakes, as if I keered.

JEREMIAH. Jest thought I'd tell you, since we're allus tergether fer the first dance. You know what Miss Mel'cint wants me ter do?

CINDY. I'd be plumb curious to know.

JEREMIAH. She wants me to larn her the dancin' step.

CINDY. Then go ahead! Larn her!

JEREMIAH. Wall, I 'lowed as how I would. Since she's comp'ny.

CINDY. Ef you want to cut didoes in front of a city gal, go ahead. Hit don't make no nevermind to me. I am—complete in—indiffrunce. I'll be flittin' around with the others.

JEREMIAH. Now, don't go gittin' sassy. Say, you got a rag I kin shine my shoes with?

CINDY *(smoldering).* Over thar on the porch. *(While* JEREMIAH *goes over to the porch,* CINDY *mutters to herself.)* I don't hev to act mad. I *am* mad!

JEREMIAH *(from the porch).* Whadja say?

CINDY. Nuthin'.

JEREMIAH. Here you go gittin' sassy as a pullet jest fryin'-size! And jest 'cause I'm bein' perlite to comp'ny. I hev to be perlite, don't I?

CINDY. You don't hev to be so bodacious perlite!

JEREMIAH. I niver saw a gal so riled! *(Feeling cocky over the whole thing.)* It wouldn't be 'cause you like me, maybe, more'n usual.

CINDY. Like you? I hate you! To me you're jest—jest—a pan o' blinky milk! You don't mount to no more'n—*(She snaps her fingers.)*—a hill o' beans.

JEREMIAH *(taken aback)*. Is that-all the way you feel about me? A hill o' beans?

CINDY. A last-year's hill o' beans, that's parched, wormy, and ruint!

JEREMIAH *(going)*. Well! I know somebody that don't feel that way, and if that's the way *you* feel 'bout it, Miss Priss, awright! That's all I hev ter say! Awright! *(He leaves.)*

CINDY *(to herself)*. Stubborn! *(She sings "Captivatin' Critter.")*

> He's so stubborn,
> He's as stubborn as can be;
> He's so sassy,
> He's even sassy to me;
> He's the contrariest, delayinest, the see-you-laterist
> Man that ever wuz.
> He makes me furious,
> And ain't it curious,
> That's why I love him so—

JEREMIAH *(speaking off-stage)*. Cindy! I picked some vi'lets fer *you,* too. Here! Ketch! *(A bunch of violets is tossed on, but CINDY doesn't make a move. She lets them lie there.)*

CINDY. I don't want any of yer old violets, Jeremiah Jones! *(She makes sure JEREMIAH is out of sight, then goes over and picks up the violets and continues singing.)*

> He can be so nice—
> Ever, ever so nice—
> He can make a girl
> Forget to think twice;
> He's the plumb provokinest, make-you-chokinest,
>   captivatinest
> Man that ever wuz!
> But when he's tender,
> He's mighty tender,
> And I guess at last I know

Why I put up with the critter,
It's 'cause I love him so.

CINDY *walks off smelling the violets.* PAW *appears on the porch, followed by the* FOUR BOYS.

PAW *(picking up two liquor jugs from the porch).* You boys better git your fiddles tuned up fer the dancin'.

Four MOUNTAINEERS *enter.*

FIRST MOUNTAINEER. Howdy, Ab.
PAW. Howdy. I know why you four come early. *(He gives them a jug of liquor.)*
SECOND MOUNTAINEER. Is that your new White Lightnin'?
PAW. Yep. Kinda potent. Jest one day old.
THIRD MOUNTAINEER. That's good.
PAW. And besides, hit's third-run.
FOURTH MOUNTAINEER. That's *real* good.

The MOUNTAINEERS *leave and* PAW *starts to join them, as the* PROFESSOR *comes out of the house with notebook in hand.*

PROFESSOR. Oh, Mr. Higgins.
PAW *(trying to escape to the liquoring session).* Professor, you ready fer the frolic?
PROFESSOR *(walking over towards Devil's Drop).* Ah! the grandeur of those endless blue ranges. Do you realize, Mr. Higgins, that those mountains are six million years old?
PAW *(as he finally escapes with a jug of liquor).* Six million years! That's a right smart spell. Makes you feel no biggern a minute, don't it?
PROFESSOR *(thinking* PAW *is still there).* The exact age would be a lifetime study.

CORETTA *enters and comes up behind the* PROFESSOR.

PROFESSOR *(pacing back and forth in meditation, and not seeing* CORETTA). Some of these boulders are pre-Cambrian, you know. The Paleozoic and Triassic periods are of particular interest.
CORETTA *(coming up to him).* Whadja say?
PROFESSOR. Oh, hello, my dear. *(Still meditating.)* I was saying that these naked, underlying formations are interesting geologically. Tell me, my dear, in your Triassic beds, have you ever come across an old fossil?
CORETTA *(wide-eyed).* Do I have to answer that?
PROFESSOR. I'd like to know. You are familiar with the Triassic bed?

CORETTA *(warily)*. Well—they's beds and beds.

PROFESSOR. Yes, but if you had run across an old fossil, you would have known it.

CORETTA *(even more warily)*. Reckon I would hev.

PROFESSOR *(shaking his finger at her)*. I can even tell which old fossil, by the footprints.

CORETTA *(indignant)*. Now, you kin nosey about all you want to. I ain't tellin' ye nothin'! *(She exits.)*

ZEKE *comes out of the door, fiddling a phrase. A crowd of people start arriving.* MRS. VAN DEVERE *appears with* MAW'S *gingham apron over her party dress.*

MRS. VAN DEVERE. Professor, I've been learning to slice pies. And it's so easy. You just stack up fourteen pies, slice them, and serve them on the same plate.

A MOUNTAIN WOMAN *(to* PAW*)*. Hope you'uns is well.

PAW. Fair to middlin'.

The PROFESSOR *leaps into action with his notebook, following* PAW *around and taking notes on dialect.*

A MOUNTAIN WOMAN *(to* MRS. VAN DEVERE*)*. Howdy.

MRS. VAN DEVERE *(shaking hands, graciously)*. How do you do?

PAW *(to* ANOTHER WOMAN*)*. Did you bring your young'uns?

ANOTHER WOMAN. Nary ary of 'em. They's too pestiferous!

The MOUNTAINEERS *ad lib "Howdys."*

PAW *(greeting someone else)*. Wall, look who's here! By George!

PROFESSOR. By George! That expression, Mr. Higgins, dates back to King George III, and I've heard others that go back still further— pestiferous, nary-ary and—young man *(to* MOUNTAINEER*)*, didn't you say this afternoon, "he spoke mighty short to me"?

MOUNTAINEER. Wall, he did!

PROFESSOR. That phrase "spoke mighty short" is in Shakespeare.

MRS. VAN DEVERE. That is very interesting.

PROFESSOR. My dear Mrs. Van Devere, it is remarkable! I have a wealth of material here for my book on Anglo-Saxon.

PAW *(turning on him)*. I been hearin' all day about that thar Anglo-Saxon. Whut in the name of common sense is it?

PROFESSOR. Well, I'll explain. *(He sings "It's Anglo-Saxon.")*
      Chaucer was wont to pronounce his words
      In much the same manner that you do.

If he should return he could be understood
Only by people like you.
The folks in his day called a child a "bairn,"
And bringing it up was a process called "rar'n,"
That little word ain't, is not only quaint,
It's Anglo-Saxon.

MOUNTAINEERS *(singing)*.

That little word ain't—it ain't only quaint— Hit's
Anglo-Saxon.

PROFESSOR.

Chaucer formed plurals the way that you do,
His pies were always pasties.
An Englishman taking a taste of wine
Said "Thanks, I'll take two tasties."
Your girl, when she sews, is not being rural,
She's merely using Chaucerian plural—
Whenever she says she "basties her waisties,"
It's Anglo-Saxon.

MOUNTAINEERS.

She ain't bein' rural, she's just bein' plural—Hit's
Anglo-Saxon.

PROFESSOR.

The English were free in their choice of sounds,
Their choices weren't always consistent;
Their inch was an eench, Their pinch was a peench,
But their wench was always a wench!
An Englishman never did touch—he tetched,
An Englishman never did catch—he ketched,
An Englishman never did reach—he _____
It's Anglo-Saxon!

MOUNTAINEERS.

Well, whaddye know—if all that's so—we're Anglo-Saxon!

PROFESSOR.

It is a language that's spoken, not written,
And all its expressions are somehow more fitten;
To Anglo-Saxons a hoist was a h'ist,
Like you, they added a T on twice't,
Whenever they whipped, they whipped with a whallop,
Whenever they tripped, they tripped with a tro_____,
Suffice it to say, our best language today
Is Anglo-Saxon!

MOUNTAINEERS.

> We vow and declare, we're somethin' rare! We're
> Anglo-Saxon!

MRS. VAN DEVERE *(coming forward).* When do they begin the house-raising?

PAW. Wall, I thought we might as well hev a little dancin' first. We usually dance awhile and work awhile.

MILLICENT *appears on the porch, with a large cluster of apple blossoms in her hair and dressed up in a party dress.*

A MOUNTAINEER. Thar's Miss Park Avenoo!

JEREMIAH *(rushing over to her).* Good evenin', Mis Mel'cint.

MILLICENT *(walking the fence rail again).* Help me down.

Several MOUNTAINEERS *rush over, trying to be there first, but* JERE-MIAH *wins.*

A MOUNTAINEER. Could I hev the first dance?

ANOTHER MOUNTAINEER. Could I?

JEREMIAH *(after* MILLICENT *comes down in his arms).* You shore are purty tonight. That shore is some dress—I mean—Well, whut I'm tryin' to say is—*(He sings "I Admire the Way You Look.")*

> I admire the way you look;
> In fact, I think I'll take another look;
> And if I look right past you,
> 'Cause I dassent ast you,
> Would you kindly hev this dance with me?
> I could whirl you 'round and 'round;
> Bet I could even lift you off the ground;
> And after we finish dancin',
> Would you take a chance, and
> Git-to-gether in a corner nook?
> 'Cause I admire the way you look!

The music continues as JEREMIAH *escorts her upstage.* CINDY, *who came out on the porch during the song and saw* JEREMIAH *singing to* MILLICENT, *sits down on the step and looks forlorn.*

A MOUNTAINEER *(speaking over music).* Hey, Cindy! Come on, be my partner!

CINDY. No, thankee. I'll jest sit here and watch.

PAW *(speaking over music).* Git yer partners, folks, and I'll call a set!

ANOTHER MOUNTAINEER. All the gals ain't hyar yit.

PAW. Whar air they? We cayn't wait all night.

ZEKE. Lookee!

ZEB. Lookee yander!

ZACK. Lookee thar!

All the MOUNTAINEERS *give long wolf-whistles, and, during the last half of "I Admire The Way you Look," there is a regular parade by the five girls:* GENEVA, IVADIE, LURAINE, PEARLAMINA, *and* MOSSY BELLE. *As each appears, the* MOUNTAINEERS *whistle their approval. One girl has an ankle-length dancing dress, but worn with bare feet; one has a dress on backwards; one has on high-heeled sandals, and her feet are killing her, etc. However, all the girls have large clusters of crabapple blossoms in their hair, exactly like* MILLICENT'S.

A MOUNTAINEER (*directing attention to* MAW). Have you ever—? (*The* BOYS *all whistle their wolf-whistle again, as* MAW *appears on the porch, just in time to be the tag-end of the parade.* MAW *is in her old gingham dress, but she has* MRS. VAN DEVERE'S *dowager dog collar around her neck, ostrich feathers in her hair, and she is holding a lorgnette.*

ZEKE. Look at Maw! And after the way she fursed this mornin'!

MAW (*as she models*). Shuckins! Ain't no use of folks gittin' so set in their ways.

As the GIRLS *parade, the* MOUNTAINEERS *sing "I Admire the Way You Look."*

MOUNTAINEERS.
>I admire the way you look;
>In fact, I think I'll take another look!
>And if I look right past you,
>'Cause I dassent ast you,
>Would you kindly hev this dance with me?
>I could whirl you 'round and 'round;
>Bet I could even lift you off the ground;
>And after we finish dancin',
>Would you take a chance, and
>Git-to-gether in a corner nook?
>'Cause I admire the way you look!

PAW (*beginning the dance-calling*). Strike up a tune, boys! Big ring!

A HILLBILLY BAND *plays a barn dance rhythm of "I Admire the Way You Look," and the* MOUNTAINEERS *select partners,* JEREMIAH *choosing* MILLICENT. CINDY *does not dance. She looks on wistfully.*

PAW *(ending the dance).* Take a breathin' spell!

A MOUNTAINEER *(coming up to* MILLICENT *and* JEREMIAH). Miss Park Avenoo, you promised I could git you some supper.

MILLICENT *(as she leaves).* Don't go away, Jerry.

JEREMIAH *(seeing* CINDY *on the step).* Oh, Cindy, thar you are. Reckon we could hev this next dance, now that I showed Miss Park Avenoo the dancin' step.

CINDY. And sung her the song you allus sung to me! No, thankee, Jeremiah Jones, I got all my dances promised. And from now on, I ain't a-speakin'! *(She rushes out.)*

JEREMIAH *(following her).* Why, Cindy! *(He goes after her.)*

The BOYS *begin house-raisin', while the* GIRLS *watch them.*

FIRST MOUNTAINEER. Come on, fellers, let's get on with the house-raisin'. Help me with this log.

SECOND MOUNTAINEER. We'll git Cindy's cabin raised ternight, ef the White Lightnin' holds out!

THIRD MOUNTAINEER. Reckon this cabin's gonna be large enough fer all the kids Cindy and Jeremiah will be a-havin'?

CINDY *and* JEREMIAH *re-enter. The* MOUNTAINEERS *raise a short log up to a window of the unfinished house.*

FIRST MOUNTAINEER *(seeing* JEREMIAH). Come on, Jeremiah, we've started the house-raisin'!

JEREMIAH. House-raisin'? Oh. No use goin' on with it, boys. *(He looks over at* CINDY.*)* Don't seem to be no call for it no longer. And I don't keer! I'd like fer a certain somebody to know I ben talking terday to the city folks. I ben hearin' that thar's other ways of livin', and I aim to find out whut they air. Just leave it, boys.

The MOUNTAINEERS, *surprised, put the log back down on the log pile.*

MILLICENT *(walking in, comes between* CINDY *and* JEREMIAH). Jerry, will you teach me the Gooseberry Twirl?

JEREMIAH *(defiantly).* Shore. Line up, fellers fer the Gooseberry Twirl!

CINDY *(as she watches* JEREMIAH *put his arm around* MILLICENT, *escorting her into place).* Somep'ns gotta be did! *(She rushes away.)*

The dance begins again. MILLICENT, *a good dancer, comes into her own as she is twirled high in the air by* JEREMIAH *in the Gooseberry Twirl. The music swells around the lively dancers.*

CURTAIN

ACT TWO

The scene is the same. Daybreak can be seen coming over the mountain peaks, and there is all the stillness of early morning. CINDY *comes out of the house, barefooted, carrying a long loop of rope. She looks furtively about to see that no one is near. In pantomime, to music ("Morning on the Mountain"), six mountain girls, all barefoot, come from around the cabin and from the thickets of laurel. Their tiptoeing and darting about, beckoning for others to come, their yawns of early morning sleepiness, is all in rhythm to the music.*

CINDY *(calling out over the bluff, over music)*. Yahoo!
ECHO (PEARLAMINA, *with voice off-stage*). Yahoo!
CINDY. Wake up!
ECHO (PEARLAMINA). Wake up!
CINDY. Pearlamina!
ECHO (PEARLAMINA) Pearlamina! (PEARLAMINA *enters, dancing as she sings.)*
PEARLAMINA *(singing).*
    When it's mornin' on the mountain,
CORETTA *(joining in singing as she dances in).*
    Things are stirrin' at the bust of dawn;
CINDY *(calling as music continues)*. Ivadie! Luranie! Mossy Belle! *(No echo.)*
MOSSY BELLE *(entering sleepily, speaking over the music.)* Landsakes, Cindy, whatcha mean slitherin' around wakin' us all up. It ain't sun-up yit.
CINDY. Sh! I got somep'n to tell you.

IVADIE *and* LURANIE *enter.*

IVADIE. Whatcha want, Cindy? We-all come hot-footin' it, lickety-split!
PEARLAMINA *(dancing around)*. And I feel good this mornin'. Hit looks like a real purty day.
PEARLAMINA, CORETTA, IVADIE, LURANIE, MOSSY BELLE *(dancing as they sing).*
    When it's mornin' on the mountain
    Things are stirrin' at the bust of dawn,

And there isn't even time to yawn?
'Fore the dew has started dryin',
The birds have started flyin',
The bees have started hummin', 'cause
A brand-new day is comin';
When it's mornin' on the mountain,
There is somethin' makes you kinda wanta sing;
If you're courtin', then as sure as you are born
You'll be his'n and yer feller will be yourn,
When it's mornin' on the mountain, in spring.

GENEVA *(entering, speaking, without music)*. Great day in the mornin', Cindy. Whaddye mean wakin' a bawdy up even afore milkin'-time?

CINDY. Sh! Come over here to the new place. I tell you I got somep'n I wanta say.

CORETTA. At daybreak! It 'ud better be good.

CINDY *(as she sits on the cabin steps, with the girls clustered around her)*. You know that Miss Park Avenoo? Wall, she's tuk a shine to Jeremiah.

IVADIE. Yeah, Pears like it.

CINDY. And he's goin' hawg-wild!

IVADIE. Cindy, why don'tcha jest fergit about Jeremiah? Give him the go-by and go on with yer cookin'. Jest push him to the back of the stove.

CINDY. I wish I could, but I reckon he'll always be right out thar in front fer me. I tried to act like I didn't keer. The Professor told me that a bird gits whut she wants by actin' indiffernt. But hit didn't work. Birds are birds, and Jeremiah's Jeremiah.

GIRLS *(nod sadly and sing reprise of "Captivatin' Critter")*.
[Bar 13 of music after break]
He's so slippery
He's so ketch me if you kin
He'll allus hev the gals, a-pinin' after him.

ONE GIRL.
He's the hoaxinest, the coaxinest, the plumb pervokinest
Man that ever wuz.

GIRLS.
But Jeremiah *(They sigh.)* is Jeremiah; *(They sigh.)*

GENEVA *(sung comically, in a cracked voice)*.
I shore would like him fer my beau—

GIRLS.
He kin act so high and mighty
'Cause wimmen love him so.

IVADIE *(speaking)*. You're shore havin' bad luck.

CINDY. Yeah. 'Course I had bad luck comin' to me. Day before yestiddy, I set backards in a cha'r.

GENEVA. You shoulda known better. A girl sets backards in her cha'r, loses her luck right then and thar.

CINDY. Yeah. And yestiddy I unthoughtedly laid a bresh broom on the bed.

IVADIE *(gasping)*. A womern might as well be dead, as lay a bresh broom on the bed.

CINDY *(rising)*. But then 'n ag'in, I'm kinda hopeful. This mornin' my last potater peelin' fell in the letter, "J".

IVADIE *(rising)*. "J"—Jeremiah. Well, whatcha aimin' ter do?

CINDY. I got ter get rid of her somehow.

IVADIE. Wall, Cindy, I'm right handy with a gun. *(She motions aiming a gun.)*

CINDY. Thankee, Ivadie, but no.

CORETTA *(rising)*. Let Ivadie go ahead. Nobawdy 'round hyar would think a thing about it.

CINDY. Hit's sorta messy.

IVADIE. Oh—not much.

CORETTA. Ivadie wouldn't hev to hurt her none. Jest fire up a little mess of buckshot—to show her whut's whut.

CINDY. No! What I aim to do is this. I'm a-goin' to New Hope afore anybawdy gets up, and use that telyphone they keep talkin' about.

IVADIE. You don't even know how to use a telyphone.

CINDY. I kin find out. And the name, if I ain't mistook, wuz Cornelius Van Devere. I'm a-goin' to telyphone that Mr. Cornelius to send after her.

CORETTA. I heerd it costes a heap o' money.

CINDY. That's why I got you over here. Somebody help me. *(With the help of two girls,* CINDY *brings a hope chest from the porch. The chest is painted with a mountain design of hearts and flowers.)*

IVADIE. Land sake! Air ye a-sellin' your hope chist?

CINDY *(rubbing the top of it lovingly as she opens it)*. I am.

GENEVA *(looking at it greedily)*. And you had right much stuff.

CINDY. With Jeremiah, I had right much time. Well, here's my quilt. I'll give it to the first buyer that offers fair. Who'll give whut? The pattern is "Hearts and Gizzards."

IVADIE. Cindy! Shorely you ain't sellin' your "Hearts and Gizzards!"

CINDY. I'm a-sellin' it. Somebody speak up.

GENEVA. A dollar.

IVADIE. Dollar-and-fifty.

CORETTA. I could use it fer my souv'nir stand. One dollar and eighty cents. (CORETTA *produces the money.*)

CINDY. Anybawdy else? *(Looking around, receives the money, then hands the quilt to* CORETTA.) It's yours, Coretter. *(She picks up a small coverlet from the chest.)* Now, who wants this kiverlet? I carded the wool myself, all light and fluffy.

GENEVA *(carefully casual).* I'll give you a dollar.

CINDY. Genever Hicks! Only a dollar!

GENEVA. Wall—two dollars—No!—ain't wuth it!

CINDY. Ain't wuth it, with you a-settin' your cap fer Lee Tompkins? And you can't spin or weave or nuthin'.

GENEVA. You don't hev ter keep tellin' me.

CINDY. And Lee Tompkins a-thinkin' all this time you kin.

GENEVA *(almost persuaded).* Well—uh—Naw, I ain't interested.

CINDY *(softly and persuasively).* Hit would look mighty purty on the bed. Betcha Lee would like it.

GENEVA. I ain't gonna take it!

CINDY. The pattern is "Lee's Surrender"!

GENEVA. I'LL TAKE IT! *(She hands over the money.)*

IVADIE. But, Cindy! What if you sell your hope chest and get yer man. Hit ain't gonna do you no good effen you git married and ain't got nothin' to start on.

CINDY. We can start on love, cayn't we? *(She takes a ruffled apron from the hope chest and looks fondly at it as she sings "We Can Start On Love.")*

> Some day we'll have a house of our own
> With all the things that we've been dreaming of,
> But 'til that happy day, when we see it under way,
> I know that we can start on love.
> Maybe it won't be terribly grand,
> Its roof won't reach as high as the pines above,
> But with each morning star, we'll be glad we're where we are,
> 'Til then, we'll have to start on love.
>
> To dream a dream doesn't mean it's bound to come true,
> To scheme a scheme is just a way of keeping dreams in view.
>
> Some day we'll leave our troubles behind
> And find the sunshine we've been dreaming of,
> But while we're waitin' here, for the clouds to disappear,
> I know that we can start on love.

(Speaking over music.) Who wants to buy this hand-embroidered nightgown? *(Holding up a white embroidered nightgown, edged with lace.)* Hit's got handmade tattin'.

IVADIE *(gasping)*. Cindy! You dassent! That's fer your weddin' night!

CINDY *doesn't answer. She only gives a demure look as she hums, "I Can Start on Love."*

GENEVA *(with an attempt to be casual)*. I don't really want the nightgown, Cindy, but—*(Greedily.)*—I'll take it for $2.15.

IVADIE. Genever Hicks! Quit being so graspin'. Two dollars and *fifty* cents! And Cindy, that's all I got.

CINDY. Hit's yours, Ivadie. *(Taking the money and handing her the gown.)* And now, you-all go on. I got to get started. *(The* GIRLS *leave with their plunder, all but* IVADIE.*)*

CORETTA *(to* GENEVA, *as they leave)*. Genever, if I wuz you, I wouldn't want Lee Tompkins to see that kiverlet you *didn't* make.

GENEVA *(with a furtive glance around)*. That's right. (GENEVA *flounces her dress back over her head, exposing pantaloons obviously made from a feed sack, since a telltale mark in red and green, "Try Purina," is still visible. She puts the coverlet in place, to form a bustle, pulls her dress back in place and follows the others in a run.)*

IVADIE. I'll help you put the chest back.

CINDY. All right.

IVADIE. And you kin put yer nightgown back in.

CINDY. But you bought it.

IVADIE. Only so's I could give it back to you. Hyar it is. It's yours.

CINDY. Thanks, Ivadie. *(They start moving the chest to the house.)*

IVADIE. But Cindy! What effen you git to the telyphone and git another flyin' machine down here. Won't she take Jeremiah away with her?

CINDY *(sighing)*. That's a chance I gotta take. Ef anybody asks 'bout me, tell 'em I've gone to pick poke, fer poke sallit.

IVADIE. They won't believe you. Hit'll take three day to git thar 'n back.

CINDY. Not the way I'm goin'. *(Holding up a loop of rope.)* I ain't goin' sixty mile by the road in a mule and wagon—I'm a'goin' to clamber down the bluff. I figger I'll be back by sun-down.

IVADIE. You mean slidin' down that boulder? The Devil's Drop? That ain't niver ben did!

CINDY. It's *gonna* be did! Now!

IVADIE. A-clammerin' down that mountainside on your hands and knees. Oh, Cindy! No man never wuz worth all that. Not no man of no kind—not never—at no time!

CINDY. This'n is!

IVADIE. I wisht I loved a man that much. Oh, Cindy, you'll never make it!

CINDY. I don't hurt easy. I'm right survivrus!

JEREMIAH *is heard in the distance, singing a refrain of the "Old Ballad."*

JEREMIAH *(singing offstage).*
　　I found my own true love
　　On a summer morning.

CINDY. There's Jeremiah. I'd better start. Don't up and tell whar I'm goin'. Promise.

IVADIE. I promise.

CINDY. Cross your heart and hope to die. *(Makes a cross over the heart.)*

IVADIE *(making the same motion and saying the phrase silently).* Oh, Cindy, ain't you a-feared?

CINDY. I'll hold on the laurel limbs when I'm gittin' my toe holds. I kin make it, excusin' I fall. (CINDY *loops the rope around a point of the bluff and disappears.)*

IVADIE. I'd be skairt white-eyed. *(Going to bluff and looking off.)* Oh, Cindy! *(Whirling around and putting her face in her hands.)* I can't look.

JEREMIAH *appears, with three fishing poles over his shoulder and a can of bait in his hand.*

JEREMIAH *(singing idly).*
　　I lost my own true love
　　On a winter evening,
　　The wind blew cold
　　All 'bout her face.

(Speaking.) Why, Ivadie! What you doin' over yere at this hour of the mornin'?

IVADIE *(flustered).* Not nothin'. Not nothin', Jeremiah. Jest on my way to the spring.

JEREMIAH. Is Cindy up yet? Hev you seen her?

IVADIE. Cindy? Yeah. She just left. Seems like she said she's a-goin' over in yon hollar—*(Pointing in the opposite direction and talking a-mile-a-minute.)*—er sommers to pick poke—you know, poke fer poke sallit—ef thar's anything I like, it's poke fer poke sallit—I wuz sayin' jest yestiddy, I shore wisht I had some—uh—*(Finishing lamely.)*—you know—*poke.*

JEREMIAH. Then I guess she'll miss the fishin' trip. And fishin's best when the dogwood's in bloom. *(Calling.)* Oh, Miss Mel'cint!

IVADIE *(still in a dither)*. I'll—I'll be gittin' on over to the spring.

JEREMIAH. Whar's yer water bucket?

IVADIE. Landsakes. Ain't I a goose! I plumb forgot and come off without the water bucket! *(She laughs, glances at the cliff, looks worried, and darts off.)* Great liver and lights!

JEREMIAH. Miss Mel'cint! *(He throws a pebble against the house.)* Wake up! Time to go fishin'. *(He starts whittling.)*

The PROFESSOR *comes out of the house, dressed in business shirt, coat, and tie, but wearing baggy walking-shorts, his knobby knees fully exposed.*

PROFESSOR. Good morning, Jeremiah! Beautiful morning! *(Calling back in the house.)* Mrs. Higgins, did you find my binoculars?

MAW *(entering from the house.)* Is these the contraptions ye wuz a-lookin' fer?

PROFESSOR. Ah, yes, thank you. They're for bird-gazing. Don't look for me back, Mrs. Higgins, until late afternoon.

MAW. Wall, now, Professor, you want to be keerful and don't overdo. I'm remembering that census taker up hyar last summer. He come in one day, bright as a button, bouncin' around all over these hills. The next day they carried him out of hyar feet first.

PROFESSOR. Don't worry. I'm used to exploring the woodland. (MAW *goes back in the house.)* Ah! Just breathe this mountain air. It's crisp and cold, and yet there is so much sunshine in these protected coves. This would be good apple country.

JEREMIAH. Air ye a farmer?

PROFESSOR. I have a place up in Vermont. Growing apple trees is another one of my hobbies. Here are some pamphlets on orchards if you would like to look them over.

JEREMIAH *(stuffing them in his pocket)*. Thankee—*(Then calling.)* Miss Mel'cint!

CORETTA *enters, with a basket on her arm.*

PROFESSOR. I've given lectures all over the country on the apple. My most popular one is called "Adam and Eve in the Garden." Ah! My dear Miss Norton. There you are, bright and early.

JEREMIAH. Keer to go fishin' with us? Got plenty of picnic.

PROFESSOR. Oh, no, thank you. Miss Norton is taking me out in the woods. (*To* CORETTA.) And is that our picnic lunch?

CORETTA. Yep. *And* my embroiderin' fer the tourists. (*Holding up a pillow top painted with a poem.*) Another pillow top—(*Giggling.*) Thissens's "Motherhood."

PROFESSOR (*eagerly*). Let's get started.

CORETTA (*scared*). I'll—I'll go on ahead and lead the way, bein' as how the woods is so tangled.

PROFESSOR (*still admiring the scenery*). Ah! The sylvan forest! This, Jeremiah, is an inspiration to a naturalist. It's enough to drive a nature-lover wild! (*He sings "I'm Wild About Wild Life."*)

> I'm simply wild about wild life,
> Wild life is the life for me;
> What I like about Flora, I like about Fauna,
> They're both lovely as can be;
> And when I hear some Turdus migratorious
> Tell another robin she's glorious,
> I'm wild about wild life
> It fills me with intoxicating glee;
> I seem to want to tarry in some wild life sanctuary,

(*Looking at* CORETTA.)

> Nature comes so natural—
> Nature comes so natural—
> To me.
>
> Oh, I'm wild about wild life,
> Wild life is the life for me;
> I get mental upheavals
> In forest primevals

(*Looking at* CORETTA.)

> There's *so* much wild life to see!
> And when I breathe fresh air, I feel so primitive
> I could even split an infinitive!
> I'm wild about wild life,
> I have a yen for every glen I see;
> Oh, when a lady ruffled grouse
> Say's "Yes" unto her eager spouse

(*Pawing the ground, getting ready to chase* CORETTA.)

> Then I know it's Springtime,
> Then I know it's Saptime,
> For me!

The PROFESSOR *runs out chasing* CORETTA.

PROFESSOR *(singing an encore, if needed).*
    I'm simply wild about wild life,
    It just can't get too wild for me;
    When forests turn vernal
    One urge springs eternal
    And now it's springing in me.
    You think a hermit thrush might have mysogyny,
    Yet he turns out quite a progeny;
    I'm wild about wild life
    Enticed by all the budding slips I see—
    I feel so virile, so robust,
    I feel a sort of wanderlust—
    Nature is a ritual—
    Nature is habitual—
    With me!
JEREMIAH *(calling).* Miss Mel'cint! (MILLICENT *appears, dressed in a brief play suit.)*
MILLICENT. Coming!
JEREMIAH *(seeing her and turning his back).* 'Scuse me, marm. I didn't aim to come afore you's dressed.
MILLICENT. I'm dressed.
JEREMIAH *(wide-eyed).* Oh!

MAW *enters, bringing a bowl and a spoon. She sees* MILLICENT *and puts down the bowl.*

MAW. Good land o'livin'!
MILLICENT. I'm going fishing.
MAW *(taking a large sunbonnet off the wall of the porch).* You better take my sunbonnet. You oughta kiver up somep'n.

MILLICENT *puts on the calico sunbonnet. It covers her head completely.*

MILLICENT *(handing it back).* No, thank you. I want to get a sun tan.
MAW *(getting her churn).* Well, I giss you will. I don't see nothin' to keep you from it. *(She takes up her bowl. By the bench are a churn and a liquor jug.)*
MILLICENT. Come on, let's go.
JEREMIAH *(frozen in his tracks at the sight of her).* I—uh—I—*(He sings a reprise of "I Admire the Way You Look." As he sings,* MILLICENT *dances.)*

JEREMIAH *(singing).*

> I admire the way you look
> And I don't even keer if you can't cook;
> I can't do chores that I orter,
> I'm as weak as warter,
> 'Cause I sorta got my eye on you.
> You're as purty as can be
> And if I wuz only sure that you's fer me,
> I'd hitch the team to the waggin',
> Put you and your bag in,
> To the preacher you'd git took;
> 'Cause I admire the way you look. *(They exit.)*

MAW *brings her bowl to the bench.* MRS. VAN DEVERE *appears with a cigarette in a long holder, and a Martini.*

MRS. VAN DEVERE. Is the churning ready for me to do?

MAW. Yep. You right shore you don't mind doin' it?

MRS. VAN DEVERE. Not at all. I fixed myself a Martini to keep me interested.

MAW. Awful early drinkin'.

MRS. VAN DEVERE. Awfully big churning.

MAW *and* MRS. VAN DEVERE *get seated on the bench.* MAW *is stirring some batter in a wooden mixing bowl.* MRS. VAN DEVERE *is churning—vigorously.* MAW *smokes a pipe and has a jug down by her side.* MRS. VAN DEVERE *takes a sip from her Martini and smokes her cigarette occasionally.*

MAW. You say your name is Mistress Van Devere?

MRS. VAN DEVERE. Yes.

MAW. Niver heerd of 'em.

MRS. VAN DEVERE. The Van Deveres are a very large family. I'm Mrs. Van Devere, the third.

MAW. The third? You mean thar's another one besides you?

MRS. VAN DEVERE. Yes. There's Mrs. Van Devere, the second.

MAW. The second? And there's another one ahead of her?

MRS. VAN DEVERE. Yes. The first Mrs. Van Devere.

MAW *(clucking).* Tsk! Tsk! Tsk! Ain't that jest like a man? They'd all have twenty wives if you'd let 'em!

MRS. VAN DEVERE *(churning vigorously).* Is there butter in there yet?

MAW. Law, no! You got a spell to go. Lawsy day! You don't even know how to churn? New York shore must be different from Slippery Creek.

MRS. VAN DEVERE. Yes, it is—somewhat.

MAW. I ben wonderin' ever since you come. What kind of pipe is that?

MRS. VAN DEVERE. It's a cigarette.

MAW. Mind if I try?

MRS. VAN DEVERE. No. *(Pointing to* MAW's *corncob pipe.)* Mind if I try?

MAW. Naw. *(They exchange. They both puff, then reflect.)* Wall, terbaccy's terbaccy, ain't it? *(They sing "Terbaccy's Terbaccy.")*

MRS. VAN DEVERE *(singing).*

    I smoke tobacco in a cigarette paper,
    You smoke tobacco in a corncob pipe,
    But anyone with sense knows there's not much difference
    As long as the tobacco's mellow and ripe.

MAW *(singing).*

    Terbaccy's terbaccy, ain't it?

The music is quiet for the following dialogue.

MRS. VAN DEVERE *(speaking).* I've heard about your mountain corn. Mind if I try a little?

MAW *(speaking).* Shore. Could I have a try at that thar Martini? *(They exchange glasses and sip thoughtfully.)*

MRS. VAN DEVERE *(speaking).* Corny, but good.

MAW *(after tasting).* Hair tonic! *(Then singing.)*

    Don't know as I could be shore of whut's in it,
    Hit's sweet-scented, but I ain't agin it;
    As long as it's ferment, then I reckon I'm carntent;
    It can drown a world of troubles in a minute.

MRS. VAN DEVERE *(singing).*

    Liquor is liquor, ain't it?

The music is down again.

MAW *(speaking).* Shore is. You say your husband's as no count as mine?

MRS. VAN DEVERE *(speaking).* Sometimes Cornelius is a great trial to me!

MAW *(speaking).* Tch, tch! Don't I know! A man's a man, ain't he?

The music comes up as they sing.

MRS. VAN DEVERE.
> Mine rambles.

MAW.
> Mine gambles.

MRS. VAN DEVERE.
> Mine bickers.

MAW.
> Mine likkers.

MRS. VAN DEVERE.
> Mine rumbles and roars.

MAW.
> Mine tosses and snores.

TOGETHER.
> *Lord, what* are men for?

The music ends on an unresolved chord and is tacet *throughout the following dialogue.*

MAW *(speaking).* What do you do up in New York to pass the time o' day?

MRS. VAN DEVERE. Play bridge, so we can gossip.

MAW. Why, that's what we hev our quiltin's fer. Ain't nary gossip we don't kiver. Wall, folks is folks, ain't they?

MRS. VAN DEVERE. And of course I go to my psychiatrist.

MAW. What's that?

MRS. VAN DEVERE. A doctor. You lie down on a couch and say anything that comes to mind.

MAW. That could be resky.

MRS. VAN DEVERE. For many people it's been salvation.

MAW. We don't do nothin' like that here. Or maybe we do! Salvation! Do you go into a trance!

MRS. VAN DEVERE. Yes.

MAW. You confess things? You git all worked up?

MRS. VAN DEVERE. Yes. It's expensive, but it's so good for pent-up emotions.

MAW. That's like our camp-meetin's! When we start *(Clapping.)* a-clappin' and a-rollin'! We get real loosened-up, and it don't cost us nothin'! *(She sings.)*

> You tell your troubles to them fancy city doctors,
> I spill my troubles in the good old way,
> But ain't it too distressin', when a body gits confessin',
> Just how much comes out you never meant to say?

MRS. VAN DEVERE *(singing)*.
    Confessin's, confessin', ain't it?
TOGETHER *(in duet, with no accompaniment)*.
    Confessin's confessin', wherever you be,
    On likker and husbands we both will agree,
    And folks is folks, a body can see,
    In Central Park West, or in Tennessee!
       (BLACKOUT)

In front of a drop-scrim curtain, the PROFESSOR *and* CORETTA *enter. At downstage left there is an old iron washpot, and in it a long jabbing-pole for prodding the washed clothes as they boil.*

CORETTA. This way.
PROFESSOR. Lead on my little wood nymph. Do you mind leading me by the hand again?
CORETTA *(giggling)*. Nope. *(She pantomimes holding an imaginary tree limb out of his way.)* Tree limb! *(She releases the limb, and the* PROFESSOR *pantomimes being hit in the stomach.)*
PROFESSOR. Ouch! Thank you. Here we are in the very bosom of nature. So beautiful! So virgin!—My dear, how old did you say you are?
CORETTA. Nineteen. Tree limb. *(She holds another limb out of his way and again the* PROFESSOR *is hit in the stomach.)*
PROFESSOR. Ouch! Thank you. Ah, so this is where you live, my little wood sprite.
CORETTA. I'd better git back to work. Left my warshin'. *(She goes over to the iron washpot and starts stirring the clothes with the long pole.)*
PROFESSOR. The more I think about your coming to New York with me, the more excited I become.
CORETTA. Wall, thar's just one thing that's holdin' me back. Do they have souv'nir stands in New York?
PROFESSOR. Yes, indeed—but you could be my secretary—and help me with my book. Tell me, is there anything more stimulating than intellectual companionship?—*(He is looking at* CORETTA *as she bends over.)*—a marriage of the minds!
CORETTA *(wide-eyed)*. Reckon not.

A hound dog barks in distance.

PROFESSOR. Ah! There's a happy huntsman.

The HUNTSMAN *enters.*

HUNTSMAN. Howdy.

PROFESSOR. How do you do, sir? Is the hunting good this season?

HUNTSMAN. Tolerable. Whatcha warmin' the cheer bottoms around here for?

PROFESSOR. Young Miss Norton is assisting me in philology. However, I'm really an ornithologist.

HUNTSMAN. Ornery what?

PROFESSOR. Ornerythol—er—ornithologist.

HUNTSMAN *(looking alarmed).* Hmm. Reckon you won't be hyar when I git back for supper? *(He strides off.)*

PROFESSOR. Supper?

CORETTA. He's my husband. He's the Sheriff.

PROFESSOR. But you didn't say you were married.

CORETTA. Niver axed me.

HUNTSMAN *(coming back).* Jest happened to think. Air you one of them circuit ridin' preachers?

PROFESSOR. Oh, no, sir.

HUNTSMAN. Jest wondered. *(Looking at* CORETTA.) They wuz one of them low-down preachers through here last spring. (CORETTA *casts her eyes down demurely.)*

PROFESSOR. He wasn't all he should have been?

HUNTSMAN. Nope. Not after I filled him full of buckshot. *(He leaves.)*

PROFESSOR *(his knees shaking).* I must be on my way. I want to track down the Orchis spectabilis before dark.

CORETTA. Ef yer a mind-ter. I got to get busy warshin' on these here baby clothes. *(She holds up a baby dress.)*

PROFESSOR. Baby clothes! But you didn't tell me you had children!

CORETTA. I did so!

PROFESSOR. I beg your pardon, my dear Miss Norton, but you did not. I remember distinctly I said, "What keeps you busy all day long?" —and you said, "Sex"! *(With a fond reminiscent sigh.)*

CORETTA. Yep! Sex! *(She holds up six fingers.)* Sex kids!

PROFESSOR. Oh! But I can't believe you have six children! You're only nineteen years old!

CORETTA. Ben right active.

The bark of hound dogs grows louder.

PROFESSOR *(startled).* Yes, well, good day! *(He bows, just in time to get a load of buckshot in his rear. He jumps, and runs off as fast as he can.)*

CORETTA *(beginning to wash again and wiping the sweat from her brow)*. Men come and they go. Oh, these plague-take-it baby clothes! Year in and year out, it's baby clothes! Looks like jest one lil' thing after t'other keeps croppin' up. *(Music begins.)* And I ain't really to blame for it either. *(She sings "Yaller, Yaller Moon," with a spotlight on her and the washpot.)*

CORETTA *(singing)*.

> Oh, that yaller, yaller moon in the month of May,
> That's why I am whur I am terday,
> That's why I am whur I am terday.
>
> I'm steady as a rock in April,
> I do middlin' well in March,
> But let it come May, I git to feelin' that away,
> I'm plumb harum-scarum in May;
> I feel so harum-scarem, I'd scare 'em in a harem in May.
>
> I wisht we didn't have no moon in May,
> I wisht that moon didn't shine;
> 'Cause when it gets yeller
> I git to feelin' meller,
> Along comes my feller, and gosh, all heller,
> That's why I'm whur I am terday,
> With this washtub full, and more on the way,
> That's why I am whur I am terday.
>
> The whale wuz a-waitin' when Jonah went swimmin',
> Thar's allus a man on the lookout fer wimmen;
> Thar's nets for them fishes that swims in the sea,
> Thar's traps for the b'ars, but that moon's whut gits me!
>
> I wisht we didn't have May blossoms,
> With all them sweet-smellin' scents;
> 'Cause I git so blessed tired of a-bein' bless'd
> With so blessed many blessed events.
> Oh, every January
> I wisht I'd been less merry
> In May!

(Encore, if needed):

> I wisht we didn't have no ruffles,
> I'm skeer't of lookin' purty in May;
> Them form-fittin' dresses kin git you into messes,

They're apt to git you feelin' too gay.
I don't need to be a charmer,
What I need's a coat of armor
In May!

(BLACKOUT)

The scrim curtains part to reveal again the Higgins cabin. The FOUR
BOYS *appear in coats—a tight squeeze for all four—stiff, ugly coats,
bursting at the seams. They are gathered around* PAW.

ZEKE. Paw, look what Maw done gone and made us do. We gotta
war these coats ever' time we' come into supper. Jest 'cause them
townfolks do.

PAW. Since them city folks come, Maw's shore been puttin' on airs.

ZEB. And I'm a-favorin' 'em goin' home.

ZACK. Yeah. We spent the past two days a-waitin' on that gal—totin'
wood, totin' water—totin', a-totin' and a-totin'—

ZO. She ain't let us set down wunst.

ZEKE. If we could only git Noo York to come after them.

MAW *(appearing on porch with a long cigarette holder).* Is Lucinda
back yit? *(She flicks ashes from the cigarette over the railing with all the
dignity of a dowager.)*

PAW. You mean Cindy?

MAW. I mean *Lu*-cinda.

PAW. No.

MAW. Then, Zeke, Zeb—*(Suddenly remembering.)*—Naw, I mean—
Ezekial, Zebedee, Zacharias, Zo—uh—Zodiac—effen you got your
coats, you can come into supper. Dinner is sarved. *(She flicks the
cigarette once more and goes in the house.)*

ZEKE. Did you hear that, Paw? She called me Ezekial. I allus thought
my name was Zeke. You writ it in the Bible jest plain Zeke, didn't you?

PAW. Shore, I did. Maw,—she's shore gone hi-falutin'. The next
thing you know she'll be callin' me Abner fer Ab. Now, 'at'll be somep'n.
Abner for Ab!

MAW *(coming out on porch and flicking ashes from her cigarette).*
Absalom! *(She goes back in.)*

PAW. It ain't to be put up with! We gotta do somep'n.

ZEKE. Paw, mabbe we could mail a letter to whur they come from
and tell 'em to come after them folks.

PAW *(indignantly).* Mail a letter! Use givernment mail! After the
givernment strung up my pappy! You know that fer forty year, we ain't
spoke to the givernment.

ZEKE. But, Paw! Wearin' these tight coats ever' day liable to squez us up to nothin'. Mabbe we ought to start speakin' to the givernment agin.

PAW. And hev that President of the United States a-goin' 'round braggin' to folks that us Higginses spoke first?

MAW *(calling off-stage)*. Absalom!

PAW. Go on in. We'll work out somep'n. We just pint-blank got it ter do! (ZEB, ZACK, *and* ZO *go in.* ZEKE *stays behind.)*

ZEKE. Paw! I jest thought. Mabbe we can git word through by pid-gin.

PAW. Naw. That cayn't be did!

ZEKE. Paw, lemme try. Dad-blast it, my coat's the tightest one.

PAW. Now whar would you find a pigeon?

ZEKE. I could try.

PAW. Ain't no pigeon.

ZEKE. Please, Paw!

PAW. I don't want to hear no more about a pigeon!

MAW *(coming out on porch)*. Absalom! Afore you come in, you git a razor and try to stall off your beard.

PAW *(starting up the steps)*. I shaved last week, and I ain't gonna do hit.

MAW *(reaching inside the door of the house for a gun and blocking him in the doorway by pointing the gun straight at him)*. Absalom! I said to stall off yer beard.

PAW *(grabbing a shaving brush and mug on the porch shelf and angrily starting to work up lather; then, turning and shouting to* ZEKE *)*. Whatcha standin' there fer? I told you what to do. *(He pauses.)* Find a pigeon!

PAW *follows* MAW *into the house.* ZEKE *leaves on his mission, but meets* MILLICENT *and* JERRY *returning from their trip.* JERRY *stands the fishing poles by the cabin and holds up a string of fish.*

JEREMIAH. Hey, Zeke! Look at the trout we ketched.

ZEKE. Do you-all know whur I could ketch a pid-gin?

MILLICENT. A pigeon? What for?

ZEKE. Send a message.

MILLICENT. Oh, what fun! I've always wanted to do that. I'll help you.

ZEKE. Oh—uh—I ain't right shur you'll want ter.

MILLICENT. Yes, I do. What is the message?

ZEKE *(gulping)*. Well, uh—first, I gotta find *(Drawling.)* a pid-gin. *(He backs out in confusion.)*

MILLICENT. Jerry, those songs you were just singing to me as we walked beside the creek—they were so nice. You sang them beautifully.

JEREMIAH *(bashful but pleased).* Aw—twarn't nuthin'.

MILLICENT. Jerry—have you ever thought of getting a job, singing in New York?

JEREMIAH *(staring at her).* No, marm. Thet idy ain't *niver* occurred ter me.

MILLICENT. You could.

JEREMIAH. Git a job? In New York? A-sangin'!

MILLICENT. Yes. I think you would be a sensation. Do you play the guitar?

JEREMIAH. You mean the *git*-tar? Why, shore, don't everbawdy?

MILLICENT. Then, I *know* you can get a job.

JEREMIAH. A job that pays money?

MILLICENT. Mmm.

JEREMIAH. Do you mean jest a-sangin' with a *git*-tar kin make money?

MILLICENT. It has, yes.

JEREMIAH. But how would I go about gittin' a job like that?

MILLICENT. I know several theater people in New York. If you go back with me, I'll see what I can do.

JEREMIAH *(eagerly).* Ye would? Thankee, marm! *(Upon sober reflection.)* Naw, I giss not, thankee jest the same.

MILLICENT. Why not?

JEREMIAH. I'd shore like to make some money, but I don't thank much of thet sangin' idy. Hit don't sound ter me like *man's* work.

MILLICENT. But think of all that money?

JEREMIAH *(gloomily).* Yeah, I'm a-thinkin' on it. Maybe a hull hunert dollars.

MILLICENT. Maybe a thousand dollars.

JEREMIAH. A thousand dollars? Did you say a *thousand* dollars? Dang it, I'll—I'll go!

MILLICENT. Oh, Jerry!

JEREMIAH. A thousand dollars! Why, thet would buy that river-bottom farm down thar in the valley.

MILLICENT. We have farms up there, too. I have a country place in Connecticut.

JEREMIAH. Ye hev? *(Excited.)* Say—do ye own a tractor?

MILLICENT. Yes.

JEREMIAH. Thank of thet! Would you let a feller like me drive it around—jest wunst?

MILLICENT. Sure, we'll have fun.

JEREMIAH. Man, effin I could only git my hands on a tractor!

MILLICENT. If I could only get an airplane we could get out of this place.

JEREMIAH. But you'll never get an airplane around hyar.

MILLICENT. I'll get one somewhere. I always get what I want! *(She goes toward the house.)*

JEREMIAH *starts off, singing the last phrase of "River-Bottom Farm." The zooming noise of an airplane is heard. Everybody rushes out of the house, both front and back doors, and neighbors begin to gather.*

PAW. Miss Mel'cint. Your airplane. Hit's up again. Hit's circlin' around. Duck everybody. *(Everybody ducks as the noise zooms louder.)*

MILLICENT. It couldn't be mine. It's another one. It's larger. It's a rescue plane. I wonder how they found us?

MRS. VAN DEVERE. Your uncle Cornelius must have sent a searching party.

MILLICENT. Yes, but how would he know? *(She shrugs.)* Well, anyway it's wonderful. Oh, Jerry! Here's a rescue plane. Now we can leave.

JEREMIAH. A flyin' machine! You allus said you got what you wanted.

MILLICENT *(to the* FOUR BOYS). Boys, do you mind carrying out the luggage?

MAW. I'll go pack for you. *(She starts for the house.)*

MRS. VAN DEVERE. We must tell the Professor. Where is he?

MAW. I'll tell him. *(She nods toward cabin.)* He's in the bed. He kinda overdid hisself today.

MRS. VAN DEVERE. In the bed? Can he travel all right?

MAW. Shore. Jest a few scratches. He jest ain't feelin' up to snuff. (MAW *goes into house.* JEREMIAH *walks along, looking up at the sky.)*

JEREMIAH. Look at that flyin' machine. Hit's a big'n.

PAW. Hit's a whopper!

MOUNTAINEER. Hit's a-landin'! Come on!

The crowd runs to see the plane, leaving MILLICENT, JEREMIAH, *and* MRS. VAN DEVERE.

JEREMIAH. I gotta see that!

MRS. VAN DEVERE. Oh, Jeremiah, if you don't mind I'd like to take some things from the mill when I leave.

JEREMIAH *(rushing off).* Sure. Take anything you want. Jest junk.

The BOYS *come from the house.*

MRS. VAN DEVERE. Thank you. *(Seeing the* BOYS.) Boys, when you get through with the luggage, do you mind coming with me over to the mill and lifting a few things.

The BOYS *return to the house as a uniformed* PILOT *enters.*

PILOT *(tipping his cap).* Southern Airlines. Are you the people this plane was chartered for?

MILLICENT. We must be. This is Mrs. Van Devere, and I am Mrs. Tucker Beaumont.

PILOT. How do you do? I'd like to leave as soon as possible.

MILLICENT. You'll have to wait until we get packed.

PILOT. Of course. I'll be waiting in the plane, Mrs. Beaumont. *(He leaves.)*

MRS. VAN DEVERE. Millicent, I'm going over to the mill. There are some ladder-back chairs that I want, some Early American glass, and the sweetest old pine chest.

MILLICENT. Aunt Phyllis, don't clutter the airplane with a lot of stuff. We won't have a place to sit, Jerry and I.

MRS. VAN DEVERE. Jerry!

MILLICENT. Yes, Jerry! He's going back with me.

MRS. VAN DEVERE. Have you told him—you are married?

MILLICENT. Of course not.

MRS. VAN DEVERE. You and your movie stars, cowboys, baseball players,—always the big and brawny. First one then the other—until you get bored, and then it's someone else. I don't know why Tucker puts up with it.

MILLICENT. What else can he do? I'm keeping up that precious, antique family of his.

MRS. VAN DEVERE *(as she leaves).* This little mountain boy doesn't know what he's letting himself in for. I hope he doesn't go with you. I'll bet a thousand dollars he doesn't.

MILLICENT. A thousand dollars! I'll take that bet. *(She shrugs.)* He will! Money buys everything.

JEREMIAH *(re-entering).* That shore is a purty airplane!

MRS. VAN DEVERE *(leaving).* Jeremiah, are you sure you want to go with us?

JEREMIAH. Yess'um. Go flyin' in that plane! Golly Moses, yes.

MRS. VAN DEVERE *leaves, shaking her head sadly.*

MILLICENT *(rushing over to prevent further conversation).* I'll teach you to fly one, Jerry.

JEREMIAH. You will?

MILLICENT. Hurry and get packed.

JEREMIAH *(looking up surprised).* We gotta wait for Cindy.

MILLICENT. Cindy!

JEREMIAH. You mean—uh—you hadn't meant fer Cindy to go?

MILLICENT. We won't have room.

JEREMIAH. Oh, you won't? Well, I gotta ask her first.

MILLICENT. You don't have to ask her. Come on.

JEREMIAH. Oh, yessum. I couldn't go nowhar without askin' Cindy. Won't take but a minute.

MILLICENT. Well, hurry. I'll change clothes and meet you at the plane. *(She goes into house.)*

JEREMIAH *(calling).* Cindy! CINDY! Wonder whar she went traipsin' off to? (IVADIE *appears.)* Ivadie, whar's Cindy?

IVADIE. I told you she went to pick poke.

JEREMIAH. But she ain't never been gone this long a'fore.

IVADIE. Said she'd be back by sundown.

JEREMIAH. It's past sundown. Hit's almost dark. Come on, I gotta find her in a hurry. *(They leave, back of the house.)*

IVADIE *(looking over the bluff as she follows him).* Great liver and lights!

MRS. VAN DEVERE *enters, as* MAW *sets out a packed bag on the porch.*

MRS. VAN DEVERE. Oh, Mrs. Higgins, will you tell Jeremiah I'm going over to the mill to get some of those cured hams?

MAW. Go right ahead. Law, he's got so many, he'll be glad to give you some.

MRS. VAN DEVERE. And I wonder if I might ask a favor of *you.*

MAW. Why, shore, whut is it?

MRS. VAN DEVERE. I've been nominated as district chairman of the Garden Clubs—and I was just thinking, if I could distribute along the Atlantic Seaboard a little of this—White Lightning—

MAW *(handing her a jug).* Why, shore, hyar it is.

MRS. VAN DEVERE. It might bounce me right into the presidency! *(She starts out, then stops suddenly.)* Oh! On second thought, I had better take *two* jugs. (MAW *walks over to her with another jug.)* I'm climbing up from corresponding secretary. *(She goes out with a jug under each arm.)*

MOUNTAINEERS *come in.*

FIRST MOUNTAINEER. I can't find Cindy. She's not acrost the Creek.

SECOND MOUNTAINEER *(entering).* She ain't in the field.

THIRD MOUNTAINEER *(entering).* She ain't back of the mill.

JEREMIAH *(appearing with* IVADIE *and other* MOUNTAINEERS*).* Ivadie, which way did she go?

IVADIE. I—I don't know. She said she wuz goin' a long way off.

JEREMIAH. Listen, fellers, better divide up. Kiver all that section. I'll search around here. *(Calling.)* Cindy! CINDY! *(The* MOUNTAINEERS *scatter to search.)*

IVADIE *(beginning to cry).* I told her not to.

The music of "Old Ballad" begins and continues softly under.

JEREMIAH. Told her not to do what?

IVADIE. I can't tell you.

JEREMIAH. Can't tell me what?

IVADIE. She said not to tell—but, oh, Jeremiah! I'm skeered. I'm bad skeered. I'm gonna tell.

JEREMIAH *(thundering).* Tell what!

IVADIE *(pointing).* She went down the Devil's Drop!

JEREMIAH *(crossing upstage).* The Devil's Drop!

IVADIE *(following him).* She didn't pick poke no more'n nothin'. She started out fer New Hope.

JEREMIAH. Down that bluff? Jest tryin' to skeer somebody. *(To* IVADIE.) Now, don't be gittin' in a frenzy. I'm not skeered. Of course she could get hurt.

IVADIE. She's dead. I know she's dead. I ain't niver confessed it, but last week, I burned wood that wuz lightnin'-struck, and I ben expectin' a death on the way. And today I saw a bird a-peckin' on the winder— Cindy's winder. You know whut that means.

JEREMIAH *(to himself).* She could have lost her footin'—in the darksomeness. She could have dropped in the falls and drownded. *(Whispering.)* Cindy! *(He stands up and speaks aloud.)* We gotta find her. She might be hurt—hurt bad! *(Calling to the searchers.)* Found her? *(Echoes of "No!" "No!" and "Not here!" are heard. He crosses to the bluff.)* I'm goin' down the Devil's Drop.

IVADIE. No, Jeremiah, don't! No use of you gittin' kilt, too!

JEREMIAH. Tell 'em to keep lookin'!

CINDY *walks in.* JEREMIAH *turns and faces her.*

CINDY. Who you searchin' fer?

The music of "Old Ballad" ends.

JEREMIAH. Oh, Cindy! *(Taking her in his arms.)* I thought I'd lost you! *(Angrily flinging her out of his arms.)* You little fool! Tryin' to skeer somebody. Well, I wuzn't skeered! *(Hugging her again.)* Oh, yes. Yes, I wuz, Cindy. My stomach caved in. *(Angrily flinging her out of his arms again.)* What in tarnation did you go down there for?

CINDY. Jeremiah, I have a lil', ol', bitty confession to make. I went down to—

JEREMIAH. I know! Jest wanted folks to go a-lookin' fer you. Wall, they didn't. *(He remembers the searching party.)* Oh. *(Calling.)* FOUND! *(Echoes of "Found!" "Found!" "Found!" come back.)*

The music of "Old Ballad" begins again.

JEREMIAH *(singing joyously).*
    I found my own true love
    On a summer evening—
(speaking, as the music continues softly.)
Oh, Cindy, you wuz gone a long time. You know somep'n? Hit's the onliest time you've ever been gone, and daw-gonit, I miss you when you ain't underfoot. Cindy, whensomever I kin git some money saved up, how about you and me gittin'—you know—

CINDY. Gittin' married?

JEREMIAH. Yeah.

CINDY. Land sakes alive. I don't know. I ain't niver studied about it one way or t'other.

JEREMIAH. Well—what about it?

CINDY. I don't know effen you're in love with me. You ain't niver named it to me.

JEREMIAH. Aw, you been knowin' it, Miss Priss. You knowed it since we wuz twelve years old and I give you my June bugs.

CINDY. Then say it, say, "Cindy, I love you."

JEREMIAH *(pleading).* Aw—it ain't manly.

CINDY. Then I ain't a-fixin'.

JEREMIAH. All right, you ornery cuss. I like you. I shore don't know why, but I like you a hull lot. Thar! Does that suit you?

CINDY *(sighing).* I giss hit'll hev ter do.

JEREMIAH *(tenderly).* Oh, Cindy! Cindy, honey! *(He kisses her, and the music fades.)*

CINDY *(coming out of a trance, with a deep sigh).* That does!

JEREMIAH. And Cindy, why else would I do jest whut I said I wuzn't gonna do. Settle on nuthin'.

CINDY. Some day we'll have somep'n. You know what I allus used to sing.

They sing a reprise of "We Can Start on Love."

CINDY *(singing).*

> Some day we'll have a house of our own,
> With all the things that we've been dreamin' of;

CINDY AND JEREMIAH.

> But till that happy day, when we see it underway,
> I know that we can start on love.

JEREMIAH.

> To dream a dream doesn't mean it's bound to come true;

CINDY AND JEREMIAH.

> To scheme a scheme is just a way of keeping dreams in view.
>
> Some day we'll leave the shadows behind,
> And find the sunshine we've been dreaming of;
> But while we're waiting here for the clouds to disappear
> I know that we can start on love.

JEREMIAH *hugs her again.* MILLICENT *appears, in time to see* CINDY *in* JEREMIAH's *arms.*

MILLICENT. Jerry! The plane is waiting.

JEREMIAH *(in a trance).* Plane? What plane? Oh, yeah. I plumb forgot. Thankee, marm. Mighty nice of you. But I ain't a-goin'.

MILLICENT. You aren't going with *me?*

JEREMIAH. I intentioned to, but the way I feel jest now, I cayn't make myself leave.

CINDY *(radiantly).* Jeremiah!

MILLICENT. Well, you're the worst little yokel I've ever met! Where's Aunt Phyllis! Why in the hell don't we get started! *(Shouting.)* PROFESSOR!

MAW *comes from the house.*

MAW *(calling from the porch).* He's a-comin'.

PAW *enters from the house.*

MAW. Paw, you git the baggins. (PAW *grabs the bags eagerly and leaves.)*

The PILOT *enters.*

PILOT *(saluting again).* I beg your pardon, ma'am, but we must leave.

MILLICENT. I'm ready. *(In a seductive voice.)* Tell me, did you land that large plane in this small clearing all by yourself?

PILOT *(pleased).* It wasn't so hard.

MILLICENT. What did you say your name is?

PILOT. Samson Smith.

MILLICENT. Samson? *(Looking him over.)* Then come along—Sammy.

They go out. MOUNTAINEERS *start gathering just in time to see the* PROFESSOR *being borne out on a board by the* FOUR BOYS. *He is lying on his stomach and a patch is visible on his rear.*

MOUNTAINEER. Fellers, look at that!

MAW. Wall, Professor! You shore had yourself a time.

PROFESSOR. Yes, indeed.

MAW. You shore look like that census taker that wuz carried out of hyar. Folks jest will come to the mountains and overdo!

PROFESSOR. The census taker? He overdid?

MAW. Yeah, but his case wuz a little different from yourn. He got to overdoin' amongst the wimminfolks and got strung up to a tree.

PROFESSOR *(bolting upright on the board).* Hurry, boys. Let's get moving.

The BOYS *carry him out.*

MILLICENT *(calling off-stage).* AUNT PHYLLIS! (MRS. VAN DEVERE *enters.)*

MRS. VAN DEVERE. Coming! Goodbye, Mrs. Higgins, and thank you. We've had such a good time.

MAW. Twarn't nuthin'. We'd be glad to hev you come back. *(Looking up at the sky.)* Jest—drop down anytime.

MRS. VAN DEVERE *(shaking hands).* Thanks. Good luck, Mrs. Higgins.

MAW. And good luck to you. I hope your husband gits to likin' you better, Mistress Van Devere the Third, and moves you right up in bed.

MRS. VAN DEVERE. Jeremiah, here's an itemized bill, *(Handing him a slip of paper.),* according to the prices I've been paying antique shops. And there is the money *(Handing it to him.)*—a thousand dollars.

JEREMIAH. A thousand dollars! Jest for that junk? Thankee, marm. Lookee! Real shore-nuff cash money. Hunert dollar bills!

MILLICENT *(still louder, off-stage).* AUNT PHYLLIS!

MRS. VAN DEVERE. You and I had better hurry, Jeremiah!

JEREMIAH. I decided not to go.

MRS. VAN DEVERE. You're not going? Good for you, my boy! For that, here's another thousand dollars. *(She counts out more bills.)* Millicent bet me this thousand you *would* go Ha! *(She chuckles.)*

JEREMIAH. Oh, no, we couldn't take that.

MRS. VAN DEVERE. Nonsense. I've never enjoyed winning a bet so much in all my life. Bless you, my dears. Good-bye. *(She waves to them as she leaves.)*

JEREMIAH. Two thousand dollars! Cindy! We're rich!

CINDY. Two thousand dollars. That would buy enough apple trees for that hull gulch and them two hollers.

JEREMIAH. Apple trees? Yeah! *(Thinking fast and getting excited.)* And I already got all that mountain land. Orchards! Like the Professor wuz a-tellin' me. Mountains, he said, *(Pulling out the pamphlets.)* is a good place for apples. Not one little old orchard, but four or five! *(Leaping to steps and looking over his land.)* Over here and over there and over there! And I'll use them new-fangled book-farmin' idees. Cindy, I'm shore glad I thought of them orchards. Say! We kin get married right now. Git ready! Boys! Git to house-raisin!

CINDY *leaves for the house, radiant.*

FIRST MOUNTAINEER. Whoopee! Gonna hev a house-raisin'!

SECOND MOUNTAINEER. Gonna hev a bride!

THIRD MOUNTAINEER. Gonna hev a house-raisin' fer a sassy lil bride!

JEREMIAH *(singing).*

> Come along, folks, I've something to confide,
> I need a house for a sassy li'l bride,
> So heft that log, raise it topside,
> Gotta build a house for a special bride.
> Swing a mountain axe, boys, let the hammers ring,
> All lift together, everybody sing,
> This log feels light, and I feel gay,
> It's mine and Cindy's weddin' day.

CHORUS.

> Come along, folks, git to raisin' that side,
> We're a' house-raisin' fer a sassy little bride.

The MOUNTAINEERS *begin work again.* CINDY *comes out of the house dressed in an old-fashioned, short-length wedding dress and veil.*

JEREMIAH *(with* CINDY *in his arms).*

When you build the doorway, make it good and wide,
I gotta carry through it a sassy little bride;
Better leave room fer a family,
Half a dozen kids fer Cindy and me,
Fix it up nice so I'll burst with pride
When I carry in my sassy little bride.

JEREMIAH *holds the high note, while the chorus sings.*

CHORUS.

Swing that mountain axe, high and wide!
We're house-raisin' fer a sassy little bride,
Singin' and praisin' at this house-raisin'—

JEREMIAH.

Split that rail,
Hammer that nail,
We're gonna hit that marryin' trail!
Cindy and me—

CHORUS.

Gonna be a weddin'—

JEREMIAH.

Cindy and me—

CHORUS.

Gonna be a weddin!

ALL.

A great weddin' day!
                    CURTAIN

Overture

Springtime in Tennessee

River Bottom Farm

It's a Matter of Taste

Millicent:

Medium bounce

mat-ter of taste, _____ And my taste is so change-a-ble. If my

love is mis-placed, _____ Then a change is ar-range-a-ble. _____ Each

time I'm sure I've got the real thing, I find it's sud-den-ly spring, and I

want a last fling, And whad-da ya know ___ there I go! It's a matter of taste, ___ And my heart is a gad-a-bout; I can nev-er be sure ___ Just which one I am mad-a-bout; I can't see the fun of con-cen- trat-ing on one And let-ting all the rest go to waste; So where men are con-cerned,

Ballad

A Gingham Dress

Maw: A gal could never learn no-thin' good from a bold piece of trash like her.

Cindy: You're wrong there, Maw, there's plenty to learn And that's what I'm here fer.

Maw: She's up to no good, that's plain to see, And besides all that, she's as brazen as can be.

Cindy: Well, if she's what you mean by a ci-ty slick-er, How do you get to be slick-er quick-er?

A ging-ham dress is all ve-ry well
ain't silk-y drape as much as the shape that will

Maw:
long as you're on the farm. And but-ton-up shoes and sen-si-ble stock-ins
turn a fel-ler's head. Jest watch a man go af-ter cal-i-co Ef the

Cindy:
Nev-er done no gal harm. But as long as I keep my hair in a braid and
fig-ger that's in it ain't bad. Now them shined up gals may glit-ter like brass, But

wear such sen-si-ble clothes, As long as my lips ain't red like hers And my
all what glit-ters ain't gold; And what does it matter as long as they glit-ter While this

slip oc-casionally shows, I know no-mance will pass me by.
gold just sets and gets

Now, it old. _ I know ro-mance will pass   me   by.

Thar's Gold in Them Thar Hills

spin-nin' wheel in the cor-ner And a wash-pot set-tin' out chere, Why, this

plain board shack ain't a plain board shack—It's got at - mos - phere! I'll sell 'em straw brooms that's

home-made, Straw flow-ers fer their win-der-sills._____ Lit-tle dolls that's are made of

corn-shucks, Shucks, that's gold in them thar hills!_____ I'll sell 'em Pink flam-in-goes

pil-lows all purt-y and paint-ed, And print-ed with a bee-yoo-ti-ful pome, I'll sell

fish to the men that ain't been fish-in' fer fish And need a string of fish to take home! Oh, I'm

fresh and un-spiled, she said so; In my ging-ham purt-ied up with frills, ____ If they

pay, they can take my pitch-er, ____ Thar's gold in them thar hills!

Captivatin' Critter

Cindy:

He's so stub-born, ____ He's as stub-born as can be; He's so

sas-sy, ____ He's e-ven sas-sy to me; He's the con-tra-ri-est, de-lay-in-est, the see-you-la-ter-est man that e-ver

wuz. ____ He makes me fu-ri-ous, And ain't it cu-ri-ous, That's

why I love him so ____ He can be so nice ____ E-ver,

e-ver so nice, He can make a girl for-get to think twice; He's the plumb pro-vok-in-est, make you chok-in-est

cap-ti-va-tin-est man that-e-ver wuz! But when he's ten-der, He's might-y

ten-der,___ And now I guess at last I know Why I put up with the crit-ter, It's

'cause I love him so.___

It's Anglo-Saxon

Professor:

Chau-cer was wont to pro-nounce his words In much the same man-ner that you do.____ If he should re-turn he could be un-der-stood On-ly by peo-ple like you.____ The folks in his day called a child a "bairn," And bring-ing it up was a pro-cess called "rar'n," That lit-tle word ain't is not on-ly quaint____

I Admire the Way You Look

I could we fin-ish danc-in' Would you take a chance and get to-geth-er in a cor-ner nook? 'Cause

I ad- mire the way you look!

Springtime in Tennessee
Square Dance Version - for Finale, Act I

Organ:
Fast

Piano: vamp accompaniment to "Springtime in Tennessee"   Repeat ad lib until curtain

Morning on the Mountain

Remainder of this part of first chorus
consists of dialogue and action over music.

Chorus:
bees have start-ed hum-min', 'cause a brand new day is com-in'; When it's morn- in' on the

moun-tain, There is some-thin' makes you kind-a want-a sing;—— If you're court-in', then as

sure as you are born You'll be his'n and yer fel-ler will be yourn, When it's morn- in' on the

moun-tain in spring. spring.

We Can Start on Love

dream a dream doesn't mean it's bound to come true, To scheme a scheme is just a way of

keep-ing dreams in' view. Some - day we'll leave our trou-bles be-hind And find the

sun - shine we've been dream-ing of,_____ But while we're wait-in' here for the clouds to

dis - ap - pear, I know that we can start on love._____

I'm Simply Wild About Wild Life

Professor:

Vivace - razzmatazz

I'm simp-ly wild ___ a-bout wild life, ___ Wild life is the life for me; ___ What I like a-bout Flo-ra, I like a-bout Faun-a, They're both love-ly as can be; ___ And when I hear some Tur-dus mi-gra-to-ri-ous Tell an-oth-er Rob-in she's glo-ri-ous,

con 8ve

con 8ve

Terbaccy's Terbaccy

Yaller, Yaller Moon

Coretta:

Not too fast - well-accented

Oh, that yal-ler, yal-ler moon in the month of May,

That's why I am whur I am ter-day, That's why I'm whur I am ter-day.

I'm as stead-y as a rock in A-pril, I do mid-dlin' well in March, But let it come May I git to

feel- in' that- a- way, I'm plumb har- um scar- um in May; I

feel so har- um scar- um I'd scare 'em in a har- em in May I

wisht we did- n't have no moon in May, I wisht that moon did- n't shine; 'Cause

when it gets yel- ler I git to feel- in' mel- ler, A- long comes my fel- ler, and

traps for the bars, but that moon's what gits me! I wisht we did-n't have May blos-soms, ____ With all them sweet smel-lin' scents; ____ 'Cause I get so bless-ed tired of a- be- in' bless'd with so bless-ed man-y bless-ed e- vents. Oh, ev-'ry Jan-u-ar-y I wisht I'd been less mer-ry in May! ____

Duet: We Can Start on Love (Act II)

Cindy: Some day we'll have a house of our own, With all the things that we've been dreaming of;

Both: But till that happy day, when we see it under way, I know that we can start on love.

Jeremiah: To dream a dream doesn't mean its bound to come true; to scheme a scheme is

Cindy: just a way of keeping dreams in view

Jeremiah: Ah — Some day we'll leave the shadows behind, — And find { the } the sunshine we've been dreaming of; —

But while we're waiting here for the clouds to disappear, —
we're waiting here for clouds to disap-

— I know that we can start on love. —
pear we can start on love. —

Entire accompaniment should be transposed to Eb.

House Raisin'

Jeremiah:

Strong & cheerful

Come a-long, folks, I've some-thing to con-fide, I need a house for a sas-sy li'l bride, So heft that log, raise it top side, Got-ta build a house for a spe-cial bride. Swing a moun-tain axe, boys, let the ham-mers ring, All lift to-geth-er ev'-ry-bod-y sing. This log feels light, and I feel gay, It's

A LITTLE TO THE LEFT

by Brock Brower

A scene from *A Little to the Left,* by Brock Brower. Originally produced by The Carolina Playmakers in 1959.

THE AUTHOR: *Brock Brower*

The author of *A Little to the Left,* Brock Brower, is a native of Westfield, New Jersey. He attended public schools there and went on to Dartmouth where he was graduated in 1953. The next two years he spent in England, where as a Rhodes Scholar he took a First in the Final Honors School of English Language and Literature at Merton College, Oxford. Returning to the United States, Mr. Brower worked briefly as a first reader for Viking Press, and then went into the Army as a private. While at Fort Bragg, North Carolina, in the Special Warfare Center, he wrote manuals on guerrilla fighting. In 1959, he came to Chapel Hill and was employed by The University of North Carolina Press in an editorial capacity. And it was here that he enrolled in a playwriting course being taught by Professor Thomas M. Patterson.

The play included in this volume is not the author's first. While at Oxford he wrote a one-act verse comedy, *The Tender Edge,* which was later published in *New World Writing #11.*

Regarding *A Little to the Left* the author wrote in reminiscence to this editor on November 2, 1967: "I wrote the first version of the play in 1955 while I was a student at Oxford. It was the second play I'd tried doing, and, to some extent, amounted to an effort to excrete all the George Bernard Shaw I'd ingested. It had a terribly inappropriate death-of-a-little-child ending at that time, and the one dramatic reading it was given at Oxford convinced me *that* had to be changed. However, no new ending occurred to me—until I got to UNC and reworked the entire play in Tom Patterson's playwriting class. Tom liked the results enough to suggest the play's being produced the following year. [But] by that time, I'd left Chapel Hill under the mistaken idea that a grant-in-aid of some $5,000 from CBS-TV was going to open up a career rich in residuals for me. [However,] I returned for some weeks of rehearsal and the production of the play.

"It was a marvelous experience: righteous ire at the audience for not understanding what a funny play I'd written; anger at myself for dropping or mangling funny lines in the original writing; delight in the sets, pleasure in the cast, [and] respect for Tom's skill at holding the shambles together. . . . I learned an incredible amount about *what worked* on the stage, and one sorry total lesson: that, as hard as I'd tried to 'mature' the play, it still bore a certain unhappy tint of juvenilia, like a faded diaper stain."

During the almost ten years since Mr. Brower saw his first dramatic work become a play, he has been busy as both editor and writer. Two assignments have been as an assistant editor of *Esquire* and associate editor of *The Transatlantic Review*. He has written more than fifty articles for *Esquire, Life, The Saturday Evening Post, Holiday, New York Times Magazine, American Scholar,* and practically every leading magazine in the country. He has also written short stories—one in the 1968 *O'Henry Memorial Awards* volume. His recent novel, *Debris,* appeared under the Atheneum banner with excellent reviews, and a collection of his reportage, *Other Loyalties,* was published this fall. A long one-act play, *The Social Eumenides,* he is holding back from production until he writes a companion piece to make a full evening of theater.

Brock Brower and his family live in Princeton, New Jersey, and he will be Lecturer in Creative Arts (Writing) at the University there for the school year 1968–69.

PREMIÈRE PLAYBILL CREDITS

A Little to the Left, by Brock Brower, was originally produced by The
Carolina Playmakers on November 18, 19, 20, 21, and 22, 1959, in the
Playmakers Theatre, Chapel Hill, North Carolina, under the direction of
Thomas M. Patterson. The settings were by John Sneden, the costumes
by Irene Smart Rains, and the lighting by John Stockard.

THE CAST

HARRY DILBY	Robert Elston
FRANCIS P. MORAN	Gordon Clark
FIELD MARSHALL ALFONSO FERNANDO DE MALAGONA	Charles Nisbet
JOHN MORAN	Allen Hayward
PEDRO MENDOZA	Bill File
HELENE MUGGINS	Mary Lawrence
ISHMAEL BOODLEHEIM	Bob Merritt
CARLOS SEGURA	Glenn L. Vernon
JULIANNA MORAN	Marilyn Zschau
SOLDIERS AND GUARDS	Jerry Walker,

Robert Thornburg, John Chase, Bill Hannah,
Chenault Spence

SCENE AND TIME

The Republic of Costa Bona. The present.

ACT ONE: Headquarters of the Costa Bona Revolutionary Army.
ACT TWO: Scene One. The same, an hour later.
          Scene Two. The same, ten minutes later.
ACT THREE: The main cell of Political Prison, after midnight.

ACT ONE

The scene is the headquarters of the Revolutionary Army of the Free People's Republic of Costa Bona. It is in a jungle. An open tent, sagging between its poles like Spanish moss, occupies whatever space the ferns, mango trees, monkey vines, plantains, and other equatorial greenery leave it. Inside the tent there is a crippled cot, an ancient field telephone with a mouthpiece like a daffodil, a desk constructed unevenly of shipping crates, a rusted mimeograph machine, and a mossy water bucket. Two SOLDIERS, *dressed in castoff U.S. Army fatigues, are asleep, almost spread-eagled, beside the water bucket.*

HARRY DILBY *enters, attired in dirty suntans, pith helmet, and an old revolver the size of a small howitzer. He notices the two* SOLDIERS *asleep.*

HARRY. Blimy! Asleep on guard again! *(He makes as if to kick them, then changes his mind. He takes the ladle from the water bucket.)* Damn good thing bananas can grow all by their bloody selves. *(He starts to drink from the ladle, sees something in the water, and stops short.)* Now ain't you the cute little bugger? Paddlin' around on your little tummy— Bloody hell, if you can drink it, I guess I can. *(He catapults the bug out of the water with a snap of his finger, sips, then throws out the rest. Now he goes to the telephone, jangles it.)* Hello. Johnny?—Hello?— Uhh?—Viva la Republica yourself, you sillyarse Wog! I want Johnny. —Señor Juan. Juanito. Immediamento.—Si, si. El aeroplano. Juanito.— Viva la Revolution!—And up your giggy with a stiff wire brush! *(*FRANCIS P. MORAN *enters. He is tropically tailored and carries a locked brief case.* HARRY *immediately draws his revolver on him and waves him to the cot.)* Have a seat, guv'ner. With you in a minute. *(He returns to the telephone.)* Hello, Johnny?—It's Harry. Is His Nibs at the airfield, Johnny?—What?—Well, tell him when he wakes up that his flagship just sank on maneuvers.—No, I'm serious! Right to the bottom—hit a water buffalo.—Bloody animal.—Gored it in the fantail.—I know it's aluminum, but it's still only a canoe!—No. The admiral lost a star swimmin' ashore, is all.—The buffalo? I don't know. Went back to sleep in the mud, I guess.—How do I know that you're going to tell him? Tell him when it wakes up, we'll sink it! *(He hangs up.)* Rotten revolution! Now, who are you, guv'ner?

MORAN *(formally).* I'm looking for Field Marshall Alfonso Fernando de Malagona, the leader of the Free People's Republic of Costa Bona. Is he here?

HARRY. You can bloody well see he ain't. Besides, I didn't ask you what you wanted. I asked you who you were.

MORAN. I'm afraid I can only repeat what I've already said. I'm looking for—*(Harry reaches out suddenly and pulls the brief case from* MORAN'S *hand, but it is locked to his wrist.)*

HARRY. Like I thought. Righto, guv'ner. Long as I know you're here on business. *(He returns his revolver to the holster.)* His Nibs is at the airfield. He likes to take his siesta, leaning up against an oil drum. Reminds him of the city. Johnny says he's on his way over. Make yourself comfortable.

MORAN. Thank you. *(He adjusts himself and the brief case on his wrist.* HARRY *continues to stare at him.)*

HARRY. Now I wonder if you're a Communist or a banana man? *(*MORAN *shifts around, ignoring him.)* A couple of years ago I could spot 'em like that. Now you can't tell a bloody agitator from a bloody capitalist. *(Imitating fingering money.)* I hope you brought along a little of the ready in that thing.

MORAN. Speaking officially, there's nothing in this brief case but my socks and a few Costa Bonan travel folders.

HARRY *(slightly envious).* Socks? Clean socks?

MORAN. Two pair.

HARRY *(nodding knowingly).* Must be a banana man.

MORAN. But, speaking unofficially, do you need funds?

HARRY. Need funds? Guv'ner, I've been mixed up in a lot of low-budget struggles, but this is the first time I ever had to fight under my own pajamas! *(He points to a flagpole at the top of the tent, where a pair of red-striped pajamas is hanging limply.)*

MORAN. It is that bad?

HARRY. Not half! Guv'ner, let me just tell you about this little social upheaval we're running. First place, it started three weeks before it was supposed to, because the underground radio got careless. I wake up one morning, and people are breaking my windows in. I snap on the underground radio, and a damn record's stuck in a groove! *"Arriba laboras!—annh!—Arriba laboras!—annh!—"*

MORAN. In St. Luis?

HARRY. In St. Luis. Well, I whip on my pants, and yank His Nibs out of bed to lead the thing, and we pulled it together pretty well. At least they were all throwing rocks in the same direction and heading for the Presidential Palace. Then some arse—some Wog carrying a big sign with something on it in Spanish about being downtrodden—went left—when he should've gone right. Before we could stop 'em, they captured two buildings. American Express and the Convent of the Immaculate Conception.

MORAN. I see.

HARRY. American Express wasn't so bad—they thought we were a big tour group—but that nunnery! I'm here to tell you, guv', nothing breaks up a mob quicker than a lot of females wailing to organ music.

MORAN. So you retreated —

HARRY. Advanced, guv'ner. We always advance. We strategically advanced out of sight.

MORAN (with an edge). To prepare for a glorious return?

HARRY (hesitantly). Well, I'll tell you guv'ner, there ain't much left to return with.

MORAN (efficient by questioning). How do you stand then? How many troops do you have? Are they supplied? Artillery? Transport? Air support? Intelligence? And where the hell is your headquarters?

HARRY. You're at headquarters, guv'ner.

MORAN (rising in surprise and walking around the tent and area). This? This Boy Scout tent?

HARRY. It ain't even that. It's an awning we picked up during the uprising. (He pulls down the fringe flap of the tent, which says clearly "AMERICAN EXPRESS.") As for a strength report—(He takes out a dog-eared notebook and begins checking it through with a pencil stub as he talks.) this morning we had twenty-seven enlisted men. But that figure is subject to change. We don't see 'em again 'til pay call. They're on temporary terminal leave, you might say. (Turning a page.) Small arms. We've got fourteen Springfield rifles—all of them with pitted barrels, and four with no bolts—six forty-five automatics, and clips for two of them—five pitchforks—and a mattock. (Turning a page.) Officer personnel includes five generals—nothing below general, in fact, except me—and a three-star—(Makes a correction.)—make that a two-star admiral now. Intelligence. We've got—ah—(He turns a page quickly.) Artillery. Two dozen shells for an eighty-millimeter howitzer, and if we can figure out how to fire them through a bazooka, we'll be hell on time on target! (He turns a page.) In the way of transport, we had, until recently, an aluminum canoe. (Crossing out a word in notebook.) But we ain't no longer a naval power.

MORAN. Incredible. How do you expect to hold out? Why bother to hold out?

HARRY (apologetically). I didn't make the revolution, guv'ner. I just work for it.

MORAN *(looking* HARRY *up and down).* You look like a reasonably intelligent man. You can read and write—point a gun in *approximately* the right direction. Why are you mixed up in this—this—*Putsch?*

HARRY *(helplessly).* I needed work, and it was the only *Putsch* with an opening! I'm sort of an itinerant revolutionary, guv'. Been in thirteen, counting a change of side in one or two of 'em. It's how I feed myself. I can usually find a position as a technical sergeant.

MORAN. And what are you in this one?

HARRY *(uneasily).* Well, being as they're short of men, and somewhat lacking in practical experience—they're all heart, guv', all heart— so-o-o-o they made me a noncommissioned lieutenant-colonel. *(He salutes.)* Colonel Harry Dilby at your service, guv'. Late of Her Majesty's Navy.

MORAN. Deserted?

HARRY *(uneasily).* Bowed out, guv'.

MORAN *(sharply).* Well, Colonel, offhand I'd say you'd be better off with a little less rank and a lot more army.

HARRY *(trying to recoup).* Maybe I put the colors on a little black. It ain't so bad. We've still got the airplane. A spanking little jobbie, that airplane.

FIELD MARSHALL ALFONSO FERNANDO DE MALAGONA *enters with a flourish. He is dressed in fatigues a la Castro and burdened with armaments. He is accompanied by several* SOLDIERS, *and there is a smart show of military courtesy.*

HARRY *(saluting).* Viva la Republica!

FERNANDO. Viva. Viva, Colonel Dilby. Are we still at full strength?

HARRY. Two more gone this morning, Marshall.

FERNANDO. Let them go. Let them go! It is patriots we want. Only patriots! Give me fifty men with hearts. They are worth ten thousand cowards who do not love their country. Knees like the castinets, eh? Fifty men with hearts, Colonel.

HARRY. Then we're still twenty-three short.

FERNANDO *(looking at* MORAN). Who is this? *(With disapproval.)* Out of uniform! Shoot him! *(Immediately the* SOLDIERS *raise their Springfields to their shoulders, aiming at* MORAN.)

MORAN *(speaking quickly).* My name is Moran, Marshall. Francis P. Moran, of the Associated Banana Corporation.

FERNANDO *(turning quickly).* Ah-h-h-h! We are delighted to see you, Señor Moran. You are welcome. Forgive me. I am a very emotional man. *(To* SOLDIERS, *harshly.)* Cease fire! Go shoot each other! *(The* SOLDIERS stand bewildered.) I am only sorry we must meet at this little outpost. But the main camp is across the river. And there is—some small difficulty with—an enemy gunboat. It sank one of our destroyers this morning.

MORAN *(going along with the* MARSHALL). I'm sorry to hear that, Marshall. Have you attacked it?

FERNANDO. That is difficult, señor. The enemy gunboat is still reported to be asleep.

MORAN. How's that?

FERNANDO. It—is lying in a backwater where it is protected. It's like the *Turpitz,* that animal. Please be seated, señor. *(As* MORAN *takes a seat,* FERNANDO *whispers to* HARRY.) Bring Lieutenant Carter. Tell him to be impressive. Very impressive. (HARRY *goes out.)* I have heard much about you, Señor Moran. Lately—from friends everywhere.

MORAN *(frowning).* Yes. We've rather overextended ourselves. In fact, I warn you. We expect solid returns from the next revolution we go into.

FERNANDO *(darkening).* Señor, you should show more respect for the Republic.

MORAN. Things are very tight in our department right now, Marshall. I'm speaking very frankly. It's easy enough to dream up a governmental overthrow, but how many of them do you know that really succeed? There's no money to throw away on cannon-cracker revolts!

FERNANDO *(looking at the brief case).* But there is money—

MORAN. Only if there is a going, profit-making republic that you can sell to the people.

FERNANDO *(suddenly emotional).* The Republic! The Republic *is* the people, señor! It is the flood that beats in their hearts. Their love of freedom, that is the Republic. Carlos Segura! Carlos Segura sits in St. Luis, smoking his bad cigars, drinking his magnificent wines—*(He begins to slip into an inadvertent revery of his own future.)* Kidnapping little girls from the streets for his pleasure—Some of them are only thirteen!—Little girls out of the cradle—like rosebuds—with their sweet, innocent—*(Catching himself.)* Carlos Segura is a dictator! He presses the people under his heel! The people cry for freedom! They flock to my banner!

MORAN. What *is* your banner?

FERNANDO *(hesitating).* It is like the flag of the United States. Not so many stars—*(Glancing over his shoulder at the flagpole that is out of* MORAN'S *vision.)* But lots of stripes!

MORAN. And if people are so ardent for your cause, why did you fail in St. Luis?

FERNANDO *(in a quick answer).* Only because of the spies of Carlos Segura. Señor, it is impossible to trust anyone in this world. Our closest friends betrayed us. *(Sadness comes into his voice.)* My own mistress, señor. My own mistress was in his pay. He corrupted her! A little girl of eleven. *(Angered.)* Hundreds are working for him. They misled our followers. Then a band of his secret police attacked us!

MORAN. In religious garb?

FERNANDO *(pleading).* Señor, I offer you 20 per cent of the revolution. With voting rights, and a three-for-one split three months after I take office.

MORAN *(shaking his head).* I'd be buying a paper hat and a popgun, Marshall. The truth is your revolution fizzled five minutes after it started. You've got a hell of a nerve, asking us for support.

FERNANDO. The revolution did not fizzle! It will never fizzle! It is the spirit of the people! It is in my heart. And his heart. *(Pointing to one of the sleeping* SOLDIERS *by the water bucket.)* And his! *(He indicates the other* SOLDIER. *Then, irritated at the failure of the tableau properly to punctuate his speech, he kicks one of the* SOLDIERS. *The* SOLDIER *wakes, bestirs himself, yawns, and goes back to sleep. Now* FERNANDO *changes his tone.)* All right. It is true we are weak. If we are attacked, we will be wiped out. Five minutes, and the revolution is finished. But if that happens, Señor Moran, it will not be so good. Not for you, will it?

MORAN *(noncommittal).* Go on.

FERNANDO. Not so good for you. Because then there will be nobody to fight with Segura, and he will have all the bananas to himself. *(He pauses, waiting for a reaction.* MORAN *does not crack.)* That is a lot of bananas, señor. It was possible once to pay him a little money, and he would let you have all the bananas. He was a lazy man. But now he has become industrious. He gets up early in the morning and goes to parliament and tells them to nationalize all the plantations.

MORAN. And you propose to get them back for us?

FERNANDO. I do not propose anything. I only say that if you do not help us, the bananas are lost.

MORAN *(angered).* And how do we know what you'll do, once you've got your feet up on Segura's desk—if—mind you—if we let you put them up there?

FERNANDO. If you *let* me? *(Sharply.)* You do not control things the way you used to, *amigo!* You need a friend.

MORAN. I control more interests right now than you think, Marshall. And you're not a friend. You're a big, fat scorpion. We want to be sure we know who you're out to sting.

FERNANDO *(wheedling again).* That is not flattering, señor.

MORAN. And I'm not so sure you've got any sting left.

FERNANDO. I have a sting. A sting that Segura will soon feel!

MORAN *(with an edge).* A naval assault perhaps?

FERNANDO. *El aeroplano!* That is my sting!

MORAN. An airplane?

FERNANDO. Yes. And a bomb. A big bomb! And a pilot who can drop it in just the right place.

JOHN MORAN *enters, followed by* HARRY. *He is nineteen-years-old, tall, dressed also in fatigues, and covered with motor grease. As he enters, father and son instantly recognize each other, but they say nothing, give no sign.*

FERNANDO *(introducing them).* And this is our pilot. Señor Moran— Lieutenant Carter. Of the Costa Bonan Republic Air Force.

MORAN *(nodding stiffly).* I'm pleased to meet you, Lieutenant— Carter—*(Imitating* FERNANDO'S *pomp.)*—of the Costa Bonan Republican Air Force! (JOHN *does not move or speak.)*

HARRY *(prodding* JOHN). Go on, Johnny! Shake the man's hand. This is moneybags!

FERNANDO *(worried).* He is a fine boy, Señor Moran. He learned flying in your country. He flies the airplane like a little bird of Paradise!

HARRY *(enthusiastic).* Oh, he's a tyke coming over them trees, guv'ner! He could put her down in Piccadilly if he had to! Bash in, he comes!

MORAN *(coldly).* I'm sure Lieutenant—Carter is an excellent pilot.

JOHN *(breaking his silence).* What is he doing here?

HARRY *(shocked).* Johnny! This is the Exchequer—the Old Lady of Threadneedle Street—

JOHN. Get him out of here!

FERNANDO *(very formally).* Señor Moran is a friend of the Republic, Lieutenant Carter. I wish you to treat him as our guest. He is here to discuss—

At this point, the ear-splitting roar of a low-flying airplane is heard above their heads. All cower back and look up. The two SOLDIERS *jump to their feet. One of them fires his rifle into the air and shouts, "Viva la Republica!"*

FERNANDO *(to* SOLDIERS). *Estupido!*

MORAN *(disturbed).* It can't be Segura. It can't be!

FERNANDO. But it may be, señor. If he has discovered our camp__

HARRY. Hold on, chappies! There's a parachute!

FERNANDO. Yes, and it is going to drop by the airfield. If that is a Segurista, we are in trouble!

HARRY *(bringing out a pair of binoculars)*. Let's have a peek—can't see much—but whoever it is, he's coming down with a bloody lot of gear.

FERNANDO. Quickly! We must investigate! *(To the* SOLDIERS.*) Arriba! Arriba! Vamos!* (FERNANDO *goes out with* HARRY *and the* SOLDIERS. MORAN *now turns upon* JOHN, *who fidgets uneasily, avoiding* MORAN'S *stare.)*

MORAN. So this is where you've been for the last month! *(*JOHN *still avoids him.)* Did Harvard give you a little time off we didn't hear about? Field research, maybe? Or is this just your idea of a little break between semesters? (JOHN *still avoids him.)* Do you realize we've had detectives looking all over the country for you? Your mother is practically in the bughouse! You know what she does? She keeps washing that laundry you sent home by mail in October! Over and over, she does it. Then she looks for holes in your socks, or buttons off your shirt. She's in seventh heaven if she can find something, anything of yours to mend! She's got *me* almost looney! *(Another pause. No reply.)* Do you think you can deign to speak to me, Lieutenant Carter? Nick Carter, I presume.

JOHN *(sarcastically)*. Nick Carter's your generation, old boy. Not mine.

MORAN. Then what is this? Your idea of a joke?

JOHN. It's no joke!

MORAN. Then what are you doing down here—mixed up with this bunch of pikers?

JOHN. What are *you* doing down here—with the pikers? (FERNANDO *returns.* MORAN *and* JOHN *break apart.* FERNANDO *sensing hostility, tries to smooth things over.)*

FERNANDO. The parachute landed in a tree. Colonel Dilby is leading a party to cut down the tree—and catch the fruit. We shall see. *(Trying for peace.)* You have had a discussion with each other maybe? A few little words? *(Silence.* FERNANDO *points to* JOHN, *speaking to* MORAN.*)* He is a brave man, señor. I tell you from my—

MORAN. He is not! He's a damn dropout. Ran away from college with his semester's allowance! Nine hundred bucks of his father's hard-earned dough! *(To* JOHN.*)* Yes, we checked the bank—and you bounced four checks with that stunt! Idiot kid can't even keep his stubs straight! *(To* FERNANDO.*)* Nine hundred bucks, which he's frittering away, playing barnstormer in your side show!

JOHN. I didn't spend a cent of that money on myself! I worked my way down here on one of your banana boats, if you want to know!

FERNANDO. Please. I do not understand. Lieutenant Carter—

MORAN. His name isn't Carter. It's Moran. John Sylvester Moran—after his maternal grandfather, may his ghost forgive us.

FERNANDO (to MORAN). He is your son? (To JOHN.) He is your father? This is wonderful!

MORAN. Like hell it is! What did you do with that nine hundred dollars?

JOHN. I invested it in the Republic. All of it.

MORAN. You blew nine hundred dollars on this—this—(He points at the flag pole.)—pajama party?

FERNANDO. It was used to buy the airplane, señor.

MORAN (to JOHN). What's the matter with the flying lessons I'm paying for? You have to come all the way down here to put in air time?

JOHN. I'm not putting in air time! I'm fighting in a revolution to build a free country—based on a few simple principles you never heard of!

FERNANDO. Your son has been chosen to write the constitution.

JOHN. And don't think you're going to buy into this revolution. We don't want a damn penny from you!

FERNANDO. Lieutenant, do not be hasty.

MORAN. I wouldn't put company money in this revolution if this fruit peddler offered me every banana in Central America. Peeled!

FERNANDO. Señor Moran. Please.

JOHN. By the time we're finished, the ABC won't have enough bananas to cover a bowl of cornflakes with! This is a people's fight!

MORAN. People? What in the hell do you know about people?

JOHN (defiantly). Just try me! Just try me!

MORAN. I'm listening.

JOHN (a little more humble). Well, you're not going to like this.

MORAN. Get on with it!

JOHN. The people—the people down here—they're helpless against a tide of backwardness that's washed them under since they were born. And, Dad—(His voice threatens to crack.) it's all your fault!

MORAN. My fault!

JOHN. Yes. I'm afraid so. (He stops uncertainly.)

MORAN (encouraging JOHN to continue). No, no. Go ahead. I can take it.

JOHN. The Associated Banana Company's robbed these people! All they have is bananas, and the only money they get is from loading them on your boats, shipping their own riches out of the country. They've got nothing; and to live they have to help you steal from them! It's a social crime! But after the revolution, it's going to be a lot different. A whole new face on things!

MORAN (*pointing at* FERNANDO). That face, I suppose—(FERNANDO *smiles uneasily.*)

JOHN. It's a spirit that's sweeping the whole world! People everywhere are rising up and demanding their rights as men! It's something I've got to be a part of! It's a shame—(*Directly to* MORAN.) a shame your generation has to miss out on it!

MORAN (*shaking his head*). My God, no man has a drop of sense until he's forty!

JOHN. You used to say thirty!

MORAN. I'm changing it to fifty! (*Really yelling.*) What about your poor mother? She hasn't eaten anything but scrapple since the Dean called. You got room on your social conscience for a mother starving to death on scrapple?

JOHN (*uneasy*). That's different—

MORAN. How different? How?

FERNANDO. Gentlemen, we are forgetting ourselves.

MORAN. And what's that you've got smeared on your upper lip?

JOHN. A moustache.

MORAN. Don't wipe it off on your sleeve!

PEDRO MENDOZA, *a Latin youth, a contemporary of* JOHN'S, *enters. He is in rich but ragged clothes, covered with grease, and comes in astride a large bomb which is being drawn in a rusty playwagon by another* SOLDIER. *He is listening to the bomb with a stethoscope.*

PEDRO (*extremely excited*). Johnny! Johnny! At last. It is ticking!

All except JOHN *cower back instantly.* JOHN, *however, jumps to the wagon and puts his ear to the casing of the bomb.*

JOHN. By God, you're right, Pedro. How did you do it?

PEDRO (*the smile suddenly falling from his face*). Oh. It stopped again.

FERNANDO. Pedro. You must keep the bomb in the demolition area. Not here.

PEDRO. I just want to show you that the bomb will work. I said it would work, and it did. It was ticking, wasn't it, Johnny?

JOHN. It was.

PEDRO. And I will make it tick again! *(He takes a screwdriver and a hammer out of his pocket and menaces the bomb with them.)*

MORAN. Stop him! *(To* PEDRO.*)* Maniac!

PEDRO *(speaking with hurt pride.)* Señor, who do you call a —? *(Then brightening.)* Ah, Señor Moran! I am so happy to see you again! *(He hops off the bomb and shakes hands with a bewildered* MORAN.*)* I am Pedro Mendoza. Last year I lived across the hall from Johnny.

JOHN. You remember Pedro, Dad.

MORAN. The stolen bus?

PEDRO *(on his dignity)*. I repaired it, señor. I got it to do seventy-five on the Massachusetts Turnpike. The transit company could never do that!

MORAN. But your father—I've had dealings with him—

PEDRO. Yes. The filthy pig. He grinds the people into dust. Is that not right, Johnny?

JOHN. Exactly. Dust. He's the worst of the Seguristas.

PEDRO. He was angry when I flunked out. A very ugly purple, he was. "No more money," he said. "To Australia," he said. "To work," he said. But he will learn that it is a brave man he tries to send to work!

FERNANDO. Pedro has been chosen to try his father.

PEDRO. But first we bomb his bank. We destroy all the money with his ugly picture on it. Such an ugly face to put on pretty money.

MORAN *(to the heavens)*. Dear God, protect us from our children!

FERNANDO *(sternly)*. I must warn you, Pedro. That bomb does not belong here, and our plans are still secret. There is a mysterious parachute in the area.

PEDRO. We must hurry with the bomb then. Do not worry. I am sure it will work now.

MORAN *(commandingly)*. Where did that bomb come from?

FERNANDO. We bought it from Panama.

MORAN. Panama? Panama doesn't make bombs like this!

FERNANDO. Yes, but Panama got it from Guatemala. Guatemala dropped it on Panama. It did not explode. So Panama sold it to us.

PEDRO. And we will make it work! Boom! Pretty money everywhere!

MORAN. But Guatemala doesn't make bombs either!

PEDRO *(shrugging)*. Then somebody must have dropped it on Guatemala. Very bad for the clock—all that bouncing.

MORAN *(genuinely concerned)*. John. Are you serious about flying this—this homemade blockbuster to St. Luis?

JOHN *(proudly)*. Yes. Right in the middle of your banana republic— *(Pats bomb.)*—our little tarantula.

MORAN. What if it goes off in the plane? My God!—Come to think of it, what kind of a plane have you got?

PEDRO. It is like a little sparrow, señor. It blows around in the wind like this. *(He makes graceful, swooping movements with his flattened hand.)* Almost upside down sometimes. It is wonderful!

MORAN. John. What kind of a plane?

JOHN *(hesitatingly).* Well—the body is sort of—sort of an old Piper Cub. And the motor—

MORAN. The motor. Go on.

JOHN. Ummmm—I'm not exactly sure, but I think it's off an old *Volkswagen.*

MORAN *(holding his head).* Oh no! You can't possibly—

At this point, there is a commotion offstage. Then the SOLDIERS, *apparently terrified, run in, yelling, "El diablo! Santa Maria!" Then* HARRY *backs in, half shielding himself from some danger.)*

HARRY. Blimy, lady! Calm yourself! Nobody's going to lay a hand on you! Watch her. She's crackers!

HELENE MUGGINS, *a female war correspondent, enters. She is dressed in a jump suit and trailing the stringers of a cut parachute. She has an abundance of camera equipment strapped about her, and at the moment, she is wielding a long tripod like a warrior's club.*

HELENE. Come near me, I'll clong you! So help me—one more of you monkeys tries to climb me—I'll cold-conk him! *(Everybody shrinks back.)* Who's in charge here?

FERNANDO *(politely).* It is possible you are looking for me. Field Marshall Alfonso Fernando de Malagona, at your service.

HELENE. You're my man all right. I'm Helene Muggins. The New York *Tribune-Star.* Call off your apes, and let's have a little talk.

HARRY. Watch her, Marshall. She's potty! Soon as we cut her down, she starts swinging at us! She's balmy!

HELENE. These *bolos* claim I'm a prisoner! What about it, Marshall?

FERNANDO. There has been some mistake. You are welcome as my guest.

HELENE. That's better. *(Lowering the tripod.)* Brother, is it a job finding you! I've had a Texas friend buzzing this damn jungle since yesterday noon. We finally spotted those pajamas up here. *(She points to the flagpole.)* What's the matter? You can't sleep dry around here?

FERNANDO *(embarrassed).* Colonel Dilby, will you please strike the colors?

HARRY. She's potty, I tell you! *(He goes over and brings the "colors" down their lanyard.)*

FERNANDO. Please be seated, señorita. What can I do for you?

HELENE. Well, it's this way. The *Daily Mirror* says you've taken political asylum in the Cuban embassy. The Los Angeles *Times* says you landed in Geneva yesterday with two overnight bags and a jungle parrot. The Detroit *Free Press* says you're shacked up on the Riviera with a bit of jailbait. The Kansas City *Star* says your body washed up on Miami Beach three days ago, considerably filled with holes. I say you've been lying on your belly in the swamp mud ever since the St. Luis fiasco. Guess who's right?

FERNANDO *(mystified)*. But what do you want?

HELENE. I'm a war correspondent, Marshall. I just want to know if there's a war on, that's all.

FERNANDO *(responding)*. The revolution will continue as long as I have a breath in my body!

HELENE. Hallelujah, buster. Up and at 'em, all right, all right. *(She takes out a pencil and pad.)* Now who's financing this deal for you?

JOHN *(butting in)*. Nobody. It's our own fight! And we don't need any publicity from that yellow sheet you run errands for!

FERNANDO *(brightening)*. Publicity!

HELENE *(to* FERNANDO, *pointing at* JOHN.) Who's this headstrong youth?

FERNANDO. This is the chief of our air force. Lieutenant—eh—Lieutenant—?

JOHN *(quickly interjecting)*. Carter. John Carter.

HELENE. What do you fly, Lieutenant? A box kite?

JOHN *(equally sarcastic)*. No. We've got a whole squadron of MIGS back of the mangoes.

HELENE. It's a hell of lot more likely you've got all your Dinky toys back there.

At this point, there is a fearsome blast on a bugle off stage. Then a SOLDIER *appears, holding the battered bugle. Other* SOLDIERS *appear behind him. All look at them in puzzlement.*

HELENE. Who are these jokers?

FERNANDO. Our loyal troops, returning from the front—flushed with victory—

HARRY *(running in from the tent)*. Marshall, that little son-of-a-bitch just blew pay call again! *(The* SOLDIER *with the bugle is smirking.* HARRY *shakes his fist at him.)* That's the second time this week, you kinky Wog!

I catch you again, I'll—*(The* SOLDIER *with the bugle giggles, and the other* SOLDIERS *begin to mutter* "Diñero. Mucho diñero. Por favor. Diñero.")

FERNANDO *(with sudden realization)*. Caramba! We have not printed any money since the last pay call! Quickly, Colonel Dilby!

FERNANDO *begins to soothe his muttering troops with a loyalty speech in Spanish. Meanwhile,* HARRY, JOHN, *and* PEDRO *run to the mimeograph machine and start it operating in abrupt, military fashion.* HARRY *stands up on a chair with his notebook in hand, counting the troops.* PEDRO *is ready at the crank of the mimeograph machine, and* JOHN *is stationed by a small paper cutter.*

HARRY. —twenty-three, twenty-four, twenty-five. Two more men missing, Marshall!

FERNANDO *(interrupting his flow of Spanish)*. Shoot them! They are pigs!

HARRY. Roll her, Pedro! We need—*(With quick calculations in his notebook.)*— thirty-seven thousand dollars!

PEDRO *starts cranking the mimeo, and* JOHN *grabs the sheets as they come off the roller, then slices them into approximately dollar-size on the paper cutter. He picks up a bill, and holds it out for inspection.*

MORAN *(to* FERNANDO*)*. What is this supposed to be?

FERNANDO. Costa Bonan Republican dollars. One of them is worth five of your American dollars. Official rate.

MORAN. Who set the rate?

FERNANDO. I did.

MORAN. What do they bring on the black market?

FERNANDO. Four cents a hundred, I think. Ask Pedro. He runs the black market for me.

MORAN *(to* JOHN, *at the paper cutter)*. You hear that?

JOHN *(going on cutting)*. Some sacrifices have to be made!

MORAN *goes over and sits down dejectedly on the bomb. The* SOLDIERS *meanwhile have begun negotiations among themselves with their currency. Some are paying back debts, others are shooting craps in a circle, and* HARRY, *right next to* FERNANDO, *has a line-up of boxes and containers, the age-old collection at the end of the pay line.*

HARRY *(as the newly paid* SOLDIERS *pass him by)*. Soldiers' Relief, chappies! Stuff it in there!—That's for the Regimental Smoker, end of this month!—Bundles for Bolivia! Remember you ain't the only buggers struggling for liberty! *(If they don't contribute, he grabs the money out of their hands.)* Cough up, you Chinaman! This is voluntary!

Among those in the pay line is someone vaguely naval, his uniform still soaked. When he arrives in front of FERNANDO, *there is a torrent of Spanish abuse. Then* FERNANDO *rips off all but one of his remaining stars and hands him no pay.*

FERNANDO *(to* HARRY). Admiral Iyaso Pedro Rodriguez de Panalito is reduced in grade to civilian! Third class!

HARRY *(writing in his notebook)*. Righto, Marshall!

As the ADMIRAL *goes past* HARRY, HARRY *pulls off his last star and drops it in Soldiers' Relief.* HELENE, *who has been wandering around in confusion, finally goes over and sits down beside* MORAN *on the bomb.*

HELENE *(to* MORAN). What *is* this?

MORAN. A fight for freedom.

HELENE. Sure. What's in it for you? *(She is taking out a typewriter, preparing to write a dispatch. She sets the wafer-thin machine on her lap.)*

MORAN. Me? *(Pointing over his shoulder at* JOHN.) I'm the father of the revolution.

HELENE *(looking back over her shoulder.)* Carter? He's your kid?

MORAN. Moran. His name's Moran. We're disowning each other.

HELENE *(catching the name)*. F. P. Moran! Associated Bananas! *(She begins furiously pounding her typewriter.)*

MORAN. We can have that story stopped easily.

HELENE. Where are we? *(She looks around.)* Somewhere to hell and gone. Time, approximately—you got the time?

MORAN *(morosely)*. You got a watch.

HELENE *(showing her wrist)*. It stopped when those monkeys pulled me out of the tree.

MORAN. I can hear it ticking from here.

HELENE. No, it's stopped. Look.

MORAN. Well, something's—*(He looks down at the bomb they are sitting on, and jumps up.)* Pedro!

CURTAIN

ACT TWO

Scene One

The scene is the same, an hour later. A heavy tropical rain has fallen and passed on. The jungle is breathing a steady mist, like a suspiring green pot. The same two SOLDIERS *are asleep beside the water bucket, in much the same postures.*

HARRY enters. This time he simply ignores the sleeping SOLDIERS, *takes off his pith helmet, and shakes rain off it.)*

HARRY. Bloody rain. Every five minutes you're wringing out your *hanky!* (*To* SOLDIERS.) Don't you blokes ever mildew? (*Now he goes over to the water bucket and bends over it inquiringly. Then he takes a small can of fish food from his pocket, opens it, and pinches up a mite between his thumb and forefinger.* HELENE *enters, with camera.)*

HELENE. Hey! What're you up to there Harrykins? Trying to poison the water?

HARRY. It's fish food.

HELENE. You got fish in there?

HARRY. Had to put one in for sanitary purposes.

HELENE (*leaning over the water bucket*). I don't see him.

HARRY. Under that bit of mossy stuff there. (*Pointing.*) See? Regular kipper, he is.

HELENE (*with disgust*). You really drink this water? Kipper and all?

HARRY. It's safer with a fish in it, lady. A fish'll eat what bugs he can that land in it. And if the water goes bad, you can tell right away— because he curls up and dies.

HELENE. Thanks, but no thanks!

HARRY. Well, this ain't no frilly little tea party you plopped your girdle into!

HELENE (*sharply*). Just what do you mean by that crack?

HARRY. Like I say—it ain't no frilly tea party.

HELENE. Listen, Harrykins, you ever drink water from a goatskin?

HARRY. Can't say as I ever—

HELENE. Well, I did. Forty-two, in Algeria. It tasted like camel dung and battery acid. This water is pure crystal compared! (*She grabs the ladle, scoops it into the water bucket, lifts it to her mouth, and gulps*

mightily.) Thanks for tea. *(She drops the ladle back into the water bucket.*
HARRY *is silent a moment, simply peering into the water.)*

HARRY. Funny. Don't see the kipper around anywhere—

HELENE. *What! (She gags, staring wildly into the bucket.)* What d'you
mean? He's right there!

HARRY. So he is. Must've been hiding when I looked. *(He pinches up
another mite of fish food and sprinkles it over the water bucket.)* Cute
little tyke.

HELENE. Very funny. (JOHN *enters.)* Hey. I want to talk to you,
Lieutenant.

JOHN. Well, I haven't got time to talk to you. *(To* HARRY.) Go give
Pedro a hand with the Tarantula. We're taking off as soon as the ground
dries.

HARRY. Today?

JOHN. Today. Plans have changed.

HARRY. But nothing else is ready! No guns, no men. We can't strike
now. It's pay day.

JOHN. It's got to be now! If we wait, the old boy is going to buy it
right out from under us. Plans have changed.

HARRY. You won't have enough light.

JOHN. We'll have enough light to reach St. Luis and make our drop.

HARRY. And what about getting back, Johnny?

JOHN. The moon'll get us back. The Marshall has men laying fire
along the strip now. *(Slapping* HARRY *on the shoulder.)* Don't worry. It's
a soup run!

HARRY. You ought to wait, you know·that.

JOHN *(shaking his head).* We can't, Harry. Ever since she parked
herself on the Tarantula—*(indicates* HELENE.) It's been ticking like a
bum heart.

HELENE. Now wait a minute—

JOHN. Pedro says it'll go off at six o'clock, no matter what. That
gives us a little over an hour—

HARRY. Six o'clock, whammo? Even if you're still carting it around
up there? *(He points to the sky.)*

JOHN. Maybe before. Pedro thinks the clock is running fast now.

HARRY. Forget about it, Johnny!

JOHN. I can't! Don't you see? It's all I've got to fight with!

PEDRO *enters. This time he is wheeling the bomb in the play wagon
himself.* HARRY *jumps up, steadies the bomb in the wagon.*

HARRY. Blimy! Watch the bloody rock! You want to decimate us?

PEDRO (*to* HELENE). Thank you, señorita. You give the Tarantula the old hip, huh? *(He executes a bump.)*

HELENE. Oh, shut up!

JOHN. Get it over to the air strip, Pedro. Harry—

HARRY. Righto.

PEDRO *(showing a rope).* We use this to hang her over the side. *(He pats the bomb on its casing.)* And then—bongo, bongo!

HARRY (*to* PEDRO). You pulling or pushing?

PEDRO *(grabbing the handle of the play wagon).* Pulling. *(He starts out.)* Hurry, Johnny. We must get there before the bank closes.

HARRY *(offstage).* Easy there Pedro. This ain't a marimba! (JOHN *and* HELENE *are alone on stage.)*

HELENE. Your father know about this?

JOHN *(quickly).* That's been taken care of.

HELENE. I'll bet it has. *(Pause.)* Look. What are you? A peacenik or something?

JOHN *(indignant).* A peacenik?

HELENE. No, I guess you'd be more of a leftnik.

JOHN. Why does everybody have to be a *nik* these days? It used to be *isms.* Now it's *niks!*

HELENE. Take it easy! I'm only trying to peg you. You're good copy.

JOHN *(warning her).* My father can have anything you write stopped.

HELENE. Oh I see! It's *okay* if he helps you out there—

JOHN *(caught).* All right. What do you want to know?

HELENE. How did you get hung up in this revolution?

JOHN. I came down here to look for it.

HELENE. *This* revolution?

JOHN. *Any* revolution!

HELENE. You're just not particular, huh?

JOHN. Any revolution that could be used to give the people of the world a new life. Or a new start on a new life.

HELENE. The people of the world? All two—*(She makes circles with her finger.)* zero-zero-zero, zero-zero-zero, zero-zero-zero *billion* of them?

JOHN *(indignant).* Why not?

HELENE *(shrugging her shoulders).* Sure, why not? It's a free country.

JOHN. It is not! What do you think we're fighting the revolution for?

HELENE. I'm asking! I'm asking! *(She takes out notebook.)* How old are you?

JOHN. Nineteen.

HELENE *(whistling)*. Been in any revolutions before?

JOHN. No.

HELENE. Any panty raids?

JOHN. You're a riot!

HELENE. Got any other interests besides revolutions?

JOHN. Poetry. I used to write it. The *Atlantic Monthly* printed one last year.

HELENE. That's damn good at your age!

JOHN. But I don't anymore. It doesn't do any good.

HELENE. Who are you kidding?

JOHN *(hypersensitive)*. Rimbaud. Look at Rimbaud. He quit writing when he was nineteen—

HELENE. Who wants to quit doing anything when they're nineteen? Half your best glands are just getting started!

JOHN. Is it any of your business?

HELENE. No, but—

JOHN. Then lay off me!

HELENE *(angered, trying to reach him)*. Look. I ran away from the family beanery when I was *sixteen*. I borrowed some guy off a counter stool to get out of there, and I've been running ever since. I suppose I'll spend the rest of my life popping out of airplanes—that kind of stuff. But it's a crazy life—and you don't have to get hung up in it—so use your head a little, kid, it's *big* enough.

MORAN *enters, glaring at* JOHN.

MORAN *(to* JOHN*)*. Is this true? *(No answer.)* Do you think I'm going to let you take off in that flying egg crate?

JOHN. You're not running this operation—*(Turning around.)* And we take off in twenty minutes!

MORAN *(to* HELENE*)*. I'd like to talk to my son alone, Miss Muggins.

HELENE. Take him. He's all yours. *(She goes out.)*

MORAN *(pacifying)*. Now let's both of us just take it easy this time. Let's talk it out nice and quietly.

JOHN. You talk then. I haven't got anything to say. *(He pulls beat-up flying togs out from under the cot.)* And I'm busy changing.

MORAN *(reasoning)*. Don't you realize you'll lose your citizenship, playing around with other people's governments?

JOHN. I'm underage.

MORAN. You're what?

JOHN. I don't think they can take it away from me. I'm under twenty-one. *(Pointing to a boot near* MORAN.*)* Throw me that boot, will you?

MORAN *(picking up the boot, holding it.)* Your mother, John! Think of your poor mother!

JOHN. You're always telling me to think of mother! Poor mother! What has she got to do with the revolution? You think about her. She's your wife. Not mine.

MORAN. But she's worried about you.

JOHN. Toss me that boot!

MORAN *(still holding on to the boot)*. She worries herself sick over you!

JOHN. Listen. Ever since I was six years old, she's been telling me *you're* worried, and you've been telling me *she's* worried. If I come home with a black eye, she says you're going to have a heart attack on the subway platform. *(He hops across in one boot.)* If I fly a plane in the middle of the jungle, you tell me—one thousand miles away—*she's* going to need an aspirin! Why don't you do your own worrying instead of each other's? *(He grabs the boot from* MORAN.*)* And gimme that boot!

MORAN. All right. I'm worried about you!

JOHN. Why? Look at me. I'm fine. *(He pulls on the boot.)*

MORAN. Because you're getting harebrained! What happened?

JOHN. What d'you mean, what happened? *(He starts adjusting straps on the goggles.)*

MORAN. We haven't been good to you?

JOHN *(uneasily)*. That's not it.

MORAN. We put you in Harvard, your mother and I. Her brains and my money. No, I'll admit it, you've done damn well for yourself. On your own. I'm impressed.

JOHN. All right, all right.

MORAN. I mean, the *Atlantic Monthly*—

JOHN. If you want to know the truth, it's really a terrible magazine.

MORAN. Beautiful. What you wrote about the sea. Beautiful!

JOHN. It wasn't about the sea.

MORAN *(insisting)*. The sea was in it!

JOHN *(exasperated)*. It just shows how much you understand—

MORAN *(baffled)*. No! I don't understand! I'm mystified, frankly. You should be happy. What do you have to run away for?

JOHN. Let's get this much straight. I didn't run away from anything. I left to come down here and *do* something.

MORAN. What's down here you can't find up there?

JOHN. If you must know—the germ revolution.

MORAN. The what?

JOHN. The germ revolution. *(His voice turns suddenly otherworldly.)* It's the first, pure, incorruptible revolution—doesn't make any difference how small it is!—that rises spontaneously out of modern man's struggle for dignity. From it—well, it's like a microcosm—from it, come all the principles for the Ideal Revolution.

MORAN *(baffled)*. The Ideal Revolution?

JOHN. Which works the final overthrow of tyranny and establishes all mankind in one peaceful polity. *(An uncertain pause.)* It's a phrase of Malcom Malcolm's.

MORAN *(even more baffled)*. Malcom Malcolm?

JOHN. Yeah. Malcom Malcolm. Author of *The Key to Chaos. (He takes a considerably thumbed poket book from his jacket and tosses it to* MORAN. *The cover is resplendent with triangles, rules, oblongs, and other symbolic crash effects.)*

MORAN. I see. *The Key to Chaos: A Student Guide to Insurrection.* The Egret Government Series. This book, I take it, has—has greatly influenced your thinking on the subject?

JOHN *(with enthusiasm)*. Tremendously!

MORAN. I see. Tell me—*(With sarcasm, waving his hand around to indicate the area.)* this great, humanitarian struggle we've got here—at present suffering from the jungle rot—is that the germ revolution?

JOHN *(bridling a little)*. It could be! It could be!

MORAN. What great social gains do you have in mind when it comes to power? I'm curious. Just curious.

JOHN *(rattling them off)*. A health program, new housing, a better wage, the franchise, tax relief, public sanitation, theater projects, schools—!

MORAN. Schools. Good, let's take schools for a minute. There's a lot of other examples, but schools will do. Do you know the company built several of them in the little villages, back of St. Luis? An experiment. Free education. Native school teacher. You know what happened? Nobody would send their kids.

JOHN. Only because they—

MORAN. Didn't know any better. Quite right. So the Costa Bonan government of the time—it was a very progressive, upstanding regime that lasted three weeks, despite all we could do for it—made a law. A good law, forcing the parents to send their kids to school. And guess what? One by one those schools caught fire at night, and every bucket in the country had a hole in it.

JOHN. Okay. It's not an easy problem.

MORAN. You're damn right it's not an easy problem! I've been faced with it for the last twenty years—and you think you're gone to solve it with a bomb and a two-bit book on running revolutions? *(He flips open "The Key.")* Logarithms of resistance, for God's sake!

JOHN. You don't know anything about that book! Read it at least, before you burn it.

MORAN. I don't have to read it! *(He points to the sleeping* SOLDIERS.) Can *they* read it? The proletariat over there?

JOHN. They need leaders. It's a book for the leadership!

MORAN. I suppose you and the Marshall sit up nights, reading it to each other.

JOHN. No. I read it to him. It helps him get to sleep. (MORAN *laughs, and* JOHN *grows angry.)* Look, all I know is that for years the ABC's been playing one revolution off against another, just to keep the banana export up! Only this is going to be one revolution you don't hijack!

MORAN. How do you know what I'm here for? I haven't said one word, have I? Not one word!

JOHN. Oh come on! The usual collection of travel folders, I suppose? And a special number in a Swiss bank.

MORAN. Listen. What do you know about the Marshall's intentions? Is he your idea of the—the germ carrier?

JOHN. You won't buy the Marshall.

MORAN. I see. Can't be done, huh?

JOHN *(threatening).* You won't buy the Marshall!

MORAN. Now you just listen. The Marshall is going to do what I tell him. You're going to do what I tell you. This whole movement is going to do what I tell it! No crackpot air raids on banks, understand? You're going back to Harvard in one piece. One your mother can recognize, too. So shave off that fuzz before it infects your lip or something!

FERNANDO *enters, followed by* HARRY, PEDRO, *and* HELENE. FERNANDO *is strangely serious.*

FERNANDO. The plane is ready, Lieutenant—if you insist. You must hurry.

MORAN. Nothing doing, Marshall. If you want any further dealings with me, you'd better listen damn carefully. My son is not to fly that plane. The bomb goes in the river. *(A pause.* FERNANDO *is worried.)* No monkey business. Take it or leave it.

FERNANDO *(unhappily).* I regret to say, Señor Moran, that you are under political arrest.

MORAN. You're joking.

FERNANDO. Please, it is unpleasant, I know. But circumstances—

SOLDIERS *enter and seize* MORAN. *The brief case is sawed from his wrist.*

MORAN *(furious)*. You watching this, John? You see what's going on? Now let me tell you something. Two hours ago this patriot had his whole revolution up for sale, and I wouldn't buy. So now he thinks he's going to steal our help! (*To* FERNANDO.) Whose bright idea was this, Marshall? All your own?

JOHN. No. Mine.

JOHN, PEDRO, HELENE, *and* HARRY *start a general exit toward the airfield.* MORAN *stands dumbfounded.*

CURTAIN

Scene Two

The same, ten minutes later. FERNANDO *is seated at the shipping crate desk, trying to prize open the lock of the brief case with* PEDRO'S *hammer and screw driver.* MORAN *is seated on the cot, minus his pants and jacket, with his head tucked sullenly in his hands. The two* SOLDIERS *are, for a change, busy. They are stuffing* MORAN'S *pants and jacket with straw.*

The engine roar of a low-flying airplane sounds swoopingly over their heads. MORAN *and* FERNANDO *look up.* FERNANDO *waves.*

FERNANDO. He is wagging his wings. I think. It is hard to tell because the plane always wags a little.

The engine begins to sputter and almost falls. MORAN *groans and ducks his head, registering that he can't bear to look.*

FERNANDO. Up, up, little sparrow! (*The engine gains heart again, and the roar trails off, out of hearing.* FERNANDO *waves gleefully.*) A fine boy, Señor Moran. You can be proud of him. A scholar, a warrior, an idealist! (*He taps the brief case with the screw driver.*) A political strategist. (*Returning to the attack on the brief case.*) Where would the revolution be without him?

MORAN. Down the drain. Where's it going anyhow—soon as he gets back.

FERNANDO *(tut-tutting)*. You must be more reasonable, señor. Your arrest is only temporary.

MORAN. So is your neck.

FERNANDO *(ignoring the threat)*. Who taught him to fly, señor? How do they teach him something so glorious?

MORAN *(sarcastically)*. By pushing him out of the nest.

HARRY *and* HELENE *enter from the direction of the airfield.*

HELENE. That kid is bats!

HARRY. Blimy, you should've seen that take-off!

MORAN. We saw it—

HELENE. He was so low over the trees, the monkeys were ducking!

HARRY. It wouldn't be so bad, guv-ner, but with that bomb—things ain't so trim. Pedro's got it dangling by a rope, and it's swinging like a pendulum.

MORAN. My God!

HELENE. You look a little piqued, F. P. What's a matter? Swallow a cartel the wrong way?

MORAN. I'm just thinking what I'm going to do to that kid if he gets back alive. (*Turning on* FERNANDO.) And what I'm going to do to you if he doesn't!

FERNANDO. He will be all right, señor. St. Luis is just over the treetops and back.

HARRY. It's a soup run, guv'. And Segura hasn't even got a paper clip to send up after him.

HELENE. Okay. So the job's a cinch. But what good is it going to do, knocking the lid off a bank? Demolish a few tellers' windows—so what?

MORAN. Exactly my thoughts, Miss Muggins.

FERNANDO. The reasons are—(*He begins ticking them off from a faulty memory.*) all part of economic reorganization. Bombing a bank— redistributes wealth—eliminates debt—reforms currency—reduces interest rates—and simplifies credit. Besides which, it signals the end of money—and the beginning of architectural reform. I think those are the reasons. They are all in that book. Appendix B. "How and Where to Strike."

HELENE. What book?

MORAN. *The Key to Chaos*—by Malcom Malcolm. (*Handing the book to* HELENE.) First edition.

HELENE. It looks like a bird book. (*She points to the egret on the back cover.*)

MORAN. That's the publisher.

HELENE (*to* FERNANDO). You mean, you get all your reasons out of this paperback?

FERNANDO. No, please, señorita. These are not *my* reasons. These are *the* reasons.

HELENE. Well, *whose* reasons?

FERNANDO. Nobody's reasons. *The* reasons. Señor Moran's son is a scholar, a theorist. He says we must have *reasons* for everything we do. All the reasons are in that book. Fortunately. It would be difficult if we had to think of them ourselves all the time.

HARRY. Let's have a peek at that. *(He takes "The Key" from* HELENE *and retires to read.)*

FERNANDO. *My* reasons are another matter.

HELENE. That's what I want to know. Your reasons.

FERNANDO. Very simple. The bombing of the bank is necessary because it is the only way to get rid of Lieutenant Moran for a little while. So that I can talk to Señor Moran alone.

HELENE. Gotcha.

MORAN *(infuriated)*. My son is out there—flying around in that condemned windmill—just so you can get him out of your way?

FERNANDO. It was necessary, señor. He is very sensitive about the Republic, your son. He wants both power and virtue. He would not let me make a deal with you. I had to arrest you before he would take off.

HELENE. A deal?

MORAN. No deal, Miss Muggins. Quote me on it.

FERNANDO. Patience, señor, patience.

MORAN *(angry)*. You put me under arrest, steal my coat, my pants, my brief case—endanger the life of my son! You think I'm still interested in making a deal? I had a real bargain for you—one you wouldn't believe, it was so good—but you're out, fruit peddler, you're out in the cold!

FERNANDO. You are still angry. Then we will wait till after the execution.

HELENE. Who's getting executed?

FERNANDO. Señor Moran.

MORAN. Why you no-good, slimy, son-of-a—!

FERNANDO. Please, señor! Only technically, we are shooting you. *(He points to the* SOLDIERS *stuffing* MORAN's *clothing.)* They are giving you your last meal now.

HELENE. You're shooting him in effigy?

FERNANDO *(shrugging)*. My men have not seen action for a long time —*(Fiddling with brief case.)* We will discuss when I finish opening— (*To* MORAN.) You know my position. I will soon know yours. Then we will discuss.

MORAN *(emphatically)*. No deals!

HARRY, *from his corner, bursts out laughing.*

HELENE. What's eating you?

HARRY. This book's a bloody lark! Listen to this. He says here, "It is tauto-tauto-"

HELENE. "Tautological," lame brain!

HARRY. "—tautological—" *(To* HELENE.) Hooked her that time, didn't I? *(Reading again.)* "—to speak of revolutionary ideas, because every new idea has led to a revolution." Ain't that a lark?

HELENE. What's the matter with it?

HARRY. It's backwards! He's got it all turned around! Revolutions don't start because chaps *think up* new ideas. They start because chaps *run out* of new ideas. It works like this. First, there's a meeting place. Life a *café,* like. A group of characters come there—and talk! Talk their bloody heads off. Yakity, yakity. New ideas all over the place, like butts. You finish smoking one, you light up another! So long as that's happening, it's okay. But one day these same characters come in, sit down—and don't say a word! Just stare at their coffee, play with the sugar—dig holes in it. Can't think of a single new idea. That's when the revolution starts!

FERNANDO. Yes, that is how it happens. I remember the day they stopped talking at the Happy Parrot. It was a terrible thing.

HELENE. How come?

FERNANDO. Because I owned the Happy Parrot. In three days I was out of business.

HARRY. Choked on its own cracker.

FERNANDO. If only they had kept talking—

HELENE. Then there wouldn't have been a revolution!

FERNANDO *(in a revery)*. No. Just talk. Long, sweet, twittering talk— that makes everybody thirsty.

HELENE. But didn't you want a revolution?

HARRY. Lady, nobody wants a revolution except kids and financiers. And maybe blokes who write books. Like Mark and Eagles. *(He shrugs.)* The rest of us prefers a cup of coffee.

FERNANDO. You think I want to be a military leader? I want to run a *café!* But for a long time, nobody comes to the Happy Parrot. I am in business for the flies! Then one day, a little man with a stare this long— comes in and asks if he can put a sign in my window. "Why not?" I say. "Maybe the flies will read it." But suddenly the cafe is full of people, buzzing, louder than the flies—all the time—heads turning, eyes bulging —I am delighted! I try to show it. I speak to each little group of flies, joke with them. Until one day—Santa Maria, I am head fly!

HELENE. That's how it happened?

FERNANDO. So now I have the revolution—and no *café*. It is a very bad exchange, but I do my best. First, we win the revolution. Then we set up the Republic, and there will be one fundamental rule!

HARRY. Freedom of speech!

FERNANDO. And everybody will be *required* to exercise freedom of speech! Anybody who sits in silence will be arrested! And whenever there is a long silence, there will be a purge!

MORAN *(with disgust)*. Ridiculous!

HARRY. Righto, guv', but it's the way of the world. I'm tired of revolutions too.

MORAN. I thought they were your bed and board.

HARRY. They are, but I'm ready to retire any time. A little corner kiosk with the leading Socialist newspapers—maybe a native girl to turn on the burner—and I'm happy. Guv', me and the Marshall, we're fighting the revolution best we know how. We're putting a bloody lot of work into it. But, blimy, sometimes it just don't seem worth the candle.

MORAN. That's because you've got no plans, no vision! *(On a new tack.)* Maybe you ought to listen to my son a little more often—

HARRY *(catching it)*. What's this? What's this?

HELENE. He's turning leftist on us!

MORAN. Everybody's a little to the left these days! Why not? And at least my son's out there, showing a little moxie—instead of sitting around a wet jungle, waiting for the regime to collapse!

HARRY *(fairly bitter)*. Come off it, guv'! A revolution's like a banana. It ain't worth a monkey's whistle down here. It's got to be sold up North! And somehow that takes all the kicks out of it.

MORAN. Go on. Get all the kicks you want this time. I said I wasn't buying in.

FERNANDO *(singing)*.

> Yes, we have no bananas!
> We have no bananas today!
> They've all been snatched by Segura,
> The people's plantations, hooray!

MORAN. And we can take care of Segura! Or you! Whichever. Don't worry.

FERNANDO. Sit down, señor. We are almost ready to shoot you.

FERNANDO *continues to grapple with the locked brief case, while the two* SOLDIERS *put the finishing touches on the effigy of* MORAN *and prop it against a tree.* MORAN *sits down, watching all this with apprehension. Meanwhile,* HELENE *sidles up to a morose* HARRY, *who has taken out a hip flask and already gurgled down a few liberal swigs.*

HARRY *(bitterly)*. You always end up fighting for somebody else. Never for yourself.

HELENE *(dejectedly)*. You're so right!

HARRY. The capitalists—the anarchists—the royalists—the loyalists —the plutocrats—the democrats—*(With an elaborate gesture.)* I've worked for 'em all, and it's the same bloody rotten gaff.

HELENE. I know just how you feel.

HARRY *(interrupting his drinking)*. Do you now?

HELENE. Yeah. It's like working for all the damn newspapers!

HARRY *(drinking again)*. Do you now?

HELENE. Do I what!

HARRY *(trying to think what)*. Want a drink?

HELENE. Sure. I'll try a nip. *(She drinks and gags.)* Man, what is this jazz?

HARRY. Revolutionary brandy. Made it in every revolution I been in. *(He drinks again.)* Usually sell it to the other side though.

HELENE. Listen, Harrykins, what about this kiosk of yours?

HARRY. What's that?

HELENE. Your kiosk—with the native girl.

HARRY. A-h-h-h—It's just a dream!

HELENE *(wheedling)*. Come on now—

HARRY. Jus' a dream.

HELENE. Come on. Where's it going to be?

HARRY. No—

HELENE. You don't know where?

HARRY *(on his toes)*. Picked out the perfect spot, I have!

HELENE. Well, where?

HARRY. Right directly opposite—Number Ten Downing Street!

HELENE. Can you do that?

HARRY. Don't know, but it's the spot! *(He gets into his dream.)* There I am—wearing my busby and beating the fog out of the London *Times* —a proper Coldstream toff, I am—it's morning—and the Prime Minister himself comes walking out of Number Ten with sixpence in his grubby hand. To buy the morning paper! *(He smiles wildly.)* Don't you see what an opportunity I've got? (HELENE *shakes her head, puzzled.*) I don't give him just any paper! I keep special ones in store! Like now if he comes out with egg on his tie—too chipper, cocky—I hand him one, it says, "WAR DECLARED—H-BOMB LEVELS PARLIAMENT." It takes him down a peg right away—Or if he comes out a bit off his color, I give him one to perk him up, like—"PRIME MINISTER WINS FOOTBALL POOL." Oh, I could keep a proper check on the little ponce! Stability. That's what I'd be. National stability. What do you think of that?

HELENE. It's—it's revolutionary!

HARRY *(sinking back)*. It ain't likely either.

HELENE *(encouraging him).* Why not? Why not?

HARRY. Jus' a bloody dream—*(He takes a drink.)*

HELENE. Come on. All you need is somebody who knows the newspaper game!

HARRY. You're right.

HELENE. Somebody to turn on the burner—

HARRY. You're smack on! You're—*(Suddenly realizing the implications.)* Never mind.

HELENE. What's the matter?

HARRY *(getting up and moving away).* Just leave off. I'll fiddle with the burner. *(To* FERNANDO.*)* Let's get cracking here.

FERNANDO *(wrenching at the lock).* We are almost ready.

MORAN. I said, no deal, Marshall. It still goes.

HARRY *(conciliatory).* Have a heart, guv'. We need the coin.

MORAN. Sure you do. But I'm not going to let you double-deal my son!

HARRY. He don't understand these things! He's still a kipper.

MORAN. He wants a pure, unadulterated revolution, and by God, he's going to get one. Where he's concerned, I don't skimp!

HARRY. No. You only cut our throats, that's all!

FERNANDO. Señor Moran is playing the wise parent, Colonel Dilby. Only he is playing it with the heavy hand. He thinks, if there is no deal, the revolution will soon be over. Right? Then his son will come dragging home. Right? With his tail between his legs, maybe.

MORAN. I'm not going to let you sell him out!

FERNANDO *(angry).* No. You are going to starve him out instead! But I do not want to starve, señor. The revolution is all I have left in the world. It is my business, and I am going to be a success in this business. *(The lock on the brief case finally gives way.)* Now we will deal, señor. *(Holding up the brief case.)* And this will be—how do you say?—your option money! *(He lifts up the brief case, shakes it, and out fall some socks and a cascade of travel folders.)* Caramba! Travel folders!

MORAN. I warned you.

HARRY *(leafing through the folders quickly).* Not one rotten security! *(He holds up a pair of socks.)* And I'll bet these are too bloody small for me!

HELENE *(picking up a travel folder and reading).* "Welcome to Costa Bona. Where the bananas wear only their skins."

FERNANDO *(in a towering rage).* Shoot him! Shoot him!

The two SOLDIERS *fire into the effigy, which falls limply to the ground.*

FERNANDO *(still fuming)*. Now. You are dead, señor, and can be useful to us. *(To the* SOLDIERS.) Bury him!

MORAN. Marshall, I've got you coming and going!

The SOLDIERS *begin digging.*

FERNANDO. No. You are going, señor. Right back up to your Wall Street and get us money!

MORAN. I can't! I'm dead! *(He laughs.)*

FERNANDO. Yes, and when your son returns, I will show him your grave. And if you don't get us the money, I will show you *his* grave!

MORAN. What are you trying to pull, you—

FERNANDO. I'm holding your son as a hostage, señor. We will fight the revolution—as long as you keep us supplied. If not—(FERNANDO *makes a motion as if cutting his throat. It is impressive, but when it is finished, a very real knife appears at his own throat. Somebody is behind him. He looks at the knife.)* I do not understand! (*Suddenly out of the jungle comes a ring of smartly dressed troops, guns leveled. They surround the little group, and the man with the knife steps around in front of* FERNANDO.) Seguristas! We are discovered!

SEGURISTA. Line up, all of you. I am placing you under political arrest.

MORAN. This can't be! Something's gone wrong!

SEGURISTA *(to* MORAN). In line, señor!

There is a great deal of confusion as the prisoners are lined up and marched off the stage. Everybody babbles. Then the stage is empty, silent. Suddenly HARRY *reappears, running across the open space to the water bucket. As he grabs it up with a smile, two* SEGURISTAS *seize him and drag him back into the line-up—still with the water bucket.*

CURTAIN

ACT THREE

The scene is the main cell of the political prison in St. Luis, after midnight. At present, there is only one inmate, ISHMAEL BOODLEHEIM, *who is off in one corner, clattering away furiously at a typewriter. He and the typewriter are each on a box, the only two pieces of furniture in the cell, except for a long bench against the left wall. His tie is loosened and hangs just out of range of the flying typewriter keys. Now, however, the keys stop flying, and* ISHMAEL *yanks the copy out of the machine with a squeak from the roller. He begins separating carbons and copies hastily. Then he holds up one piece of carbon paper to examine its condition. It is shot through.*

ISHMAEL. Goddamn. *(He crumples up the carbon paper, rises from his box, and goes to the barred window.)* Guard! Hey, Pablo!

The GUARD *appears at the window, a face dominated by a shaggy moustache over an inane grin. During the ensuing scene, his stupid expression does not change. The head only nods, and* ISHMAEL *increasingly tries to shout his way over the language barrier.*

ISHMAEL. Pablo. *Importanto. Muy Importanto.* See this? *(He holds up a crumpled piece of carbon paper.)* Carbon paper. See? Car--bon pap--er. Yes?
GUARD *(nodding).* Si, señor, si. *(But he does not move.)*
ISHMAEL. Well, go get it then, you idiot! *(The* GUARD *does not move.)* You *go! (Gesturing.)* You go get *me (Pointing again.)* car--bon pap--er! *(He points to the piece in his hand.)* Car--bon pap--er, you wall-eyed moron! CAR--BON PAP--ER! *(No response.)* Look, Pablo. *Me.* Me, me. *You.* *(The* GUARD *pokes a tired finger through the bars, pointing at* ISHMAEL, *who takes this gesture as a complete victory over Spanish.)* Yes-yes-yes! Me, you. Writer, author. Need car--bon pap--er. For typewriter. *(He begins a wild imitation of typewriting, which puzzles the* GUARD *no end.)* Now just listen, Pablo. Everything will be clear. *(He points to himself.)* Me, writer. Author. Book. Write books. Like Cervantes. Cervantes. Don Quixote!
GUARD *(puzzled, and pointing a finger through the bars at* ISHMAEL). Don Quixote?

ISHMAEL *(exasperated)*. No, no, no! Me, writer! You, fathead! *(He breaks down.)* I've got a publisher's deadline to meet. A copy has to go in the mail by six this morning. It's after midnight now. I've still got another chapter to write. *Comprendez?* Another whole chapter! I need CAR--BON PAP--ER!

GUARD. Si, señor! *(But he does not move.)*

ISHMAEL *(giving it up)*. Oh, go to the devil! *(He stomps back to his typewriter with the old piece of carbon, and begins reassembling paper and tattered carbons for a fresh start.)*

GUARD *(vaguely, at the window)*. Car--bon--pap--er—*(Then he is gone.)*

ISHMAEL *(jumping up)*. He got it, by God! *(Then, sitting down again.)* What the hell? He probably thinks I want a woman. *(He rattles keys, thinking hard.)* No, I haven't got time for it! *(He begins typing again.)*

Very soon, the cell door opens, and MORAN, HARRY, *and* FERNANDO *are thrust rudely into the room. After a long trip through the jungle to St. Luis, they have begun to look like captives, ragged and slightly unconscious of what's happening to them.* FERNANDO *exchanges Spanish profanities with his captors, but they are routine.*

MORAN. What *is* this filthy place?

HARRY. The St. Luis political prison, guv'. Ain't been cleaned out since the last time I was chucked in it either.

MORAN. Somewhere there's been a tremendous blunder!

HARRY *(sitting down on the bench)*. Maybe so. Anyway, it's put us away for a while. *(He settles the water bucket down beside him and feels in his pockets.)* Ruddy hell, forgot the fish food!

MORAN *(beside himself)*. A monstrous blunder!

HARRY *(misunderstanding)*. It's all right. He's off his feed anyway.

MORAN. I'm not talking about your idiot fish!

ISHMAEL *(rising suddenly from his box)*. Pardon me, gentlemen, but one of you wouldn't happen to have a piece of carbon paper?

HARRY. Sorry. Pencil help?

ISHMAEL. No, no. Thank you. Never mind. *(He plunges back to his typewriter.)*

MORAN. My son, Marshall! There was nobody to light the fires!

FERNANDO. I am worried myself, señor. I am not positive, but I do not think the bomb has fallen on St. Luis. I hear no talk—

MORAN *(rubbing his hand on the prison wall)*. This place is a pig sty!

FERNANDO. It cannot be helped. It is a political prison. If you clean it up one day, they are writing all over it the next!

HARRY (*pointing to writing on wall above the bench*). Here's some bloke who's all for you, Marshall! Only it's written in Wog.

FERNANDO (*scrutinizing the writing*). He's not for me! He's *against* me!

MORAN. I'm holding you personally responsible for my son's safety, Marshall!

FERNANDO. And what am I to do, señor? Pull him out of the air?

MORAN. You never should've let him go up! Never!

HARRY (*suddenly realizing*). What about *her?*

MORAN. Who?

HARRY. Helene. Where's she gone to?

FERNANDO. The pigs! They have taken her to Woman's Wear.

MORAN. Woman's Wear!

FERNANDO. Where they wear out the woman—I am afraid—

HARRY (*shaking his head*). Jolly good luck to them! They want bloodshed—Jolly good luck to them!

ISHMAEL. Goddamnit, shut up! (*This expletive takes everybody a-back.*) I mean, *please* shut up. Goddamnit. (*He whirls back to his typewriter.*)

HARRY (*annoyed*). Now what's your trouble, shipmate? This is a public prison. I've a right to talk whenever I please. That's what they put blokes in here for!

ISHMAEL. Can't you see I'm trying to write?

HARRY. And I'm trying to talk!

ISHMAEL. Listen. It's *all* got to be in the mail in another five hours. And I've still got one whole chapter to write. One whole chapter!

HARRY. Go ahead and write it then!

ISHMAEL (*clipping his words*). Thank you. I will. If you'll only please —shut—up! (*He hits the keys again.*)

HARRY (*after a pause, in an awed tone*). You mean—you're a *writer?*

ISHMAEL. Yes. Yes. I'm a writer. (*He abandons his machine.*)

HARRY. What're you doing in prison then?

ISHMAEL. That's where society puts all writers!

HARRY. What's your name? I bet I never heard of you.

ISHMAEL. Well, I've got a lot of names. I'm sure one of them has crossed your ken. D. D. Van Dine, author of *The Nether Man* mysteries? (HARRY *shakes his head.*) How about Dr. Arthur Merrydown, M.D., discoverer of home hypnosis—the housewife's trance for kitchen tasks? (HARRY *shakes his head.*) Katherine St. John—*The Final Dahlia?* It ran in *Modern Romances* for a year and a half—(HARRY *still shakes his head, and* ISHMAEL *becomes irritated.*) Perhaps Johnny Jupiter is more in keeping with your reading level. *Rum Tum, the Rhinoceros,* or the *Noodle Bunny?*

HARRY. Come off it! What's your name now?

ISHMAEL. At present, I'm Malcom Malcolm.

MORAN. Malcolm? *Malcom* Malcolm?

ISHMAEL. Researcher for the Committee for the Advancement of Worldwide Struggle. I thank you. And good evening. *(He turns back to the typewriter.)*

MORAN. You wrote *The Key to Chaos?*

ISHMAEL *(lighting up).* You've read my book?

MORAN. No.

ISHMAEL *(his face dropping).* Oh.

MORAN. But I know someone who's been influenced by it—quite a bit.

ISHMAEL. Who, for God's sake?

MORAN. Someone—at Harvard.

ISHMAEL. I'll be damned! I thought those boys were a lot smarter than that. Suppose a professor can be just as big a chump as the next guy, though.

MORAN. Oh?

ISHMAEL. I wrote that thing in two weeks. Out of *Das Kapital,* Bernard Shaw, a little Milton for quotations, and *The Businessman's Guide to Corporation Success.* Smooth bit of compilation.

MORAN. Indeed?

ISHMAEL. Wanted to publish it as the Revised Edition, but it's selling okay as a first work. We'll hoke it up again when the market slumps.

MORAN. Tell me—is there any worthwhile revolutionary guidance in this work of yours?

ISHMAEL. Of course! Especially in the parts I cribbed out of the corporation manual. Those jokers know how to organize! My basic idea is a dictatorship of the proletariat, run by the best brains in industrial management!

MORAN. Perhaps I ought to read it.

ISHMAEL. Hell no! That's just hack work. Not that there's anything wrong with hack work. It can be great stuff. Look at the Bible! There's no telling what you can throw together out of good source material. But for the real me, read this one when it comes out. Empirical, that's what it is.

MORAN. What's it about?

ISHMAEL. *Notes from a Political Prisoner,* that's the title. The methods of modern tyranny. Segura, the big cheese here, we cooked up a deal. He lets me rot for a month in his prison in return for one quarter of the royalties. *(Standing up.)* Look at me! Lost twelve pounds already. *(He holds out his hands.)* See those fingernails? Jaundice. You know, just a touch.

HARRY. How do you feel?

ISHMAEL. Crackerjack. This is gonna be a really honest piece of work. I've even got my mind to wander. Not too far you know, sort of over to the corner and back. Delirium—claustrophobia—erotic fancies —recollections of a happy childhood—What-I-might-have-been-if-the-world-was-not-against-me—the whole shebang! They're gonna torture me, too.

MORAN. For real?

ISHMAEL. Oh, just a little bit, so's I get the idea. Realism. That's what this book is gonna have. I could've pinched it all from Lord Byron, but— *(He holds up his hand, as if taking an oath.)* I've decided to go straight, man!

MORAN. I'd like you to meet my son, Malcom. Very much, I'd like it—*(To* FERNANDO.*)* If I still have a son!

FERNANDO *(to* ISHMAEL*)*. Señor, has there been an explosion in town today?

ISHMAEL. Didn't hear any. Expecting one?

FERNANDO. Perhaps—

ISHMAEL. Is that what they nabbed you guys for? Sabotage?

FERNANDO *(with dignity)*. I am Field Marshall Alfonso Fernando de Malagona! I am above sabotage!

ISHMAEL. Fernando? The Free People's Republic?

FERNANDO. Yes, señor!

ISHMAEL. You poor son-of-a-bitch! (FERNANDO *splutters.*) I've heard of you, buddy! The revolution that went five blocks and took a leftist deviation. You know what they call it around here? The Morning of the Screaming Nuns.

HARRY. Aw, have a heart.

ISHMAEL. Have you seen the propaganda job Segura did on this monkey? He murdered him! After they burned down the Happy Parrot—

FERNANDO. O-o-o-h-h! He did not! He *could* not!

ISHMAEL. Right to the ground.

FERNANDO. An atrocity!

ISHMAEL. Then he made a speech from the balcony. He pulverized you! "You have nothing to fear from the Antichrist!" he told them. That's you, buddy!

FERNANDO. He will suffer for this! I will have him dragged into the streets! I will—

ISHMAEL. I'd stay out of the street if I were you. There's a lot of talk about burning you at the stake.

FERNANDO. Me? A stake? A real stake?

ISHMAEL. And a real fire. Oh I don't think he'd do it—but the people might.

MORAN. So that's how people feel about the Republic?

ISHMAEL. Friend, I'd forget I even knew the word—

FERNANDO. They have been deceived. It is shameful to play on the people's ignorance!

ISHMAEL. Oh I don't know. Sometimes playing on people's ignorance is the only way to make a buck. Appeal to their intelligence, they put you in jail. For debt, if nothing else. *(An idea occurs to him.)* Listen, you're ripe, buddy! If they burn you, there's a wow biography in it. You'll be dead, of course, but maybe I can get you an advance on the rights!

FERNANDO. You are too kind.

ISHMAEL *(looking at his watch)*. Jesus, it's two o'clock! *(Running to the typewriter.)* Kind of keep the noise down, will you? It distracts me.

HARRY *(lying down on the bench)*. What about your own bloody banging! A bloke can't catch a wink—even in a ruddy jail! *(He sleeps.)*

FERNANDO *(considerably worried)*. What do you think they will do to me, señor?

MORAN *(simply)*. Light a match.

FERNANDO. That is arson.

MORAN. Fumigation.

FERNANDO *(going over to the wall and reading over the inscriptions)*. I must have a friend somewhere!

At this point, there is a commotion in the corridor, and the cell door flies open. In comes HELENE, *fuming.*

HELENE. Lay off me, you bums! I'll claw your eyes out! So help me— *(The door closes quickly.)* Boy, oh, boy! Am I gonna expose *this* place!

MORAN. You're unharmed?

HELENE *(holding her foot)*. My toe's a little sore from kicking teeth in—Yeah, I'm all right. But you should see it down there! All the girls are in business!

FERNANDO. It is a national disgrace!

HELENE. They all send their regards, Marshall. They're having a sort of fire sale.

FERNANDO. I do not understand you—

HELENE. Well—your Happy Patriot—they're all that's left over from the fire!

MORAN *(sarcastically)*. Very enterprising of you, Marshall.

HELENE. Oh, he's a bird, all right! (FERNANDO *shrinks back.*)

MORAN. Did you hear anything of my son? Or the bomb?

HELENE *(shaking her head).* Sorry. I don't think they made the drop. *(She notices* ISHMAEL *typing.)* Who's the Charlie with the type–? *(Recognizing him, she shouts out.)* Ish!

ISHMAEL *(turning and seeing* HELENE). Helene! Where'd you come from?

HELENE *(running over and embracing him).* The jungle, boy! What're you doing in jail? They finally get you for copyright violation?

ISHMAEL. No, I'm on a job.

FERNANDO. You know Señor Malcolm?

HELENE. Malcolm? *(Coyly to* ISHMAEL.) Are you Malcom Malcolm, too? (ISHMAEL *nods shyly.)* Ish, there's getting to be more of you than the Great Books! *(To* MORAN, *and* FERNANDO.) His real name's Ish. Ishmael Boodleheim.

ISHMAEL. Aw, lay off it, Helene!

HELENE. We used to be engaged. Except I wouldn't marry him with that name. So he started changing it. Every week he changed it! Pretty soon I couldn't even find him in the phone book. *(She embraces him again.)* You ran out on me, you bum, but I still love you—and all sixty-three noms de plume.

At this point, HARRY *wakes up and reacts immediately.*

HARRY. Get your hooks off her!

ISHMAEL *(surprised).* What am *I* doing to her?

HARRY *(threatening).* Get 'em off!

HELENE. Harrykins!

HARRY *(to* HELENE). Minute my back is turned, you're down the lane with any bloke what comes along!

HELENE *(almost joyfully).* You mean it?

HARRY. And him a bloody writer!

ISHMAEL. Now you take that back!

HARRY. You heard me proper!

ISHMAEL. Listen, you limey, I don't care who—

HARRY *takes a swing at him. They mix it up, and the others try to separate them. But what does separate them is the sudden opening of the cell door. In walks* CARLOS SEGURA, *accompanied by guards.*

SEGURA *(sternly, as the guards separate* ISHMAEL *and* HARRY). If you please. This is a well-ordered, if not altogether sociable, prison. It is run quietly, with some small consideration for others. Brawling is out of place.

There is a general subsidence. HELENE *takes* HARRY *over to the bench. He has a black eye.*

HELENE *(soothingly)*. Harry! Look what I remembered to bring! *(Taking out the fish food container.)* Go on! Take a pinch! *(They happily feed the fish.)*

SEGURA *(surveying the scene)*. Good evening, Señor Moran. I am sorry to act with such haste.

MORAN *(affably)*. I'm sure you have a reason, Señor Segura.

SEGURA *(to* HELENE*)*. Señorita. I apologize for my men. You are unharmed?

HELENE. Sure. I'm fine. *(To* HARRY.*)* What am I supposed to do? Curtsy to him?

HARRY *(disdainfully)*. Kiss his boots, why not?

SEGURA. They are poor, ignorant soldiers who undertake certain outrages as a point of honor. I hope you understand, señorita. *(He turns to* ISHMAEL.*)* Señor Malcolm, your torture is ready.

ISHMAEL *(nursing a sore jaw)*. Thank God!

SEGURA. I believe we have finally found something suitable. An iron boot that tightens on the foot. It is extremely rusty, much out of use. But it will allow you to say something like—"Modern tyranny will make use of any device, no matter how crude or primitive." Will that do?

ISHMAEL *(enthusiastically)*. It's a gasser!

SEGURA. The gentleman who will apply the instrument is a young priest—doing research on the methods of the Inquisition. I suggest you reach agreement beforehand—when to leave off the investigation. You follow me?

ISHMAEL. I follow you.

FERNANDO *(in despair)*. They are all his followers!

ISHMAEL *goes out with one of the* GUARDS, *exchanging glares with* HARRY.

HARRY. Give him a couple extra twists for me!

SEGURA. Señor Moran, I am sorry to have acted so abruptly— without consulting you. But the situation has become impossible. A decision must be reached immediately. May I include all those present in a discussion of our affairs?

MORAN. If we make clear to Miss Muggins that it's off the record—

FERNANDO *(losing control)*. This too? You, Señor Moran? You come to me—when you have already sold us out? Like garbage—like old scraps—!

SEGURA *(as if lecturing a child).* Alfonso, you are better off than you know—or deserve to be. I have made some rash promises to the people about you! If we can do business quietly, I may find ways not to keep them. Otherwise—

FERNANDO *(with a shred of dignity).* I will not be reduced to a fool, Carlos!

SEGURA. No! You will be reduced to a cinder! (FERNANDO *pales and falls silent.)* Señor Moran?

MORAN. Yes, we can settle it now. But first, this afternoon, did an airplane—?

SEGURA. Yes. *(There is a deadly pause.)* An airplane flew over.

MORAN. Did it? Please—my son was in it, señor!

SEGURA. I know.

MORAN. But how on earth—?

SEGURA. They crashed. *(A moan from all concerned.)* No, no. They were lucky, señor. Very lucky indeed. They are still alive to see you.

The cell door opens, and JOHN *and* PEDRO *are hurried into the room by* GUARDS. PEDRO *is mostly bandages.* JOHN *has his right arm in a sling.*

MORAN *(going up to* JOHN). Thank God, boy! You're safe! I didn't think we'd get anything back but pieces of you!

JOHN *(still cocky).* You're not *getting* me back.

MORAN *(ignoring the comment).* Your arm! Wait'll your mother sees that. She'll have a fit.

JOHN. Didn't you hear? I'm not going back! Mother can have a fit without me for once! *(To* SEGURA.) I wish to ask for political asylum in Costa Bona!

SEGURA. You are already a political prisoner here! How can I grant you political asylum?

MORAN *(trying to cover for* JOHN). I'm sure the boy didn't mean any harm—

JOHN. The hell I didn't! I meant to blow him off the map, that's what!

SEGURA. You have a very stubborn son, Señor Moran. Pedro confesses all, but these are the first words from your son since we drag him out of the wreckage. A mule, he is. And I do not think it was very nice of you to let him drop bombs on us.

MORAN. Believe me. I couldn't stop it.

FERNANDO. But the bomb? What happened with the bomb?

JOHN. The damn thing didn't go off.

PEDRO. I dropped it. You see there? *(Holding out his hands.)* Rope burns. But for nothing. It did not explode. Six o'clock, seven o'clock, eight o'clock, now midnight, one o'clock. Poof—nothing!

JOHN. A bust! A complete bust!

MORAN. John, in a way—I'm very sorry. (*To* SEGURA.) You disabled the bomb then?

SEGURA. Disabled it? We can't even find it!

PEDRO. The bank! We dropped it on my father's office!

SEGURA. Pedro. We have looked. It is not in your father's office, or in the bank, or near the bank.

PEDRO. Then it must have *rolled* somewhere.

SEGURA. You see what my life is, Señor Moran? A rolling bomb in my capital, which nobody can find.

JOHN. What the hell difference does it make? It's not going to go off. It's a bust—this whole operation!

HARRY. You're not taking this right, Johnny. You can't win 'em all.

JOHN. Yeah? Did you ever even come close to winning one? Just one?

HELENE (*defending her man*). Quit picking on him! He's a tired man —and you don't have to get snotty all of a sudden!

SEGURA. One crisis after another! Can you blame me if I lose my temper sometimes and promise to burn someone?

FERNANDO. You do not scare me now, Carlos. You are just as much the blunderer as I!

SEGURA (*quietly fuming*). You—*you* call me a blunderer? Alfonso, if you only understood what a clown you are, how amused you would be. Your blunders make mine look like *finesse!* You cannot even win a revolution against me when I help you!

FERNANDO. What do you mean, Carlos? I do not understand!

SEGURA. You are telling me this? I, who have been kept in office by your sheer stupidity? I did everything I could for you. I cleared the streets. I gave all my secret police a secret holiday. I got the only difficult cabinet minister drunk. I waited for you at the Presidential Palace, the door unlocked, the gates open—my flight for Nice arranged for. I even saw that the order was given to start the revolution! I did everything for you. All you had to do was climb out of bed, put on your slippers, and walk toward me with the crowd. But can you do that much? No. Instead you attack a nunnery—which defeats you!

FERNANDO. But—but—it's impossible!

HARRY (*offering excuses*). It wasn't our fault! We weren't prepared. You started the revolution too soon, guv'—What am I saying?

SEGURA. Even then I am willing to forgive you. You are hopeless, but I will try again. I send Señor Moran out to the jungle to ask you if you will please rouse the peasants and march back in again! And what do you do? You try to bomb me!

FERNANDO. But I didn't know. I didn't!

MORAN. It's partly my fault. I never got a chance to explain it all to the Marshall. I was whittling him down when my son walked in.

FERNANDO. Who is whittling me?

JOHN *(bitterly)*. Everybody. It's a big joke!

FERNANDO. A joke?

JOHN. Yeah. You and I—and Pedro here—we thought we were running a revolution. That's the joke. It was only a freak act my father was planning to bring to town.

MORAN. That's not fair, John.

JOHN. Show me any different!

HELENE. But why all the finagle? (*To* SEGURA.) You want to get yourself overthrown?

SEGURA. Exactly. I need the revolution as much as Alfonso does. First, there is my health. I need a long rest under the gentle hum of the roulette wheel. Then, there are the plantations. I tell you frankly, señorita, it is a grand thing to nationalize them in the eyes of the people, but financially, it is disastrous.

HELENE. Costa Bona is on the rocks?

SEGURA. No, but very near them. I am afraid I have to ask the ABC to return.

HELENE. But you just threw them out of the country.

SEGURA. That is just the problem. I must be overthrown before the ABC can come back. Therefore, there must be a revolution. Revolutions —they are always around, except when you need them. (*Looking at* FERNANDO.)

FERNANDO. I—I—still do not understand.

JOHN. Oh it's simple enough, Marshall. You're going to come to power, and you won't even need the revolution! It's all arranged, you see. Things are going to be just exactly like they were before. You'll look around and think it was yesterday.

SEGURA. Again that is not fair, Lieutenant. Your father has granted me a number of concessions—in view of my coming retirement. Schools for the people, housing, hospitals, many of the things you want for them. I do not think we shall ever reform the ABC, but we can cut its purse a little. (*Frowning at* JOHN.) It is not a joke. It is the best thing for Costa Bona—like it or not.

JOHN. Sure, sure. Now I'll tell you what I think. I think for a couple of seconds there really was a revolution. Just for two or three seconds.

That was when Pedro let go of the rope. The Tarantula was real. Wasn't it, Pedro?

PEDRO. *Si, si.* Very heavy too!

JOHN. That was it. The drop. Not even the bomb. Just dropping it —that was the revolution. The rest of it is a fraud. All of it. And I spit upon it. *(He spits in elaborate Spanish fashion.)* Now—*(Grabbing* PEDRO *by the sleeve.)* Take us out and shoot us!

PEDRO *(trying to break away).* Shoot us? *(To* SEGURA.) We are only little boys, señor!

SEGURA *(smiling at* JOHN). I am sorry, Lieutenant. I see no reason to shoot you. The bomb did not go off. Your father is Señor Moran. And somewhere you must have a mother waiting for your safe return. I cannot shoot you.

JOHN. Jesus, Pete, doesn't anybody around here believe in a goddamn thing? *(To* SEGURA.) Where the hell's your streak of cruelty?

At this moment there is a tremendous explosion off stage. It shakes the prison. There is immediate confusion. GUARDS *pour in through the cell door and out again.* SEGURA *tries to restore calm.*

JOHN. Pedro! The Tarantula!

PEDRO. I told you I would make it work! I told you!

HARRY. Where'd it land?

HELENE *(feeling the top of her head).* I felt it about here.

MORAN. What a rocker!

SEGURA. In the next block, if I am not mistaken. Please excuse me. I must see what nonsense your son has caused now.

JOHN. Nonsense? Not this time, Segura. That counted. I don't know what we hit, but we hit it! Blew it right up in your face. That counts!

SEGURA *(deadly serious).* Perhaps you are right. Perhaps this is not nonsense. Perhaps I will treat it much more seriously. *(He speaks to his* GUARDS *in Spanish, and they go out.)*

MORAN. You're a fool, John.

HARRY *(seconding the sentiment).* A bloody damn fool!

JOHN *(nervously defiant).* At least I'm not a fraud. What I do is real. *(To* MORAN.) Not a sell-out!

MORAN *(icily).* Do you have any idea how many chances I've had to buy your revolution right from under you? And didn't do it?

JOHN. You couldn't, you mean!

MORAN. Now you listen to me. Five minutes after you took off, your precious Marshall had the whole revolution back on the counter again. He's never *stopped* trying to peddle it. He sent you up in that damn airplane, just so he could work a deal while you weren't around. And he was going to hold you as hostage if I didn't deal with him!

JOHN *glares at* FERNANDO, *who smiles weakly.*

HELENE. But your old man wouldn't take it, kid.

HARRY. That's right, Johnny. He kept it straight for you. Not saying how long he would've kept it up—but that's what he did!

MORAN. You wanted a revolution. Okay, so you've had one. And no flies on it. Now you can just stop crying in your beer and start figuring out where it's got you or anybody else.

The cell door opens, and ISHMAEL *comes in with an extremely painful limp.*

ISHMAEL. That Jesuitical son-of-a-bitch played me for a sap. He put screw holes in me! *(He sits down on the bench.)* What the hell was that bang a few minutes ago?

HELENE. A bomb, sluefoot.

MORAN. By the way, John, this is Malcom Malcolm.

JOHN *(going up to him).* You're Malcolm? Are you? Really?

ISHMAEL *(sensing a sucker).* That's right, friend. You know my work?

JOHN. I sure do. Thank God, there's somebody left in the world with principles.

ISHMAEL. Unnnh? Oh yeah, sure. Thanks, friend. We try to live the good life, don't we?

JOHN. That book of yours has meant a lot to me. I'm just sorry I couldn't live up to it. What are you doing here?

ISHMAEL. Political prisoner.

JOHN. I was afraid they'd get you sometime. What's the matter with your foot?

ISHMAEL. Torture. They're trying to get me to denounce my writings. Be a propaganda victory for them, if I'd go over. They're using the boot on me, friend. Up to three times a day now. Tighter and tighter and—

HELENE. For Chrissake, Ish, level with the kid! He's getting it hard enough without your claptrap.

ISHMAEL *(after a pause).* Forget it, kid. It's the business.

JOHN. What d'you mean?

ISHMAEL. A fake. All of it.

JOHN. *You, too?*

SEGURA *re-enters, terribly grim. The* GUARDS *seize* JOHN *and drag him out.*

MORAN. I warn you, Carlos. Don't touch a hair on my son's head!

HELENE. Give the kid a chance. He's still young, huh?

SEGURA. Nothing will happen to him. Only a good scare and a good lesson. Although I'd like to shoot him. *(Banging his fist.)* What makes the young so barbaric? Pedro, don't you know your father's own bank when you see it? *(To* MORAN.) Do you know what these two imbeciles hit with their bomb?

MORAN. I suspect—

SEGURA. Yes, Señor! The banana sheds!

MORAN. I was afraid—

SEGURA. The entire street is one big banana split! Skins everywhere! Bananas everywhere. The street cannot be swept. It must be plowed!

PEDRO *(clapping his hands).* Wonderful! I must see it! *(He runs, but* SEGURA *catches him.)*

SEGURA. Oh you will see it, Pedro. Don't worry. *(He shakes him.)* In fact, you are now going to clean it up. Starting at the deep end!

GUARDS *seize* PEDRO, *hand him a shovel, and out he goes.*

SEGURA. You realize the extent of the disaster, Señor Moran? Economically?

MORAN. We'll absorb what we can. A loan—

SEGURA. That is generous. *(Wiping his brow.)* I hope this is all the revolution there will be. It is quite sufficient. I will appoint Alfonso head of an investigation into this mysterious bombing. From there he can inflate gradually to the Presidency. He will be a hero when he discovers the facts of the explosion, which Señor Malcolm will enumerate out of his lively imagination. *(To* MORAN.) And you will take your son home. Please. I am a tired man, and I might just shoot him, to get some sleep.

The cell door opens, and JOHN *comes in, a look of bewilderment on his face.*

JOHN. Dad—I've ruined the country!

MORAN. Practically.

JOHN *(to* SEGURA). Señor Segura, I didn't mean to do *that!* I really put you in a pinch, didn't I? *(To* HARRY *and* HELENE.) You know what it looks like out there? Like they dumped the whole United Fruit Company in a Waring Blender. *(Back to* SEGURA.) God, I'm sorry.

SEGURA *(coldly).* That's all right, Lieutenant. Just please—go home.

JOHN *(with resolution).* No, I'm going to make it up to you. I really am. I am going to stay here and help you rebuild.

SEGURA *(with a double-take; then to* MORAN). Señor Moran, I give you five hours to ship him home. In a box with airholes. After that, I'm shooting him.

JOHN. But I know a lot about economic reorganization. I can send home for the book right away—

SEGURA. Three hours, señor. In five, he might reorganize me!

JOHN. But—

At this point there is a hesitant knock on the cell window. Everybody looks toward it. The face of JULIANNA MORAN *appears.*

JULIANNA. Is everybody decent in there? May I please come in?

SEGURA. Who is this? *(He signals the* GUARDS *to let* JULIANNA *in.)*

MORAN *(flabbergasted).* Julianna! What in the hell are you doing here?

JULIANNA. Oh, Francis, our little boy—the detectives—they've located him. He's down *here* mixed up with some *awful* people. You've got to help me find him, I don't care *how* busy you are.

MORAN. Julianna—*(He points toward* JOHN.)

JOHN *(suffering her embrace).* Hello, mother.

JULIANNA *(all over him).* Oh you poor, dear lost soul. What is it you've gotten into? A gang? Some awful gang of Puerto Ricans?

MORAN *(harshly).* Get your claws off him.

JULIANNA *(shocked).* Why, Francis, what did you say?

MORAN. You heard me. Get your claws off him. He's just been through a revolution. He's old enough, he doesn't need you to scratch his mosquito bites for him.

JULIANNNA *(huffily).* Well, you certainly don't need to shout at me —I don't intend to *smother*—he's my own flesh and blood—and—and —*(Scrambling in her pocketbook.)* I just wanted him to have his mail. *(She hands him a stack of letters.)* The Dean is very angry with you, John. He's stricken your name. *(Pointing to another letter.)* And the government has business with you!

MORAN. I knew it. They're revoking his citizenship!

JOHN *(tearing open the letter).* Like hell! They're drafting me.

JULIANNA *(in tears).* But they can't do that. He's only a sophomore. *(Running over to* MORAN.) You'll fix it for him, won't you, Francis?

MORAN. He dropped out of school, didn't he? What's he expect?

JULIANNA. But you'll fix it, Francis! Now don't tell me you can't, I know you can.

MORAN. That's up to him. Not us.

JOHN *(in disgust).* A stinking, lousy private. *(He feels his epaulets.)*

MORAN. John. Your mother says I should fix it.

JOHN *(angrily).* You stay out of this! You've fixed enough for me already.

MORAN *(smiling, to* JULIANNA*).* You see, Julianna?

JULIANNA *(in tears again).* But he'll get into some sort of trouble! I know he will.

MORAN. What do you think he's been in for the last two months?

JULIANNA *(sternly).* Yes, John, where *have* you been? Your father's been worried sick.

SEGURA. May I take it—that something has been settled with this young man?

MORAN *(to* JOHN*).* You willing to settle for the army?

JOHN *(looking at the letter).* What the hell! It's only two years—*(He gets a dreamy look.)* And just think what you could *do* in two years. *(Off into rhetorical dreamland.)* Dad, do you have any idea what a mess our defense system is? The waste is fantastic! Congress is scared stiff of the brass—And Dad, if you could just get me assigned to the Pentagon, I know—

JOHN *trails off into a rabid plan for reorganizing the defense system, as everybody collectively moans.*

CURTAIN

THE BATTLE OF THE CARNIVAL AND LENT

by Russell Graves

A scene from *The Battle of the Carnival and Lent,* by Russell Graves. Originally produced by The Carolina Playmakers in 1967.

THE AUTHOR: *Russell Graves*

A native Pennsylvanian, Russell Graves was born in Philadelphia, the son of a prominent business executive, in 1922. He began his career in the educational theater as a student at Carnegie Institute of Technology, where he displayed a particular bent for dramatic writing. After three years, however, his studies were interrupted by a tour of duty with the military in World War II. During this time, he continued his playwriting and won a contest for service personnel sponsored by the National Theatre Conference. Following a brief stint as radio writer-director for USO, he was awarded a fellowship in 1946 as playwright-in-residence at Dartmouth College.

Returning to Carnegie in 1947 to complete work on two degrees, his play, *The Juggler,* was presented as the first full-length major production of a student-written play at that institution in a decade. Further graduate study led to a Ph.D. degree from Florida State University; and, after five years on the teaching staff of Lycoming College, at Williamsport, Pennsylvania, Dr. Graves came to The University of North Carolina at Chapel Hill in 1958. At present he is a professor in the Department of Dramatic Art and a staff director of The Carolina Playmakers.

A frequent contributor to scholarly theater journals, Dr. Graves has been chairman of the Publications Committee and the Editorial Board of the American Educational Theatre Association, and is now a member of the American Society for Theatre Research and the Shaw Society of Great Britain.

His full-length plays, which now number seventeen, have been produced in many educational and community theaters across the country. *The Magic Island,* a play constructed after the *commedia dell'arte* formula, was produced under his direction in the Forest Theatre here in 1959. *The Battle of the Carnival and Lent* was staged for the first time in the Playmakers Theatre, climaxing the forty-ninth season's bill of major productions. Professor George Savage, teacher of playwriting at the University of California at Los Angeles, upon reading the script, wrote to The University of North Carolina Press: "This is a thoughtful play, commenting clearly and dramatically on the crusades, monastic orders, and the attitudes and beliefs of the medieval world. The Russell Graves play proves that regionalism has not completely dominated the writing coming from The Carolina Playmakers."

PREMIÈRE PLAYBILL CREDITS

The Battle of the Carnival and Lent, by Russell Graves, was originally produced by The Carolina Playmakers on April 12, 13, 14, 15, 16, 17, and 18, 1967, in the Playmakers Theatre, Chapel Hill, North Carolina, under the direction of Thomas M. Patterson. The settings were by Tom Rezzuto, Jr., the costumes by Douglas L. Barger, and the lighting by Christopher Parsons.

THE CAST

THE DOCTOR	Kai Jurgensen
THE CAPTAIN	William Ellington
PANTALONE	S. Terrence Gregory
FRANCESCHINA	Betty Setzer
THE LEPER	Tom Kindle
THE JEW	Gary Weathersbee
PULCINELLA	Benjamin Keaton
BROTHER SILENUS	John Marshall Jones
BROTHER MARTIN	Shawn Smith
THE PRIOR	Tom Marriott
THE KING	William Watson
SIR GERALD	William Huf
MASTER DUDLEY	Ross Prevost
TERRIBLE TOM	Foster Fitz-Simons
ARNOLD THE GOATHERD	Julian Hartzell
BROTHER THOMAS	Rick Dula
BROTHER AMBROSE	Paul H. Crouch

MONKS, TOWNSPEOPLE AND CRUSADERS......Judith Andrews, Paul Baker, Madge Bunce, Alison Cain, Arthur Cain, Terrence Fitz-Simons, Robert Hardison, Brenda Ann Hauser, Kathryn Howell, Roger Howell, William McDaniel, Dallas M. Sprinkle

SCENE AND TIME

In and near a monastery in northern Europe.

ACT ONE: The late Middle Ages.
ACT TWO: The same.

ACT ONE

Scene One

A roadside. A bank runs along the side of the road. A milestone, very weathered, even at this early date, sits by the road on one side of the stage. On the other a cowled figure is seated. It might be a monk or a plague victim: its face is concealed, making it impossible to tell. Presently a voice is heard off stage. It is deep and masculine, loud and strong, singing a song which is at first unclear, but shortly becomes more distinct.

THE DOCTOR *(singing, as he leads on a troupe of players).*
> When I dream of the devil's home,
> I dream of snow and ice;
> In heaven I may never roam,
> But wouldn't it be nice
> To see the fields of clover
> And to hear the angels sing,
> To spend eternity in an everlasting Spring.

By now the troupe has arrived on stage. THE DOCTOR *leads them. He is a robust man of middle age, heavily weighed down with various sacks and bags. He is followed by two men:* THE CAPTAIN *pulling and* PANTALONE *pushing a heavily laden cart. They seem very old and tired, thin and worn, their clothes ragged, although one suspects they are not actually any older than* THE DOCTOR. *Along the sides of the cart a series of masks hangs: those of the* commedia dell'arte *characters of* THE DOCTOR, THE CAPTAIN, PANTALONE, *and* PULCINELLA. *On the wagon a tarpaulin covers what appears to be a body, stretched along the top of the load. Bringing up the rear of the procession is a woman (*FRANCESCHINA*), perhaps a few years older than the men. She too is loaded down with bags.* THE DOCTOR *holds up his hand to stop the procession.*

THE DOCTOR. All right. This ought to be far enough away from that town and its sanctimonious son-of-a-bitch of a mayor. *(They all stop and*

AUTHOR'S NOTE TO THE DIRECTOR: Except for the one intermission, it is important that the play move forward without interruption. The staging, therefore, should be simple—basically set pieces against a black cyclorama. At the very end, however, a night sky must be made visible. The last line of one scene should act as the cue line for the next, with no gap between successive scenes.

put down their burdens. THE DOCTOR *spots the seated figure and approaches it.)* Good day, Brother. *(There is no answer.)*

THE DOCTOR. I said, "Good day, Brother."

THE CAPTAIN. Don't go near him!

THE DOCTOR *(crossing to the figure).* I'll put a civil tongue in your head!

THE CAPTAIN. It's not a monk!

THE DOCTOR. What's bothering you, Captain?

PANTALONE. They put them along the roads.

FRANCESCHINA. To warn sinners . . . like you, Doctor.

THE DOCTOR *(approaching closer to the figure.)* Sinners! I'll sinner you! *(He strikes the figure's cowl. It falls back, revealing a death's head. All step back with a gasp, and all but* THE DOCTOR *cross themselves.)*

FRANCESCHINA. Holy Mother, preserve us from sin!

THE DOCTOR. Too late, Franceschina. It's been too late for thirty years.

FRANCESCHINA. Watch what you're saying!

THE DOCTOR. Thirty years, Franceschina. Thirty years the biggest whore from Genoa to Bergamo . . . until you got so old and fat not even a blind man with a hard-on could stomach you.

FRANCESCHINA. Shut your foul mouth!

THE DOCTOR *crosses and takes up the death's-head in his hand. The others withdraw farther away, crossing themselves.*

THE DOCTOR *(pretending to toss the skull).* Here . . . catch. It's a bone for you to gnaw on.

PANTALONE. You're damned for sure!

THE DOCTOR. We're all damned for sure . . . only I know it. You fools still have hopes. *(Speaking to the skull.)* You know better, don't you, old man? You're turning on a spit right now, eh? Here . . . I'll put you back together again. *(He places the skull back where it was, but he does not replace the cowl.)* And I wish I was burning right along side you. You could tell us, couldn't you? Is it hot there or is it cold? Is the song right or wrong? *(He sings as the others throw themselves to the ground, exhausted by their efforts and the horror of the doctor's actions.)*

> The devil's heart is frozen
> And his soul is solid stone;
> His food is icy sinners
> And his knives are human bone.
> His domains are the coldest
> In the universe, I fear;

That's why I wish I could stay warm
As long as I am here.
End of concert; beginning of digging. Get out the shovel, Captain.

THE CAPTAIN *drags himself up and takes the shovel from the cart.*

PANTALONE. I've never been so cold in all my life. Once when I was
a baby we traveled for days, and we went into the mountains. It was
cold there, but not like this. There were icicles on the trees, and the
birds were frozen in the snow.

THE CAPTAIN. Where abouts?

FRANCESCHINA. Make it a good grave.

THE DOCTOR. The ground's frozen. That ditch ought to be softest.
Here, Pantalone, give him a hand.

PANTALONE. Aren't you going to do any digging?

THE DOCTOR. Not if I can help it. Let's get going. We've a long way
ahead of us.

FRANCESCHINA. Where *are* we going?

THE DOCTOR. North.

FRANCESCHINA. That's all you ever say . . . north! A lot of help that
is!

THE DOCTOR. We won't go anywhere, unless the Captain gets a move
on.

PANTALONE. I'd almost rather catch the plague than have to go
where it's as cold as this.

THE DOCTOR. Colder!

PANTALONE. Colder?

THE DOCTOR. The nights last for six months and the ground is
covered with ice all year round.

PANTALONE. I'd rather catch the plague. What's it worth if you're in
misery all the time?

THE DOCTOR. You're forgetting what they look like. You forgot how
their faces look. How black they are. How they stink. Think about that
before you decide to turn around. *(He points to the shape on the cart.)*
Think about him before you bitch too much about how cold it is. Think
about what he looked like before we covered him up. Remember how he
moaned day and night. Remember that, Pantalone.

*A bell is heard ringing from the direction from which the troupe
entered.*

FRANCESCHINA. What's that?

THE CAPTAIN. The monks are going to mass.

THE DOCTOR. They'll be holding a mass for you, if you don't get that hole dug.

FRANCESCHINA. It's getting closer.

PANTALONE. You don't suppose . . . ? *(He and* FRANCESCHINA *look at one another fearfully.)*

FRANCESCHINA. What would one of them be doing out here?

A cowled figure (THE LEPER) *enters. His costume resembles that of the seated figure except that it has a distinct character to it that would set it off from that of any monk or priest. He is ringing a hand-bell. His face is completely hidden from us.*

FRANCESCHINA. It is!

All four of them draw as far away from the figure as possible.

THE DOCTOR. Get away from us.

THE LEPER. Please let me join you. I'll keep my distance.

THE DOCTOR. On your way!

THE LEPER. Just let me rest here a moment.

FRANCESCHINA. God's put his curse on all lepers.

THE LEPER. I've been walking for weeks. *(He slowly takes up his journey, wearily ringing his bell as he goes.)*

PANTALONE. Doctor!

THE DOCTOR. What?

PANTALONE. He's going the same direction we are!

THE DOCTOR. I can't help that. Come on, Captain, it's getting late.

THE CAPTAIN. Why do I have to do all the work? Why doesn't Pantalone do anything? Why don't you?

THE DOCTOR. What did you have to eat last night?

THE CAPTAIN. You know very well what I had.

THE DOCTOR. And where did you get it?

THE CAPTAIN. I didn't get it.

THE DOCTOR. Exactly . . . I got it.

PANTALONE. You stole it.

THE DOCTOR. I stole it.

FRANCESCHINA. Another sin to put down in the book.

THE DOCTOR. I stole it, and you ate it . . . without any complaints that I noticed.

FRANCESCHINA. It's a sin . . . stealing.

THE DOCTOR. And eating stolen food isn't? They call it "accessory after the fact."

PANTALONE. What's the use of arguing with him?

THE CAPTAIN. You're not doing the digging!

PANTALONE. Neither are you!

THE DOCTOR. That's right . . . back to it, Captain. You don't want our beloved, departed brother here . . . *(He gestures to the covered body on the cart.)* not to have a Christian burial, do you?

THE CAPTAIN. I don't mind doing my share. . . .

THE DOCTOR. If you don't hurry we'll be spending the night here . . . with that leper wandering around.

During the following, THE CAPTAIN *tries to dig in several places, but they all prove too hard.*

FRANCESCHINA. You and your talk against God. We'll all die of the plague or leprosy or of just plain evil. *(She crosses herself.)*

THE DOCTOR. That's right, Franceschina, brush the sins off that stained breast of yours. Brush off all the heads that have gone to sleep snoring there. Wiggle your fingers and everything will be all right. You've had enough practice wiggling them in the wrong places, you bet!

FRANCESCHINA. You'll freeze in hell for sure. You're a damned soul if ever there was one.

THE DOCTOR. I was damned the first time my father climbed in the hay beside my mother. *(To* THE CAPTAIN.) Haven't you started yet?

THE CAPTAIN. You couldn't break this ground with a pick, and all we've got is this old shovel.

THE DOCTOR *(crossing to* THE CAPTAIN *angrily).* Not a one of you can do anything . . . including getting yourselves enough to eat.

He takes the shovel from THE CAPTAIN, *but before he is able to do anything with it, a man* (THE JEW) *enters from the same direction as that used by* THE TROUPE *and* THE LEPER. *He, too, is in a cowled robe. It is similar to that worn by the dead figure, except that his has a Star of David prominently displayed on it. His face is also hidden by the cowl. He stops upon seeing* THE TROUPE.

THE JEW. Some bread, for the love of God!

FRANCESCHINA. For the love of God!

THE DOCTOR. Be on your way, Jew. We want nothing to do with you.

FRANCESCHINA. You killed OUR God, and now you want our bread!

THE JEW. I haven't eaten for two days!

THE CAPTAIN. Good! Another day and there'll be one less Jew on earth.

THE JEW. May you all be damned!

THE DOCTOR. We are already . . . you don't scare us.

THE JEW. May all your sons be cursed!

THE DOCTOR. All our sons! That's a good one. I've got sons from one end of Italy to the other . . . and I've never seen a one of them. Curse away! It doesn't make any difference to me.

FRANCESCHINA. Send him on his way, Doctor. He makes my spine creep.

THE DOCTOR. On your way, Jew!

THE JEW *(as he leaves)*. And your sons' sons through all the generations.

THE TROUPE *stares after him.*

PANTALONE. They say they're wizards; that they're in league with the Devil himself.

THE DOCTOR. Aren't we all!

PANTALONE. He scares me!

THE DOCTOR. You're scared of your own shadow. Come on, let's get this done with. Now we've got a leper and a Jew to avoid in the dark. (THE DOCTOR *tries digging, but he, too, finds the ground impossibly hard.)*

THE DOCTOR *(throwing down the shovel).* Damnation! It's like solid rock!

FRANCESCHINA *(pointing to the covered body on the cart).* What are we going to do with him?

PANTALONE. We can't just leave him lying there.

THE DOCTOR. Do you have a better suggestion?

FRANCESCHINA. Out in the rain!

THE DOCTOR. It isn't raining.

FRANCESCHINA. But it will! And snow, too. That's no way to leave him.

THE DOCTOR. That's the way we're going to leave him. Captain . . . take off the cover.

FRANCESCHINA. NO!

THE DOCTOR. You didn't think I was going to waste good canvas on a dead man, did you?

PANTALONE. It wouldn't be right, Doctor.

THE DOCTOR. We need it for the new backcloth.

FRANCESCHINA. You won't take it off.

THE DOCTOR. Oh yes I will! Captain!

THE CAPTAIN. She's right, Doctor.

THE DOCTOR. So you're all as gutless as ever! All right, I'll do it myself. *(He goes up to the cart and puts his hand on the canvas-covered body.* FRANCESCHINA *grabs him from behind and pulls him away.)*

FRANCESCHINA. Come and help me.

THE CAPTAIN *and* PANTALONE *make ineffectual movements in her direction. Finally,* THE DOCTOR *throws her to the ground.*

THE DOCTOR *(looking at her, bewilderment written on his face).* Does it mean that much to you? You'd have thought he was your own flesh and blood.

FRANCESCHINA. If we don't watch out for each other, it's sure nobody else will.

THE DOCTOR. That's true enough! All right . . . leave it. What a waste!

He starts to lift the body. THE CAPTAIN *helping him, while* FRANCES-CHINA *hovers over them.* PANTALONE *mounts the bank in search of a good spot. Suddenly* PANTALONE *calls out.*

PANTALONE. Doctor!
THE DOCTOR. What now?
PANTALONE. There's someone here!

The others mount the bank beside PANTALONE.

THE CAPTAIN. He's dead!
FRANCESCHINA *(getting down into the ditch beside the still unseen man).* No, he's not; he's still breathing.
THE DOCTOR *(getting down beside* FRANCESCHINA*).* Here. Let's lift him out.

FRANCESCHINA *and* THE DOCTOR, *with the help of the others, raise the body of a man from the ditch and lay it on the bank. His clothes are torn and covered with dirt, his eyes are closed, and there is dried blood around his mouth.*

THE DOCTOR. He might as well be; he's on his last legs.
FRANCESCHINA *(wiping off his mouth).* Bring some wine.
THE DOCTOR. Don't waste it.

PANTALONE *gets a wine flask from the wagon.* FRANCESCHINA *takes it and holds it up to the lips of the unconscious man. He chokes on it and stirs restlessly.*

THE DOCTOR. That comes out of your share, Pantalone.
FRANCESCHINA. It comes out of mine!
THE DOCTOR *(shrugging).* It's no skin off my ass.
THE CAPTAIN. He's opening his eyes.
FRANCESCHINA *(very solicitously).* There, there. You'll be all right.
PANTALONE. What happened to you?
THE CAPTAIN. Who are you?

THE DOCTOR. And what are we going to do with you?

PANTALONE. He's a shepherd . . . here's his flute.

FRANCESCHINA. Give him a chance, all of you. He's almost dead.

THE DOCTOR. Better for us if he was!

THE CAPTAIN. Look! He's trying to say something.

THE DOCTOR. He's trying to say: "Give me something to eat," you can bet.

FRANCESCHINA. Doctor! He can't talk! *(She looks puzzled. Then she pushes his head back and forces open his mouth.)* Doctor!

THE DOCTOR. Now what?

FRANCESCHINA *(rising and stepping away from the man)*. He's got no tongue! *(The others stare at her.)* He's got no tongue, I tell you.

THE CAPTAIN *(looking closely at the man)*. It's been ripped out!

THE DOCTOR *throws back his head and laughs.*

PANTALONE. What is there to laugh at?

THE DOCTOR *(gaining control of himself with difficulty)*. I only know two things they take your tongue out for: bearing false witness is one, and blasphemy is the other. You've found yourselves a fine one, you have!

FRANCESCHINA *(drawing farther away)*. Blasphemy!

THE DOCTOR. Blasphemy!

PANTALONE. He doesn't look like a blasphemer.

THE DOCTOR. You should know, you've heard enough of it. Come on. We're wasting too much time. It'll be dark soon. *(They go on about their business of removing the body from the cart, a very quiet group. From time to time they return to glance at the man lying on the bank, now with his eyes closed again. They take off the tarpaulin and carry the canvas-covered body up the bank. They lay it in the ditch, some distance from the man.)* There! That's done. Now we can be on our way.

FRANCESCHINA. Without a word?

THE DOCTOR. There have been enough words already. Let's get going.

FRANCESCHINA. You said a Christian burial.

THE DOCTOR. I was joking.

FRANCESCHINA. I won't budge an inch until we've done it right.

PANTALONE. It won't take more than a minute, Doctor.

THE DOCTOR. A bunch of sanctimonious old ladies, that's what you are!

FRANCESCHINA. Not an inch!

THE DOCTOR. All right. Go ahead. But hurry up. We've a long distance to go.

THE DOCTOR *goes to the wagon and takes out a lantern, which he lights. Then he goes to the skeleton, to which he speaks while the others are praying. The others gather around the body and kneel, murmuring prayers.* THE MUTE *(later called* PULCINELLA*) has awakened and watches them curiously. He seems at first uncomprehending, but then he follows the murmured prayers, mouthing them silently to himself.*

THE DOCTOR *(to the skeleton, holding up the lantern).* You and me prefer light, don't we, old man? None of their muttering for us, eh? You know what? They think it'll get them to heaven; but it won't, will it? You know, don't you? *(Calling to the others.)* Hurry up; it's almost dark! *(To the skeleton once more.)* When it thunders, they pray; when it lightnings, they pray; when a flea gets in their lousy breeches, they pray. *(He puts the cowl over the death's-head.)* Here, I'll cover you up for the night. *(To the others.)* Come on!

They finish their praying and cross themselves. THE MUTE, *without thinking, follows suit.* FRANCESCHINA *catches this out of the corner of her eye.*

FRANCESCHINA *(as* THE CAPTAIN *and* PANTALONE *clamber down from the bank).* Doctor! He crossed himself!
THE DOCTOR. Good for him. Now let's get moving.

The men busy themselves with preparations for moving. FRANCES-CHINA *crosses beside* THE MUTE.

THE DOCTOR. Make sure everything is secure; you can't see the ruts when it's dark.
FRANCESCHINA *(to* THE MUTE*).* Did you commit blasphemy? *(He answers with a shake of his head: "No.")*
FRANCESCHINA. Or bear false witness? *("No.")* What was it then?

THE MUTE *tells his story, entirely in pantomime. The others are arrested by the beauty of his narration and stop their work to watch it, spellbound.*

THE MUTE'S STORY

I was a shepherd, wandering in the hills, playing my flute, and taking care of my sheep. It was a lonely life and people don't want to talk with shepherds. But it was rewarding, too. In the winter it is cold, and in the summer it is hot, but in the spring everything is reborn and the world is beautiful.

A short time ago, I was sitting on a hillside, playing my flute and tending the sheep, when suddenly I was attacked from behind by a band of brigands. I struggled with them, but they were too many for me and they were strong. They soon had me overpowered and lying on the ground, all trussed up. They took my sheep, and then they held me down and tore out my tongue. Then they threw me in this ditch where you found me, for which I am very thankful.

He looks from one to the other. They are amazed at the beauty of his performance. The silence is finally broken by THE DOCTOR.

THE DOCTOR. A pack of lies! It's blasphemy, I tell you, or lying. One or the other.

FRANCESCHINA. I believe him!

THE DOCTOR. But it doesn't matter. For all I care, he can be the antichrist.

PANTALONE. Doctor!

THE DOCTOR. Or anything else. I've an idea.

FRANCESCHINA *(suspiciously)*. What idea?

THE DOCTOR. Pulci! *(He indicates the ditch where they have placed the body.)*

PANTALONE. What about Pulci?

THE DOCTOR. We've just buried him, haven't we?

FRANCESCHINA. If you can call it burial. I don't.

THE DOCTOR. And that means we're one member short, doesn't it?

THE CAPTAIN *(pointing at* THE MUTE*)*. But he can't talk!

THE DOCTOR. He talks better without a tongue than you do with one.

PANTALONE. He did make himself very clear.

FRANCESCHINA. I think it's a fine idea!

THE CAPTAIN. You would . . . you'd mother every stray dog that came down the pike.

THE DOCTOR *(crossing to* THE MUTE, *who hasn't moved throughout the discussion)*. We're actors, do you know what that means? *("Yes.")*

THE DOCTOR. Good! Now we've just lost one of our players . . . *(He points to the spot where they placed the body.)* That's him over there. . . .

FRANCESCHINA. He was a fine man! Too good for us.

THE DOCTOR. He was too good for life. That's why he's over there in that ditch and we're still on our feet.

THE CAPTAIN. But there's never been a Pulci who couldn't talk! The audience will never stand for it!

THE DOCTOR. Where we're going the audience won't know the difference.

FRANCESCHINA. Be quiet, Captain. It's a good idea.

THE DOCTOR (*to* THE MUTE). How would you like to come along with us and take his place? *("Me?")*

PANTALONE. Do you think he'll ever learn all the business?

THE CAPTAIN. A shepherd? Never!

THE DOCTOR. We'll stop before we get to the next town and teach him enough to get by. He'll do all right. (*To* THE MUTE.) How about it? *("Yes.")* Good! Franceschina . . . give our new member some bread. And let's be on our way.

FRANCESCHINA *takes some bread from her pack and gives it to* THE MUTE, *now* PULCINELLA. *He falls upon it as if he were starving.*

FRANCESCHINA. He doesn't even know who we are!

THE DOCTOR *introduces each of them. As he does so, he tosses each man the mask that goes with his character, the masks that have been hanging on the side of the wagon. Each of them puts on his mask as he is introduced. The introduction and the putting on of the masks seems to effect a transformation in the characters: there is a new air of youthfulness about them all.* FRANCESCHINA *does not have a mask, but she shares in the general air of hope that has developed.*

THE DOCTOR. Our names aren't our own, of course. Nobody is named The Captain and Pantalone and The Doctor in real life. Nobody who didn't have something to run away from would join up in the first place. These are the names of the characters we play . . . and these are the masks we wear. This is The Captain, and this scared-looking old bastard is Pantalone. Franceschina, the most motherly whore in all Europe. And I'm The Doctor.

FRANCESCHINA. The biggest sinner in all Europe.

THE DOCTOR. And you will be Pulcinella . . . and this is your mask. (*They are all masked now, except for* FRANCESCHINA. *They pick up their packs and start on their way,* THE CAPTAIN *and* PANTALONE *pushing and pulling the cart as before, but now being helped by* PULCINELLA. *As they go,* THE DOCTOR *sings his song again.*)

> When I dream of the devil's home,
> I dream of snow and ice;
> In heaven I may never roam,

But wouldn't it be nice
To see the fields of clover
And to hear the angels sing,
To spend eternity in an everlasting Spring.

And they are gone. Only the cowled figure remains.

Scene Two

A monastery in northern Europe. We are in the anteroom to the private chapel of THE PRIOR: *a bench, two stools, a prie-dieu set before a crucifix hanging on the wall, a rough desk covered with papers, pen and ink, and the appurtenances of medieval monastery administration.*

Two elderly monks are arguing. One (BROTHER SILENUS) *is very stocky in build, if not, indeed, fat. The other* (BROTHER MARTIN) *is his precise complement, to the point of being cadaverous. At this moment the fat one is seated on one of the chairs. The thin one is standing, hands held together in front of him, on the opposite side of the stage. They are facing away from one another, obviously in deep disagreement.*

BROTHER SILENUS. I won't discuss it any further. It's ten thousand, ten thousand, ten thousand! And nothing you or anyone else can say will change that!

BROTHER MARTIN. All right, Silenus, all right! Have it your own way. Ten thousand or ten million or just plain ten . . . have it any way you want. It isn't important. It isn't important at all!

BROTHER SILENUS. There! That's exactly what I mean! It isn't important! What's come over you, Martin? The world might be falling to pieces about our heads . . . indeed there is good reason to believe that's exactly what it is doing . . . and you say it isn't important!

BROTHER MARTIN. All I say is, that if God wants to make it ten thousand he can; if he wants to make it none he can; if he wants to make it infinite he can. God can make any number dance anywhere any time he wishes. Who are we to argue about it?

BROTHER SILENUS *is about to answer, but before he can say anything they are joined by* THE PRIOR. *He is older than the others, and his bearing shows the authority of one who is accustomed to command. He enters quickly, crossing to the desk, at which he seats himself, with scarcely a nod in the direction of the others. He glances over a parchment on his desk.*

THE PRIOR. At it again, you two?

BROTHER MARTIN. A slight disagreement, Prior.

BROTHER SILENUS. If you call blasphemy slight!

THE PRIOR. Blasphemy! Dear, dear! Have you been blaspheming, Brother Martin?

BROTHER MARTIN. You know me better than that, Prior.

THE PRIOR. I know Brother Silenus just as well; he's no more given to telling lies than you are to committing blasphemy.

BROTHER SILENUS. Prior, he said. . . .

THE PRIOR *(holding up his hand)*. Just a moment, Brother Silenus. Patience. *(He looks from one to the other of them and back, half amused, half irritated.)* It looks as if we have a problem worthy of Solomon himself, doesn't it?

BROTHER MARTIN. I scarcely think our little disagreement could be thought fit for Solomon. I'm afraid Brother Silenus has blown it up out of all proportion.

THE PRIOR *(becoming quite severe)*. I haven't time to settle every disagreement between two brothers. Now! What is this all about? Brother Silenus?

BROTHER SILENUS. Brother Martin here said that intellectual discussion was a waste of time.

BROTHER MARTIN. I said no such thing! I simply said. . . .

THE PRIOR. Hold your peace, Brother Martin. Let me hear Brother Silenus out; then it will be your turn.

BROTHER MARTIN. I'm sorry, Prior. It's just that he said. . . .

THE PRIOR *holds up his hand peremptorily.* BROTHER MARTIN *subsides.*

THE PRIOR. All right, Brother Silenus.

BROTHER SILENUS. He said it doesn't matter how many angels can dance on the head of a pin. He said . . . well, he said a great many things. But worst of all, he said the world is in such a terrible state it doesn't matter about the angels, and I said it is just because of the state of the world that it does matter!

THE PRIOR. Aha! Theology!

BROTHER SILENUS. Theology! Oh, no, Prior!

BROTHER MARTIN. Not theology, Prior. Just a minor disagreement. *(To* BROTHER SILENUS.*)* Now see what you've done with your self-righteousness!

THE PRIOR. Now, now, Brother Martin. *(He ponders the situation a moment, then speaks.)* Brother Silenus?

BROTHER SILENUS. Yes, Prior?

THE PRIOR. What are the vows you took when you joined this order?

BROTHER SILENUS. Poverty, Purity, and Obedience.

THE PRIOR. Obedience, yes! And Brother Martin, what are my instructions regarding theology?

BROTHER MARTIN. You forbade us to engage in theology unless we were trained for it.

THE PRIOR. Exactly! Theology is not for everybody. Leave it to Brother Ambrose. It suits him. So, no more theology, eh? And now my reason for summoning you. Or, rather, my reasons. First, the lesser. We are to be visited.

BROTHER MARTIN. More crusaders?

THE PRIOR. More crusaders. *(He holds up a parchment that has been lying on his desk.)* I have the message here.

BROTHER SILENUS. And we will be expected to provide the usual food and lodging, when we've scarcely enough for ourselves. And we certainly haven't any room to spare.

THE PRIOR. Nevertheless, we are expected to provide food and lodging and . . . entertainment.

BROTHER MARTIN. What?

THE PRIOR. Here. *(He hands* BROTHER MARTIN *the parchment.* BROTHER MARTIN *and* BROTHER SILENUS *read it.)*

BROTHER SILENUS. Entertainment! What do they mean by "entertainment"?

THE PRIOR. Not even you are so unworldly as not to know what entertainment is, although I suspect the soldier's ideas of it and ours may prove quite different.

BROTHER MARTIN. Do they expect us to dance for them?

BROTHER SILENUS. Or sing songs?

THE PRIOR. I really don't know what they expect, but I imagine the two of you will think of something.

BROTHER MARTIN. The two of *us?*

THE PRIOR. As a special privilege, I am giving you two the task of providing our brave guests with entertainment.

BROTHER MARTIN. As a special privilege?

THE PRIOR. Every brother will have to contribute to the burden put upon us by our guests. If you would rather work in the kitchen. . . .

BROTHER MARTIN. Oh, no, Prior.

THE PRIOR. Or the stables. . . .

BROTHER SILENUS. I think we should go wherever you assign us, Prior.

THE PRIOR. Good! That's settled! Now we can turn to a far more serious matter.

BROTHER SILENUS. More serious than having to take care of a thousand crusaders?

THE PRIOR. More serious than a hundred thousand. There's a soul in mortal danger. Brother Thomas. *(The two monks nod understandingly.)* Yes, I see you recognize the problem.

BROTHER MARTIN. Doubting Thomas!

THE PRIOR. Doubting Thomas is a good name for him, but I'm afraid things have moved to the point where even that harmless little joke leaves a bitter taste in the mouth. Brothers, I have called on you because you have been here longer than anyone else. We've known each other longer. We've passed through more crises together. I need your help and advice.

BROTHER SILENUS. Anything, Prior.

BROTHER MARTIN. We're here to serve.

THE PRIOR. I know you are, my friends, and I thank you. *(He searches for the right words.)* When Brother Thomas first came here, we all had such great hopes for him. He was the most intelligent, the most devout, the most . . . Christian young man I've ever known. And his first year gave us every reason to expect fine things of him: first in the Chapel, first done with his chores, first in all his studies, and the last to complain. There had never been another like him. And strangest of all, no one was ever jealous of him. That's the remarkable thing. I suppose we all recognized a spirit above and beyond our own. No one ever said a word. And now everything is changed.

BROTHER SILENUS. What has he done, Prior?

THE PRIOR. He has come to doubt his own faith.

BROTHER MARTIN. He was doing that already.

THE PRIOR. This is different, deeper. Oh, they all do, the bright ones, when they're young.

BROTHER SILENUS. I never did! *(The other two look at him until he realizes the implications of what he has just said.)* I mean. . . .

THE PRIOR. After a year or so it's expected of them. After all, aren't we enjoined to examine our faith continuously? I went through such a period myself. But this is different.

BROTHER SILENUS. How different, Prior?

THE PRIOR. He's on fire. He's being consumed by some great conflagration, some torment.

BROTHER MARTIN. I wouldn't be too concerned, Prior. As you say, most young men go through it. He'll come around.

THE PRIOR. I hope so. I devoutly hope so. But in the meantime. . . .

BROTHER SILENUS. What has he done, Prior?

THE PRIOR. He's gone into the streets . . . like a madman. He's preaching some strange gospel of his own.

BROTHER SILENUS. Preaching!

BROTHER MARTIN. In the streets?

THE PRIOR. The people are afraid of him. They hurry away when he comes near them, as if he were some sort of devil.

BROTHER MARTIN. Devil!?

THE PRIOR. He can't go on.

BROTHER MARTIN. But surely, Prior, you can simply order him to stop!

THE PRIOR. Not as simply as all that, Brother Martin. I must think of the souls of the people, yes, and they mustn't come to fear us. But, you see, there's Brother Thomas' soul, too. He must be saved for God's work.

BROTHER MARTIN. We will pray, Father. Night and day.

THE PRIOR. Something more than that is needed. I'm assigning Brother Thomas to you two, to help with the preparations for the crusaders. I want you to keep an eye on him.

BROTHER SILENUS. Is that wise, Prior? Is it wise to send him out into the town, just when his doubts are deepest?

THE PRIOR. I don't know, Brother Silenus. I don't know. But I have a feeling that whatever I do must be severe. Nothing less will do.

BROTHER MARTIN. We'll do our best, Prior.

BROTHER SILENUS. Our very best.

THE PRIOR. I know you will, my friends, I know you will. And now let us pray that God may guide us in carrying out our missions and bearing our burdens. *(The two monks kneel on either side of the* prie-dieu.*)* Brother Thomas has a very long journey ahead of him. And he will have to travel alone most of the way . . . I hope he has the strength. *(He kneels beside them and prays.)*

Scene Three

Another roadside, very much like that in the first scene, but there is a difference. Right and left are reversed: the milestone, the rock on which the figure sat (there is no figure this time), the hill, the ditch . . . all reversed right for left. They are all here, but placed as they might be seen in a mirror.

A procession is crossing the stage, entering and leaving from the sides opposite to those used by the performers in the first scene.

Although the men in the procession are obviously tired, they do not present the picture of exhaustion found in the first group. These are the crusaders: mounted knights and their attendants, yeomen, armorers, provisioners, priests, clerks . . . the whole collection of motley mankind required by an army on the move. They are strung out in single file, although some are walking and talking together, showing that they still have a long way to go before they are in any danger of encountering the enemy. THE KING, *dressed more magnificently than any of the others, rides back along the line and holds up his arms. He calls out, "HALT!" in a voice that reinforces at once the judgment one has made from his costume. Immediately upon his command, each man throws down his kit and throws himself beside it.* THE KING *calls again along the now-halted column.*

THE KING. Sir Gerald! Sir Gerald!

A distant call answers him from the direction of the end of the column, but it is too distant for the words to be distinguished. THE KING *seems satisfied, however, and he seats himself on the hill, leaning back and admiring the sunlight. As he drinks in the day, he hums a nondescript little tune to himself. Presently a knight (*SIR GERALD*) rides up, and as he dismounts we realize that he is only slightly less magnificently caparisoned than* THE KING. *He bows and then stands at attention.*

SIR GERALD. You called me, Your Majesty?

THE KING. I called you, Sir Gerald. Now don't be so stuffy. Here, sit down. We'll have a talk while we're resting.

SIR GERALD. Of course, Your Majesty. *(He sits, but he is obviously made uncomfortable by this degree of familiarity on the part of his monarch.)*

THE KING. Of dreams and things.

SIR GERALD. I beg your pardon, Your Majesty?

THE KING. I beg your pardon, Your Majesty! My pardon is granted. I'm afraid you won't do, Sir Gerald. Let's have a wrestling match. My best man against yours.

SIR GERALD. I am sorry if I don't suit, Your Majesty.

THE KING. You don't. But no one else does either. That's what it means, being king . . . no one suits. You have a hundred thousand subjects and no friends at all. What about that wrestling match?

SIR GERALD. There *is* a new man in my company.

THE KING. Good! *(Calling.)* Master Dudley!

A young squire (MASTER DUDLEY) *appears. He is obviously only too anxious to please* THE KING.

MASTER DUDLEY. You called, Your Majesty?

THE KING. I called, Your Majesty. (*To* SIR GERALD.) You see . . . only subjects. (*To* THE SQUIRE.) Do you have any idea where you can find Terrible Tom?

MASTER DUDLEY. Oh, yes, Your Majesty. He's sleeping . . . a little ahead. He sleeps whenever he gets a chance.

THE KING. You are here to learn, my boy. Well, here's a lesson: don't volunteer information . . . to a king or anyone. You won't be thanked for it.

MASTER DUDLEY. But, Your Majesty, I only thought. . . .

THE KING. Lesson number two: don't explain. You can only reveal weakness to your enemies, and you reveal nothing to your friends. There you are: two lessons in three minutes. Now off with you and send along Terrible Tom. And be fast about it.

MASTER DUDLEY. Yes, Your Majesty.

SIR GERALD *(as* MASTER DUDLEY *starts off)*. And tell one of my men I want to see Arnold the Goatherd.

THE KING. Arnold the Goatherd?

SIR GERALD. He's the best fighter I've ever seen.

THE KING. We'll see about that! And now . . . what shall we wager?

SIR GERALD. Must we, Your Majesty?

THE KING. What good is a contest without a prize?

SIR GERALD. But, some way, you always seem to win, even when you lose.

THE KING. That's one of the little prerogatives of being king . . . to compensate for the great disadvantages of office.

SIR GERALD *(resignedly)*. Very well, Your Majesty.

THE KING. What do you say to: the manuscript I saw you reading last evening against the inlaid helmet I saw you eyeing?

SIR GERALD. The manuscript! But, Your Majesty, you can't. . . .

THE KING. I can't read. I know that as well as you do. I have been too occupied with building a kingdom . . . and defending it . . . to spend hours sitting at a lectern doing something that any priest who isn't dry behind the ears yet can do just as well. No thank you! But I noticed that it had pretty pictures in it.

SIR GERALD. If His Majesty wants the manuscript, he has only to ask for. . . .

THE KING *(holding up his hand admonishingly)*. Only in fair combat, my friend. Here they come! (MASTER DUDLEY *enters followed by two*

giants, peasants of incredible size and obvious power (ARNOLD THE
GOATHERD *and* TERRIBLE TOM). *They stand deferentially to one side as*
MASTER DUDLEY *approaches* THE KING *and* SIR GERALD.) Well, that took
long enough!

MASTER DUDLEY. But, Your Majesty, I. . . .

THE KING *(holding up his hand)*. What did I just tell you? (MASTER
DUDLEY *draws back beside the peasants.)* Oh, come, Master Dudley!
You're here to learn. Don't get upset when you do. *(Beckoning the two
men to him.)* So you're Arnold the Goatherd?

ARNOLD THE GOATHERD. Yes, Your Majesty.

THE KING. And you think you can beat Terrible Tom here?

ARNOLD THE GOATHERD. I'll do my best, Your Majesty.

THE KING. Tell me, how did you ever learn to wrestle if you have
always been off tending goats?

ARNOLD THE GOATHERD. I never have, formal-like, Your Majesty.

THE KING. How did you learn . . . informal-like . . . then?

ARNOLD THE GOATHERD. When you're as big as I am, Your Majesty,
you have many chances to prove yourself. Every ambitious boy who
wants to show what a man he is already . . . every old man who wants
to show what a man he is still . . . they all use you to prove it.

THE KING. Do they succeed?

ARNOLD THE GOATHERD. Nobody has yet.

THE KING. Good! And how are you today, Terrible Tom?

TERRIBLE TOM. I'm just fine, Your Majesty, although I am a little
tired.

MASTER DUDLEY *looks quickly at* THE KING, *and then just as quickly
away, when he finds* THE KING'S *eyes upon him.*

THE KING. I saw that, Master Dudley. You were thinking "I told the
old fool so," weren't you?

MASTER DUDLEY. Never, Your Majesty!

THE KING. Never, Your Majesty! Only subjects! Well, what are we
waiting for? Let's get to it.

During the following conversation THE WRESTLERS, *assisted by*
MASTER DUDLEY, *are making themselves ready for the match . . .
stripping to the waist, warming up, etc.*

THE KING. They look in fine shape.

SIR GERALD. They do indeed.

THE KING. But it won't do any good, I'm afraid!

SIR GERALD. I beg Your Majesty's pardon?

THE KING. Nothing does any good. The days go on, one after the other, never changing.

SIR GERALD. I don't understand, Your Majesty.

THE KING. Boredom, my friend, boredom.

TERRIBLE TOM. I'm ready, Your Majesty.

ARNOLD THE GOATHERD. So am I, Your Majesty.

THE KING. Master Dudley, you'll be referee.

MASTER DUDLEY. I, Your Majesty?

THE KING. You, Your Majesty! Just tell them when to start, and separate them if it looks as if they might be about to kill each other.

MASTER DUDLEY. Separa . . . *(He is very unsure of himself and not quite certain whether or not he is being put upon.)* Are you ready? *(They nod.)* Begin!

THE WRESTLERS *proceed with their match, showing by their caution and developed skill that they are experienced fighters and not ambitious but foolhardy beginners. During* THE KING'S *speech, the patterns of the wrestling match tend to illustrate the points he is making, or even, at times, to anticipate them and actually to suggest them to him.*

THE KING *(after watching the beginning of the match and still keeping his eye on its progress).* Boredom . . . infinite, eternal, debilitating, destroying, hateful, spiteful boredom. From morning to night, from day to day, from birth to death, from one eternity to the next. Sitting on a throne gives you blisters on your bottom, and that's all it gives you. Wearing a crown makes you bald that much sooner, and that's all that can be said for wearing a crown. You can have anything you want to eat . . . fatness; any pleasure . . . mere familiarity; any woman . . . satiety. And all the time every peasant . . . probably even every goatherd . . . is that right, Goatherd?

ARNOLD THE GOATHERD *(as he and* TERRIBLE TOM *reach an impasse and freeze in a killing hold).* That's right, Your Majesty.

THE KING. That's right, Your Majesty! . . . envies you your wealth and your power, the beauty that's there for the taking, and the food. Every poacher envies you your forests with their rabbits and their deer, every peasant your fields, every knight your horses and your armor and your spears and shields and maces. And every one of them . . . from the lowest to the highest . . . envies you your . . . freedom. It is the only thing that can really make a king laugh, but it's a laugh out of the wrong side of the mouth. A king is the least free of all the souls in his kingdom, the least privileged, the most enslaved . . . by those same peasants and knights and . . . yes . . . even goatherds . . . who so envy him. And most of all, above all, by boredom, that forbids him nothing and allows him nothing.

The match has proceeded to the point where ARNOLD THE GOATHERD *has* TERRIBLE TOM *flat on his back.*

THE KING *(shaking himself as he returns from his tirade).* Stop! Don't kill him! *(To* SIR GERALD.*)* The helmet's yours. (SIR GERALD *looks at him in dismay. The two men rise.* THE KING *speaks to* TERRIBLE TOM.*)* So you finally lost, Tom!

TERRIBLE TOM. It's my age, Your Majesty. I just can't stand up to the younger men the way I used to.

ARNOLD THE GOATHERD. He's right, Your Majesty. Age gets a wrestler in the legs. Then he's not much good any more. *(To* TERRIBLE TOM.*)* If you'll pardon my saying so.

TERRIBLE TOM. Why should you be pardoned for telling the truth? It *is* the legs, Your Majesty. They go something terrible, after forty.

THE KING. And where does age get a king? In the head? In the rump? In the heart?

ARNOLD THE GOATHERD. I wouldn't know about that, Your Majesty.

THE KING. No one would know about that, Your Majesty. Come, my friends . . . the Holy Land is very far from here.

Everyone immediately picks up his gear and makes ready to move on. THE KING *speaks to* MASTER DUDLEY, SIR GERALD *by this time having gone ahead and out of sight.*

THE KING. It's warm there, they say. Maybe that won't be as boring as the cold here. Maybe there, in the warm sun, in the magic lands, there will be no boredom at all.

MASTER DUDLEY. Oh, I do hope so, Your Majesty!

THE KING. You do hope so, Your Majesty! *(He slaps the boy on the shoulder.)* Come let's be on our way. (MASTER DUDLEY *runs ahead and out of sight.* THE KING *looks after him and at the moving column.)* It may all be different where the sun never stops shining, where the seas are sand instead of water, and where our Lord walked upon this earth. Oh . . . Your Most Gracious Majesty . . . I do hope so.

Scene Four

BROTHER THOMAS *is kneeling at the altar in prayer. He is an intense young man, destined to be consumed in a fire of deep passion. It burns in his eyes. It sounds in his voice. It throbs throughout his being.*

BROTHER THOMAS. Our Father in Heaven, hear the prayer of Thomas, Thy servant. Hear the prayer of this the lowest of all Thy servants, the lowest of all Thy creations. Hear the prayer of this unworthy creature, of a slave of this earth. Hear, in Thy infinite mercy.

O Father, prepare me for the earth about me; prepare me for the sky above me; prepare me for the seas and the sun and for the coming of great winds.

And in the dark night of my soul, succor me; in the cold day of my passion, warm me; and in the passing of all years, tell me of the ages gone and of the ages yet to come.

Help me to live my days; help me to earn my death.

I have drawn away from men in order to draw closer to Thee; I have denied the world and time for Thee; I am alone in the universe for Thee.

But, O Heavenly Father, *I am human!* And the world will not be denied!

Give me the strength to live on this earth; tell me the ways to be faithful to Thee; and above all, O Divine Spirit, arm and strengthen me, that I may fight the evil in men; that I may drive the money-changers from the temple as did Thy Son, Our Lord, Jesus Christ. Until all the world is cleansed and Thy feet may once again tread on this, Thy earth. Amen.

Scene Five

A square. THE TROUPE *has set up its stage. The tiny platform and the backdrop seem to fill a great deal of space. This is more a matter of garish appearance than of size. The backdrop consists of a large canvas, painted with a pastoral scene. Although the colors are still bright in spots, time and all kinds of weather have worked their wills, and, in the main, the gay painted scene is badly faded.*

When the curtains rise only PULCINELLA *is to be seen. He is chasing imaginary flies with his slapstick: from time to time he slaps one, catches it as it falls, tears off its wings, and eats it. He has gone through this routine twice when* BROTHER MARTIN *and* BROTHER SILENUS *arrive on the scene. They watch* PULCINELLA, *entranced for a moment. He does not see them.*

BROTHER MARTIN (*whispering to* BROTHER SILENUS). Remarkable!
BROTHER SILENUS. Why do you suppose he's doing that?
BROTHER MARTIN. It must have something to do with entertainment.
BROTHER SILENUS. I thought entertainment was singing and dancing.

BROTHER MARTIN. And telling stories and playing instruments and killing imaginary flies, I guess.

BROTHER SILENUS *(applauding, after* PULCINELLA *has performed a particularly graceful piece of business).* Wonderful! Wonderful!

PULCINELLA *looks around, startled. When he sees the two monks, he picks up his properties and hurries out of sight.*

BROTHER MARTIN *(calling after him).* Here! Wait! *(Turning to* BROTHER SILENUS *when he is sure that* PULCINELLA *is gone.)* Now see what you've done!

BROTHER SILENUS. What *I've* done! What did I do? I thought he was an actor!

BROTHER MARTIN. He *is* an actor. Anyone can tell that!

BROTHER SILENUS. Well, then, if he's an actor, why did he run away? Of course, I've never seen an actor, but I've been told that when you applaud they bow.

BROTHER MARTIN. That's the whole trouble . . . you've never seen an actor, and I've never seen an actor. And we haven't seen dancers, and we haven't heard troubadors. . . . How can we arrange an entertainment? Why in Heaven's name did the Prior pick us?

BROTHER SILENUS. Why not? We're no worse off than the others.

BROTHER MARTIN. I suppose we'd better get to it; though, Lord knows, I haven't the faintest idea what to say to them.

BROTHER SILENUS. Hadn't we better wait until Brother Thomas gets here?

BROTHER MARTIN. And that's another complication!

They start off stage, but their exit is arrested by the sound of a horse approaching rapidly from the opposite side of the stage.

BROTHER SILENUS. Who's that?

BROTHER MARTIN. I've never seen anyone ride so fast. A knight.

BROTHER SILENUS. It can't be the crusaders, can it? They aren't supposed to arrive until tomorrow!

BROTHER MARTIN. And we haven't found one bit of entertainment yet!

The two men are hailed from off stage. A knight hurries on stage. It turns out to be SIR GERALD, *breathless.*

SIR GERALD. Wait, Brother! Are you from the monastery of St. Simeon Stylites?

BROTHER MARTIN. We are.

SIR GERALD. Good! May I present myself: Sir Gerald of the Cross. . . .

BROTHER SILENUS. See! I told you!

SIR GERALD. . . . Knight of the Holy Crusade. I bring a message from our king. I am to say that our forces will arrive within three hours. Where will I find your prior?

BROTHER MARTIN. Three hours!

SIR GERALD. Please! The King is right behind me. He'll be furious if I haven't delivered this message. He isn't too fond of me as it is.

BROTHER SILENUS. The monastery is right down there. You can't miss it. You can see the buttress from here.

SIR GERALD. Thank you. *(He starts out.* BROTHER SILENUS *whispers to* BROTHER MARTIN.)

BROTHER MARTIN *(agreeing with* BROTHER SILENUS*).* A good idea! *(Addressing* SIR GERALD, *who stops.)* Perhaps you can help us, Sir Gerald?

SIR GERALD. If it won't take more than a minute. We've been traveling night and day to make sure we got here before the carnival was over. Our men need relaxation. Entertainment. Rest.

BROTHER SILENUS. Night and day! Imagine that! Traveling all that time!

BROTHER MARTIN. It's that we want to ask about . . . entertainment. We have been assigned the responsibility of arranging it for your king, and we thought . . . well, it has been bothering us . . . anyway, we wondered if you could. . . .

SIR GERALD. Get on with it, man.

BROTHER SILENUS. We don't know what entertainment is!

BROTHER MARTIN. We thought you might be able to help us.

SIR GERALD. You don't know what entertainment is?

BROTHER SILENUS. Oh, we have an idea, but we've never seen any.

SIR GERALD. Well, entertainment is singing and dancing and . . . *(He looks around somewhat desperately. Finally, he notices* THE TROUPE'S *little stage with its gaudy backdrop.)* Well, *that's* entertainment! Right there in front of your eyes. It's a circus or something. It should do fine. Our king's not particular. And now, if you will excuse me. *(He starts out, stops, then turns back to them).* Perhaps they will put on a wrestling match. You might ask them. *(He leaves.)*

BROTHER SILENUS. Now all we have to do is find them!

BROTHER MARTIN. They must be here somewhere. Perhaps back of that painting. *(He points to the backdrop.)* Come along.

BROTHER SILENUS. You know, Brother Martin, I think I am going to like meeting an actor. Do you suppose they really do bow?

But before we hear BROTHER MARTIN'S *answer, they are gone. The stage is unoccupied for a moment, and then* THE DOCTOR *appears, running around the corner. He has a heavy sack slung over his shoulder. He seems to be hiding. He looks around carefully. When he sees that the coast is clear he steps boldly on to the tiny stage.*

THE DOCTOR *(calling).* Franceschina!

FRANCESCHINA *(off stage).* Yes?

THE DOCTOR. Come here. I've brought our supper.

FRANCESCHINA *(entering).* Run here! Run there! That's all I do day in and day out. What have you stolen this time?

THE DOCTOR. You can be thankful I don't have your conscience. If I did, you'd all have been dead and buried long ago. *(Opening up the sack.)* Take a look.

FRANCESCHINA *(looking into the sack).* Beef! Where did you get that?

THE DOCTOR. I got it. Now you cook it, and we'll give ourselves a little strength to perform with.

FRANCESCHINA. But peasants don't have food like that!

THE DOCTOR. No . . . we do! Get going. It makes me nervous to have it lying around in the open. *(As she goes off.)* And send Pulcinella along. *(While he is waiting* THE DOCTOR *goes through one of his routines. He stops as soon as* PULCINELLA *enters. He crosses to* THE DOCTOR *and stands patiently waiting.)* Let's see the "fly lazzo." (PULCINELLA *goes through the same routine we saw at the beginning of the scene. At its conclusion* THE DOCTOR *applauds.)* Bravo! Now, "the discovery." (PULCINELLA *goes behind one of the tree stumps on the stage. He goes through a routine of discovering someone. During the course of the scene,* FRANCESCHINA *enters. She watches the action quietly, with a professional eye. When the action is over, both she and* THE DOCTOR *applaud enthusiastically.)* Bravo! You're ready.

FRANCESCHINA. I've been telling you that for a week.

THE DOCTOR *(ignoring her).* There's a whole army of crusaders coming to town, and it's carnival time. We'll make a fortune. You can play with us when they get here.

PULCINELLA *bows.*

FRANCESCHINA. Make a fortune! HMMMPPPHHH! More likely lose our shirts! Crusaders don't give anything; they take. Remember Paris! They think that everyone owes them everything, just because they're on a holy crusade. Heaven preserve us from crusaders!

THE DOCTOR. Be quiet, woman! You talk too much, and none of it

makes any sense. Now, get the others. We have a lot of work to do before
they get here.

FRANCESCHINA *(as she goes out).* Just because they're on their way
to the Holy Land.

THE DOCTOR. Don't pay any attention to her. She's just a woman.
There isn't a one of them that's worth her keep. But the audiences insist
on them, so what are we to do?

THE CAPTAIN *comes in. He is wearing one sword and carrying another.*

THE DOCTOR. Comé on, Captain. Pulci's going to play during the
carnival, and he hasn't learned the duel yet.

THE CAPTAIN. He'll be fine. I've never seen anyone learn as fast.

THE DOCTOR. Let's get going. (THE CAPTAIN *and* PULCINELLA *begin
the duel lazzo. When they have reached the point where* PULCINELLA *is
to stab* THE CAPTAIN, THE DOCTOR *raises his voice.)* Wait! This way. *(He
takes* PULCINELLA'S *sword and demonstrates the correct way to perform
one of the movements.)* Be fiercer! Shake your head and get way back
for the run! But at the same time you've got to show the audience that
you are just as frightened as he is. (THE CAPTAIN *and* PULCINELLA *go
through the routine again. This time* PULCINELLA *does it as* THE DOCTOR
wishes.) Good! Now, Captain, that wasn't broad enough. Remember:
these are soldiers; they expect things to be said right out. Go back to the
old Venetian business. *(The two men pick up the lazzo in the middle.*
THE CAPTAIN, *in order to inspire awe, uses the classic phallic sword
business to be seen in Callot.* THE DOCTOR *applauds at its conclusion.)*
Bravo! *(Calling off.)* Come on, everybody, we've got a lot to do.
*(*FRANCESCHINA *and* PANTALONE *enter. They place themselves about the
stage, waiting for* THE DOCTOR'S *instruction.)* We'll do *THE CAPTAIN
IN LOVE.*

THE CAPTAIN. Must we? It always wears me out.

THE DOCTOR. We'll do it because it's the broadest, and these are
soldiers, crusade or no crusade. Places, everyone! Let's go!

Immediately THE TROUPE *moves into the positions required for the
performance. All of them move to different sides of the stage except* THE
CAPTAIN. *He stands to the center and takes his stance. He doesn't wait
for anyone to call curtain, but begins immediately. The others don't pay
particular attention, but they are ready when their turns come.*

THE CAPTAIN *(aside).* "The beautiful Franceschina is driving me
crazy. I don't know what I'm going to do if that old fool of a father
doesn't let her be mine. But shh! Here she comes. Now I'll find out how

my suit is progressing." *(Enter* FRANCESCHINA *carrying a broom. She doesn't see* THE CAPTAIN.) "Now to put it to her." (*To* FRANCESCHINA.) "My beautiful Franceschina!" (FRANCESCHINA *is startled by this and turns toward him, swinging the broom and knocking him down as she does so.)* "Ah! You see, lovely Franceschina, you are so beautiful, you knock me off my feet."

FRANCESCHINA. "I'll knock you right off your arse, if you don't stop pestering me."

THE CAPTAIN *(crawling to her on his knees and pleading pitifully).* "Oh, darling Franceschina! How come you treat me so unmercifully, when you know I love you!"

During the course of the scene, BROTHER THOMAS *enters. He stands to one side, unnoticed by the performers. His face at first displays no response to what they are doing, but as the scene progresses it reveals a growing anger. Indeed, his whole body displays a tension growing out of his reaction to their performance.*

FRANCESCHINA. "You have never given me any token of your love."

THE CAPTAIN. "I'll give you anything you want. Just name it."

FRANCESCHINA. "I don't want very much. . . ."

THE CAPTAIN *(becoming more excited as she becomes more coquettish).* "Name it."

FRANCESCHINA. "All I want is a little. . . ."

THE CAPTAIN. "Yes, yes . . . a little. . . ."

FRANCESCHINA. "A little bit of something I know you have a lot of. . . ."

THE CAPTAIN. ". . . I have a lot of . . . yes. . . ."

FRANCESCHINA. "If you'll just come over here . . . a little bit closer. . . ."

THE CAPTAIN. "If I'll just. . . ."

He is greatly excited by now. He gets set as a track star might. He runs furiously at her, only to have her step aside. He disappears offstage. FRANCESCHINA *looks after him, as if he had gone a very great distance.*

Then, from the way she looks, we know that he is coming back. He creeps back on stage, backward, with his hands up, PULCINELLA *forcing him ahead with his* (PULCINELLA'S) *sword.*

THE DOCTOR *(off).* That's it, Pulci! Don't let him get away with anything! *(He stalks on.)* "So-o-o!!! You are trying to steal my beloved from me!"

THE CAPTAIN. *"Your* beloved!"

THE DOCTOR. "My beloved!"

FRANCESCHINA. "I never said I was your beloved."

THE CAPTAIN. "Can I put my hands down?"

THE DOCTOR. "You can if. . . ."

THE CAPTAIN. "If?"

THE DOCTOR. "If you agree to engage with my valor in the gallant art of our greatest knights-errant."

THE CAPTAIN. "I don't get you."

THE DOCTOR. "If you will agree to a face to face confrontation on the field of honor."

THE CAPTAIN. "Will you say that again, please?"

THE DOCTOR *begins to do so when* FRANCESCHINA *interrupts.*

FRANCESCHINA. "He wants you to fight a duel."

THE CAPTAIN *(terrified).* "A duel! No thanks!" *(He starts off.)*

THE DOCTOR. "With my slave and champion here . . . Pulcinella."

THE CAPTAIN *(coming back and regaining his swagger).* "Why didn't you say so? I'll be glad to fight the little idiot."

This infuriates PULCINELLA. *He goes mad.* THE DOCTOR *gets him quieted down finally, and they prepare for the duel, with* THE DOCTOR *acting as* PULCINELLA'S *second and* FRANCESCHINA *as* THE CAPTAIN'S. *The preparations proceed to the point where* PULCINELLA *has his back to* THE CAPTAIN. *The latter is having great difficulty getting his rusted sword out of its scabbard. He has worked it around to the phallic position, when* PULCINELLA *turns and is frightened by the sword. He makes much of his fear and ends up cradled in* THE DOCTOR'S *arms. He has just been tossed to the ground by* THE DOCTOR *when* BROTHER THOMAS'S *voice thunders out. . . .*

BROTHER THOMAS. Stop!!!

The performers stop, dumbfounded. They look at BROTHER THOMAS *for the first time. He waits a moment before walking up to the edge of the stage.* PANTALONE *has joined the others, so the company is complete.* BROTHER THOMAS *looks at them fiercely for a moment, and then he speaks. His voice is a combination of deep anger and deep fear.*

BROTHER THOMAS. You must not go on!

THE DOCTOR. Must not?!

BROTHER THOMAS. It is sinful. Terribly, terribly sinful!

THE DOCTOR. We never claimed to be saintly. We leave that up to the monks.

FRANCESCHINA. Watch your tongue, Doctor!

THE DOCTOR. What did I say? I don't tell him how to pray and preach, and I don't expect him to tell me what makes a good show.

PANTALONE. We don't do any harm.

THE CAPTAIN. We're just trying to keep from starving to death.

THE DOCTOR. So you see, Brother, we. . . .

BROTHER THOMAS. Stop! Stop! Stop! I don't want to hear any more!

THE DOCTOR. What is it you *do* want, Brother?

BROTHER THOMAS *(half to himself)*. Peace! Eternal peace! Everlasting peace! Universal peace!

THE DOCTOR. So you interrupt a perfectly peaceful troupe of actors . . . just trying to earn tomorrow's bread. . . .

BROTHER THOMAS. What you were doing was a sin!

FRANCESCHINA. Oh, no, Brother! We are faithful children of the church . . . all except the Doctor, of course.

THE DOCTOR. *THE CAPTAIN IN LOVE* a sin? No, no, no, Brother. A little broad, perhaps, but that's because of the soldiers. They like it that way.

PANTALONE. A sin against who, Brother?

BROTHER THOMAS. Against God! You blaspheme all that's holy with your glorification of the beast in man.

THE DOCTOR. You see all that in *THE CAPTAIN IN LOVE?*

BROTHER THOMAS. And more! Let me ask you: do you believe God approves of what you do? *(To* FRANCESCHINA.*)* You!

FRANCESCHINA. I've never thought about it. I don't know why he shouldn't.

BROTHER THOMAS *(to* THE CAPTAIN*)*. You!

THE CAPTAIN. We're not so important God pays us much mind.

BROTHER THOMAS. None is too small for God's concern. *(To* PANTALONE.*)* And you!

PANTALONE. I've never felt what I did was wrong.

BROTHER THOMAS *(to* PULCINELLA*)*. You! You haven't said anything yet.

THE DOCTOR. And he's not likely to.

BROTHER THOMAS. Not even when faced with the wrath of God?

THE DOCTOR. Not even then.

FRANCESCHINA. He's dumb.

BROTHER THOMAS *(his interest aroused)*. A curse of God on his parents' sins!

THE DOCTOR. A curse of man on his tongue. They ripped it out.

BROTHER THOMAS *(crossing himself)*. A blasphemer! *(Then he peers at* PULCINELLA *with even more interest.)*

THE DOCTOR. A blasphemer maybe, or a bearer of false witness, or just some poor bastard that was set on by thieves.

BROTHER THOMAS. A blasphemer to be saved from eternal damnation!

THE DOCTOR. You like to jump to conclusions, don't you, Brother?

BROTHER THOMAS *(to* PULCINELLA, *very intensely).* You are a sinner, aren't you, my friend? You have denied God's word. You have glorified man and sent God away.

PULCINELLA *looks, panic-stricken, from one to the other.*

THE DOCTOR. Go ahead, tell him the truth.

They all watch PULCINELLA *to see what he will say.*

BROTHER THOMAS. The truth never hurt anyone.
THE DOCTOR. Ha!
BROTHER THOMAS *(angrily).* ANYONE!

PULCINELLA, *desperate, slowly shakes his head "Yes."*

THE DOCTOR. What does that prove? We've all admitted we weren't perfect. I guess that makes us all sinners, doesn't it, Brother?

BROTHER THOMAS. Just as some are specially blessed, so some are specially cursed.

FRANCESCHINA. NO! *(They all turn to look at her.)* Not Pulci! He's not cursed!

BROTHER THOMAS. You seem very certain of that.

FRANCESCHINA. I've known a lot of people who were damned . . . Lord, how many I've known! . . . he's not like them.

BROTHER THOMAS. Had their tongues been ripped from their mouths?

FRANCESCHINA. They should have been!

BROTHER THOMAS. Where did he come from?

THE DOCTOR. That is a question we never ask in our profession.

BROTHER THOMAS. Perhaps you should, my friend. Are you afraid?

THE DOCTOR. Afraid! No! It's just none of our business.

BROTHER THOMAS. Did you know his family?

THE DOCTOR *(amazed at the question).* His family!

PANTALONE. We found him in a ditch.

THE CAPTAIN. By the side of the road.

PANTALONE. I wonder about the figure.

THE CAPTAIN. Ah! The figure!

THE DOCTOR. It meant nothing.

BROTHER THOMAS. What figure?

FRANCESCHINA *(afraid for* PULCINELLA*).* The Doctor's right. It didn't mean anything.

BROTHER THOMAS *(to* PANTALONE, *inexorably).* What figure?

PANTALONE *(as if* BROTHER THOMAS *had him hypnotized).* It was sitting beside the road. . . .

THE DOCTOR. It was nothing . . . a joke. A skeleton dressed in robes like yours.

BROTHER THOMAS *(crossing himself).* A *memento mori!*

THE CAPTAIN. You see them a lot of places. It didn't have anything to do with him.

FRANCESCHINA. Just a coincidence.

BROTHER THOMAS. And that's where you found him? Then he is indeed damned! *(A fire lights up his eyes. He is seized with a deep religious fervor.)* He must be saved! We must pray for his soul.

The others look on dumbfounded and frightened by the intensity displayed by BROTHER THOMAS. *There is great fear on* PULCINELLA'S *face, and he shrinks back, but* BROTHER THOMAS' *grip is too strong for him to escape.*

FRANCESCHINA. Be careful, Brother. He isn't recovered yet. He's still weak from hunger and the cold.

During the course of BROTHER THOMAS' *prayer,* BROTHER MARTIN *and* BROTHER SILENUS *appear. They are at first stricken dumb by what they are witnessing; then they become alarmed.*

BROTHER THOMAS. O Merciful Father of all the universe, hear the prayer of one of Thy servants. Help this soul to find Thy way on earth, and help me to bring these sinners to see the evil of their lives. Give this blasphemer the power to see the path of righteousness, that he may leave his evil ways and join the confraternity of those who dedicate their lives to Thee. And Heavenly Father, hear me. . . .

THE DOCTOR. STOP! (BROTHER THOMAS *stops, startled at first, and then angry.)* Stop what you're saying! You can't have him. He belongs with us!

BROTHER THOMAS. You dare stop a servant of the Lord when he is praying?

THE DOCTOR. I'll stop Satan himself, if he's trying to destroy my company.

FRANCESCHINA. You can't take him away from us.

THE CAPTAIN. Until he came, we were nothing . . . just a troupe of tired, old actors who had played out their years in the countryside. But since he's come, everything has been different.

BROTHER THOMAS. You dare interrupt a servant of God at his prayers?

BROTHER MARTIN (*coming forward, since he and* BROTHER SILENUS *have not been previously noticed by* BROTHER THOMAS). *I* dare interrupt him!

BROTHER THOMAS. Brother Martin! Brother Silenus!

BROTHER MARTIN. You disgrace your vocation, Brother Thomas. Praying in the public streets like a beggar! Frightening these poor people who have done no one any harm! I'm ashamed.

BROTHER THOMAS. You condemn me, too? I would expect it of these people . . . they can't know any better; but you, Brother Martin, and you, Brother Silenus . . . to interfere with the Lord's work!

BROTHER SILENUS. You take a great deal upon yourself, Brother Thomas.

BROTHER MARTIN. Come along. The Prior must know what has happened.

BROTHER THOMAS. God understands! He *must* understand!

BROTHER MARTIN. Not another word!

BROTHER THOMAS (*as the three Brothers leave, to* PULCINELLA). I shall save you, my friend!

BROTHER MARTIN. No more! (*And they are gone. The performers look from one to the other in bewilderment.*)

THE CAPTAIN. Evil!

FRANCESCHINA (*who is cradling* PULCINELLA *in her arms*). We'll protect you, little Pulcinella. You belong with us. You belong with the actors.

THE DOCTOR (*clapping his hands and putting on a big smile*). Come on. It's carnival time, and we have a lot of rehearsing to do. From the beginning! (*He tosses them their masks, which they put on. Then they start the play from the beginning, but the heart has gone out of it.*)

THE CAPTAIN. "The beautiful Franceschina is driving me crazy. I don't know what I'm going to do, if that fool of a father doesn't let her be mine. But, shh! Here she comes. Now I'll find out how my suit is progressing."

As they rehearse THE KING *enters quietly. He leans against the wall watching them. After a particularly effective turn, he applauds.* THE TROUPE *is startled. They didn't realize anyone was watching. They hesitate a moment, but almost immediately* THE DOCTOR *steps forward, and in his most commanding voice announces.* . . .

THE DOCTOR. And now the greatest of fools, the master of silence, Pulcinella. . . .

PULCINELLA *enters, and they go on with their performance . . . considerably livelier now that they know someone is watching.* THE KING *speaks softly to himself as he watches:*

THE KING. The greatest of fools, the master of silence . . . *(He looks directly at the audience.)* . . . Your Majesty!
           ‘ *END OF ACT ONE*

ACT TWO

Scene One

THE PRIOR'S *room of Act One, Scene Two.* THE KING *is pacing back and forth. After a moment,* BROTHER THOMAS *hurries in. He throws himself to his knees at* THE KING'S *feet.*

BROTHER THOMAS. Your Majesty!

THE KING. What's this? Who are you?

BROTHER THOMAS. I am nobody, Your Majesty.

THE KING. You can be nobody on your feet as well as on your knees. Get up.

BROTHER THOMAS. I come to beg a privilege of you, Your Majesty.

THE KING. Your Majesty!

BROTHER THOMAS. Take me with you!

THE KING. Take you with me?

BROTHER THOMAS. To the Holy Land, Your Majesty. Where our Lord is most present.

THE KING. The Saracens are most present there right now, my friend.

BROTHER THOMAS. But not for long! The truth will prevail!

THE KING. It may! It does sometimes.

BROTHER THOMAS. It will! And I must be there.

THE KING. How are you with a sword?

BROTHER THOMAS. A sword?

THE KING. Or a crossbow?

BROTHER THOMAS. I am not a soldier, Your Majesty.

THE KING. Then I have no use for you.

BROTHER THOMAS. A chaplain! I can go as a chaplain.

THE KING. I'm overchaplained now.

BROTHER THOMAS. A servant, a slave! Anything!

THE KING (*raising* BROTHER THOMAS *to his feet*). Come, my young friend. A crusade is a military expedition like any other. It is still very much a matter of tactics and strategy . . . and believe me, a priest in battle is of no use. He gets in the way. You stay here and pray for our souls. You'll serve us better that way.

THE PRIOR *hurries in.*

THE PRIOR. Your Majesty! I am sorry to keep you waiting, but it was time. . . .

THE KING. For prayers; I know, Prior. Your young charge here has been keeping me entertained.

THE PRIOR. Brother Thomas! Why aren't you with Brother Martin and Brother Silenus?

BROTHER THOMAS *(very discouraged).* They sent me back.

THE PRIOR. Why?

BROTHER THOMAS. For doing the Lord's work.

THE PRIOR. Not again!

THE KING. And now he wants to do the Lord's work in the Holy Land.

THE PRIOR. The Holy Land!

THE KING. I need archers and spearmen . . . not priests. I don't suppose you have any soldiers in your flock, Prior?

THE PRIOR *(to* BROTHER THOMAS*).* What is it you're battling, my son? What do you want?

BROTHER THOMAS. Against the evil in men. For the love of God.

BROTHER MARTIN *and* BROTHER SILENUS *hurry in.*

BROTHER MARTIN. Prior, we've just . . . (*Noticing* BROTHER THOMAS.) Ah, there he is!

THE KING. I have never seen a monastery where everyone's in such a hurry! It must make it difficult to meditate.

THE PRIOR. My brothers have been upset by your visit. *(To the monks.)* You will all retire to the chapel and wait until I have concluded my business with the King. *(As they leave.)* And you might try praying for tranquility of soul . . . all three of you. *(Turning to* THE KING*.)* I must apologize, Your Majesty.

THE KING. No need, Prior.

THE PRIOR. Brother Thomas carries the Holy Cross with him always. He has begun to doubt his faith, and so he feels he must constantly prove his devoutness or it will all just disappear.

THE KING. I know. I have them, too . . . these anxious young men. Because they aren't sure, they go into battle magnificently the first morning. By nightfall they're nearly all dead.

THE PRIOR. And now for your business, Your Majesty.

THE KING. I have an army out there. As far as the eye can see there are soldiers. We've been on the march a long time, and we'll be on it a still longer time. My men need food and rest and amusement before Lent begins. I don't expect you to feed and shelter us; we can take care of that ourselves. We requisition what we need where we find it. But we still need your help.

THE PRIOR. We just don't have enough, Your Majesty.

THE KING. I know that, Prior. Whatever you can give us will be valued. But more than that, my men are restless. It's been a long march. They're tired, and they're discouraged. They need some relaxation before the Lenten season begins.

THE PRIOR. Do you think we are the best ones to turn to for that?

THE KING. There is no one else!

THE PRIOR. I've had some of my brothers looking. Just a moment. *(He goes to the entrance to the chapel and calls.)* Brother Martin, Brother Silenus . . . will you come here please? *(To* THE KING.) I am afraid we are quite inexperienced in such matters.

The two monks enter.

THE PRIOR. Brothers, his Majesty here would like to know what you've found in the way of entertainment.

BROTHER MARTIN. Actors, Prior. I think that's what they're called.

BROTHER SILENUS. Players.

BROTHER MARTIN. No, I am sure it was actors.

BROTHER SILENUS. Players!

THE PRIOR. Brother Martin! Brother Silenus! Please! *(When the two brothers have settled down.)* Players here? We've never had players here before!

BROTHER MARTIN. They're here now.

BROTHER SILENUS. From Italy.

THE KING. Do they wear masks? Four men?

BROTHER SILENUS. And a woman, Your Majesty.

THE KING. I saw them. They'll do very well.

BROTHER MARTIN. He's outside now, Prior.

THE PRIOR. Who is?

BROTHER MARTIN. Their leader. We brought him back with us.

THE PRIOR *(angrily)*. You've brought a player into the monastery?

BROTHER MARTIN. We thought you would want to see him.

THE PRIOR. Indeed, I don't. You should have thought twice before bringing him on holy ground!

THE KING. If I may, Prior? (THE PRIOR *nods, still frowning.)* Why not have the rascal in? Perhaps being in your presence will reform him.

THE PRIOR. I haven't found my presence particularly reforming, Your Majesty. But since you're our guest. *(To* BROTHER MARTIN.) Bring him in.

BROTHER MARTIN *leaves.*

THE KING. And besides, they're very good. We don't have players like that where I come from.

BROTHER MARTIN *returns, leading* THE DOCTOR.

BROTHER MARTIN. Here he is, Your Majesty.

THE PRIOR. What is your name, my son?

THE DOCTOR. I am called The Doctor.

THE PRIOR. That's no name for a Christian man.

THE DOCTOR. Christian or not . . . that's what I'm called, Your Worship.

THE PRIOR. And you lead this troupe of players?

THE DOCTOR. For twenty years.

THE PRIOR. What are you doing in this part of the world? Players have never come this far north before.

THE DOCTOR. We're passing through, Your Worship. We're going to the cold lands.

THE KING. To the cold lands! You're welcome to them! Do you have a comedy?

THE DOCTOR. We have many comedies, Your Honor. And a tragedy or two.

THE KING. It's a comedy we want . . . save your tragedies for Lent. . . .

THE PRIOR. Your Majesty!

THE KING. I'll pay you to entertain my men.

THE DOCTOR. If you'll pardon me, Your Honor, but we'd rather not.

THE PRIOR. Oh, then you aren't planning to perform in this town?

THE DOCTOR. Oh, yes, Your Worship. We'd just as soon not have His Honor pay, that's all.

THE KING. Why not?

THE DOCTOR. If you pay us, Your Honor, we can't pass the hat. However generous you may be . . . we'd rather take our chances.

THE PRIOR *(to* BROTHER MARTIN *and* BROTHER SILENUS*)*. And you saw them, Brothers?

BROTHER MARTIN. Yes, Prior.

BROTHER SILENUS. They were very good. They made me laugh.

THE PRIOR. I don't know that that is necessarily such a great accomplishment, Brother Silenus. All right, then, but only until Lent starts. And you mustn't come on holy ground again.

THE DOCTOR. Of course, Your Worship. We are as anxious to get as far north as we can. We won't be here long after the carnival, you can believe that.

THE KING. Why? Why are you going north? Do you *like* the cold?

THE DOCTOR. We hate it, Your Honor; but so does the plague.

THE KING. Ah! So that's it! Tell me, will the clown play? The one that doesn't speak?

THE DOCTOR. Of course, Your Honor. He's our Pulcinella.

BROTHER THOMAS (*appearing in the doorway to the chapel*). NO!!!

THE PRIOR. Brother Thomas! I told you to stay in the chapel!

BROTHER THOMAS. I couldn't help hearing, Prior. He must not play, whatever the rest of them may do.

THE PRIOR. Brother Thomas! You distress me greatly! What is it now?

BROTHER THOMAS. He is one of the damned . . . his soul must be saved. And it can't be if he plays.

THE PRIOR. One of the damned! Who are you to say who is one of the damned?

BROTHER THOMAS. He is a blasphemer! (*Pointing to* THE DOCTOR.) Ask him.

THE PRIOR (*to* THE DOCTOR). What does he mean?

THE DOCTOR. He's wrong, Your Worship!

BROTHER THOMAS. He has no tongue!

THE KING. Has no tongue?

THE PRIOR (*to* THE DOCTOR). Is this true?

THE DOCTOR. It's true enough. It was ripped out by brigands.

BROTHER THOMAS. Tell them where you found him.

THE DOCTOR. It didn't mean anything . . . a joke.

THE PRIOR. Where *did* you find him?

THE DOCTOR. By the side of the road. In a ditch.

BROTHER THOMAS. With a *memento mori* standing guard over him. He must seek redemption at the feet of our Lord.

THE PRIOR. We must all do that, my son!

THE KING. A what?

THE PRIOR. A *memento mori*. Some of our more zealous brothers place them by the roads to warn travelers of the Day of Judgment.

THE DOCTOR. He's a good lad, Your Worship. He is the best of our lot, believe me . . . and none of us has lost our tongues!

THE KING (*to himself*). Memento mori!

THE PRIOR. Brother Martin, you've seen them, what do you think?

BROTHER MARTIN. He doesn't talk, Prior, but that doesn't prove anything.

BROTHER SILENUS. He is very funny. . . .

THE PRIOR. We know, Brother Silenus. He made you laugh.

THE KING. He does speak, Prior. With his hands and his face and his body.

BROTHER THOMAS. You can see it in his eyes . . . fear of Hell.

THE DOCTOR. Fear of starvation!

BROTHER THOMAS. His hands are cold.

THE DOCTOR. We can't afford gloves!

BROTHER THOMAS. And he plays in this depraved comedy.

BROTHER SILENUS. Depraved, Brother?

BROTHER THOMAS. It speaks only of men. And only of the lowest in man. It is far from God.

THE PRIOR. You forget, my son, that Lent always follows the carnival. How? Far from God?

BROTHER THOMAS. It is about the evil men think and the evil men do. It says nothing about the redemption of men's souls, about the grace of our Lord.

THE DOCTOR. Well, who said it did? (*To* THE PRIOR.) We make no pretense, your worship. We preach no sermons. We save no souls. But neither does the butcher or the tailor or the farmer. We are simply trying to make our way in this world. We leave the other world to you.

THE PRIOR. If I could just see this man!

BROTHER MARTIN. You can, Prior. He's outside, waiting for The Doctor.

THE PRIOR. Bring him in. We'll see if he's damned or not. Brother Martin?

BROTHER MARTIN *exits.*

THE KING (*to* BROTHER THOMAS). And you wanted to go along with my army!

BROTHER THOMAS. There are souls to be saved there, too.

THE KING. Indeed there are! But to save a soul you must understand a man, my friend. When you are ready to embrace evil and ugliness, blood and filth, whores and pimps, sweat and flies . . . come to me then. Remember, the only path to Heaven is by way of this earth; the only companion on the journey is man. You must learn to be a man before you can be a god. You must bear man's burdens before you can bear the Lord's.

BROTHER MARTIN *enters, leading* PULCINELLA, *who looks ill and frightened.*

BROTHER MARTIN. Here he is, Prior.

THE PRIOR. This is the man?

BROTHER THOMAS. This is the man.

THE PRIOR. He's ill!

THE DOCTOR. Just tired, Your Worship. We've been rehearsing hard to be ready for the carnival.

THE PRIOR. Brother Silenus.

BROTHER SILENUS. Yes, Prior?

THE PRIOR. Fetch Brother Ambrose.

BROTHER SILENUS. Yes, Prior. *(He goes.)*

THE PRIOR. So this is your paragon of evil, Brother Thomas!

BROTHER THOMAS. A soul to be saved.

THE PRIOR. We all have souls to be saved.

BROTHER THOMAS. Some are specially blessed, and some are specially cursed.

THE PRIOR. And what is your canonical authority for that statement?

BROTHER THOMAS. My authority is in his eyes.

THE KING. Beauty, I am told, lies in the eye of the beholder. I should think the same thing might be said of evil.

THE PRIOR. Beware of the pride of humility, Brother Thomas. It is our greatest temptation. *(To* PULCINELLA.*)* And you, my son. Are you especially cursed?

THE DOCTOR. He is especially blessed, Your Worship.

THE PRIOR. Oh?

THE DOCTOR. He is, Prior. Let me show you. *(He turns to* PULCINELLA, *assuming his role in the play.)* "Where oh where has my money gone? Oh, where is my purse vanished to? Oh, woe is me! What a miserable life I lead!"

PULCINELLA *understands. He is exhausted and sick, but he slowly works into his part of the performance. They perform the "Empty Purse Lazzo." It is based on the fact that the purse has no bottom, and whenever* THE DOCTOR *places money in it,* PULCINELLA *catches it underneath.*

BROTHER THOMAS. Prior! How can you let this go on?

THE PRIOR. And this is the depth of evil from which you are going to save him.

BROTHER THOMAS. This . . . and worse.

THE PRIOR *(to the players).* That will do. *(To* BROTHER THOMAS.*)* You are so innocent, Brother Thomas, that you can judge others?

BROTHER THOMAS. I am guilty, Prior. Guilty of worldliness.

THE KING *laughs.*

BROTHER THOMAS *(angrily).* Of doubt. Of questioning. Of the flesh.

THE KING. I think he means, Prior, that he is human. Is that it?

BROTHER THOMAS. I am a son of Adam. A descendant of Cain.

THE PRIOR. A child of God!

THE KING. There we have it! It is your own soul you want to save, not his, isn't it?

BROTHER THOMAS. Both! Both!

BROTHER SILENUS *returns with* BROTHER AMBROSE, *an elderly, somewhat befuddled monk.*

BROTHER SILENUS. I had some trouble finding him, Prior. I finally looked in the stable. And there he was in the hayloft, staring at a piece of straw. He has been doing that a lot recently.

THE PRIOR. Ah! Brother Ambrose! Will you look at this young man? He is ill.

BROTHER AMBROSE. If you insist, Prior.

THE PRIOR. Do I need to insist?

BROTHER AMBROSE. I was meditating, Prior.

THE KING. On the philosopher's stone?

BROTHER AMBROSE. Of course not! I only do that on my own time and in my own cell! (*Indicating* THE KING.) Who is this, Prior? (*Indicating the players.*) And who are they?

THE PRIOR. Does it really matter, Brother Ambrose? You'd only forget, if I told you. (*To* THE KING.) He is a fine philosopher and the only monk we have trained in medicine, but sometimes he is a bit abstracted.

BROTHER AMBROSE (*looking at all of them*). Which one is it?

THE PRIOR *indicates* PULCINELLA. BROTHER AMBROSE *begins his examination. The following conversation ensues during it.*

THE PRIOR (*to* BROTHER MARTIN *and* BROTHER SILENUS). You have done very well. The King is pleased.

THE KING. My troops will be delighted. *I* am delighted.

BROTHER THOMAS. You aren't going to let these apostates perform, are you, Prior?

THE PRIOR. Apostates? You will remain silent, Brother Thomas!

BROTHER THOMAS. How can I remain silent in the face of evil?

THE PRIOR. You would do well to concern yourself with your own soul.

BROTHER THOMAS. I am, Prior! I am! I can live no other way than I do now.

THE PRIOR. I will not allow you the solace of your own misery. You speak of God's will! Are you sure it isn't your own?

BROTHER THOMAS. No, Prior, no. I am sure of nothing except that I must fight evil wherever it is. In my own soul or in another's.

THE PRIOR. You will remain silent. *(To* BROTHER MARTIN *and* BROTHER SILENUS.*)* You may go, Brothers. We still have Lent to prepare for. *(As they leave.)* And thank you. *(They go.)*

BROTHER AMBROSE *(having finished his examination).* That's all, Prior.

THE PRIOR. And the verdict?

BROTHER AMBROSE. Exhaustion and starvation. He needs rest and good food.

THE DOCTOR. He will get rest when the carnival is over. And I have just obtained some of the finest food for him. He will eat tonight like a king.

THE KING. No blessing, believe me!

THE PRIOR *(to* BROTHER AMBROSE*).* Can he wait that long?

BROTHER AMBROSE. What carnival?

THE PRIOR. He is a player. They want to perform during the carnival.

BROTHER AMBROSE. Is it carnival time again? Time flies so swiftly.

THE PRIOR. Dear Brother Ambrose. You must visit us here on earth more often.

BROTHER AMBROSE. Imagine! Lent again!

THE PRIOR. My question, Brother Ambrose!

BROTHER AMBROSE. What question, Prior?

THE PRIOR. Can he perform during these few days before Lent?

BROTHER AMBROSE. Only a few days? Dear! Perform? What does it mean . . . "perform"?

THE PRIOR *(to* THE KING*).* Perhaps you can explain, Your Majesty.

THE KING. He is a player. They sing and dance and hit each other and fall down.

BROTHER AMBROSE. Hit each other . . . dear me!

THE KING. They don't really hurt. It's for the audience.

BROTHER AMBROSE. I almost had an audience once. Long ago. When I was a student in Rome.

THE PRIOR. It's no use, Your Majesty. Let me try again. *(To* BROTHER AMBROSE.*)* Brother Ambrose . . . what can he do, and what can't he do?

BROTHER AMBROSE. Well, he mustn't be under any strain, that's for sure. And I wouldn't recommend jousting for him. His heart has a very strange sound.

THE DOCTOR. But he can perform!

BROTHER AMBROSE. As long as he doesn't joust . . . that would be very bad for him. And now I must be returning to my studies. Now what did I come here for? It must have been a manuscript I needed. That's it . . . a manuscript.

THE PRIOR. I sent for you, Brother Ambrose!

BROTHER AMBROSE. Sent for me? Oh, yes, I remember. It wasn't a manuscript after all. *(He starts out.)* The Prior wants me. If you will all excuse me, I must hurry to him. *(He goes.)*

THE DOCTOR. We must be going, Your Worship. We have much rehearsing to do.

THE PRIOR *(indicating* PULCINELLA). He is going to have some broth before he leaves this place.

THE DOCTOR. Whatever you say, Your Worship.

THE PRIOR (*to* PULCINELLA). Come along.*(They start out, but are interrupted by the hurried entrance of* BROTHER SILENUS.)

BROTHER SILENUS. Prior! Prior! It's been stolen! Somebody's taken it!

THE PRIOR. Relax, Brother Silenus. What's been stolen?

BROTHER SILENUS. The beef we were saving for the King. Somebody's taken it!

THE PRIOR. This is not a good day! We shall look into it. (*To* PULCINELLA.) Come along. *(He turns at the door.)* Brother Thomas, I should pray, if I were you. *(The three men go out.)*

THE KING. Potatoes again, I see. What I wouldn't give for a nice roast.

THE DOCTOR. And I, Your Honor. And I.

BROTHER THOMAS. It is a punishment put upon us for our sins.

THE KING. God uses thieves as his agents of punishment?

BROTHER THOMAS. Our Lord took the place of a thief on the cross, Your Majesty.

THE KING. We shall have a fine carnival, punishment or no punishment. (*To* THE DOCTOR.) Come, my friend. . . .

BROTHER THOMAS. Upon us all!

THE KING. Very likely . . . but what can we do? The beef is gone.

BROTHER THOMAS. We can learn our lesson. We can redeem the soul we are so willing to give up.

THE DOCTOR. Still the same tune. Change your flute, Brother. The world will be served. And we are its servants.

BROTHER THOMAS. Not in the final judgment. God alone will be served.

THE DOCTOR. I'll worry about that when the time comes. But for now . . . , I have my troupe, and I must rehearse, and I'll bid you farewell.

BROTHER THOMAS. The mute will not play!

THE DOCTOR. He will!

THE KING. We shall see . . . but for now . . . let the carnival commence . . . Lent is not far behind.

THE KING *and* THE DOCTOR *leave.* BROTHER THOMAS *falls to his knees in prayer.*

Scene Two

FRANCESCHINA *is washing clothes.* BROTHER SILENUS *enters, peering about him.*

FRANCESCHINA *(singing and humming to herself as she bends over the washtub).*

> When I dream of the devil's home,
> I dream of snow and ice;
> In Heaven I may never roam,
> But wouldn't it be nice
> To see the fields of clover
> And to hear the angels sing
> To spend eternity in an everlasting Spring.

BROTHER SILENUS, *who has been listening without* FRANCESCHINA *noticing him, applauds.* FRANCESCHINA, *startled at first, quickly recovers herself and bows.*

BROTHER SILENUS. Ah!

FRANCESCHINA. Can I do something for you, Brother?

BROTHER SILENUS. It's true!

FRANCESCHINA. Are you looking for The Doctor? He's out steal . . . getting our dinner.

BROTHER SILENUS. They *do* bow?

FRANCESCHINA. Who bows?

BROTHER SILENUS. Players. You. You just bowed.

FRANCESCHINA. When there is applause, we bow. Lord knows it's all we get most of the time!

BROTHER SILENUS. What's it like?

FRANCESCHINA. Bowing?

BROTHER SILENUS. Being a player. What's it like?

FRANCESCHINA. Like? It isn't *like* anything, Brother. It's just . . . It's just being a player. That's all.

BROTHER SILENUS. And you travel all over the world?

FRANCESCHINA. All over . . . and it's all the same. Northern fleas bite as hard as southern fleas. You can starve in the east as well as in the west.

BROTHER SILENUS. Sometimes I wish I had traveled. Just a little.

FRANCESCHINA. You're welcome to it!

BROTHER SILENUS. I don't think God ever meant me to be a monk.

FRANCESCHINA. Don't say that, Brother!

BROTHER SILENUS. Brother Martin thinks so, too.

FRANCESCHINA. I would give anything to stay in one place for a while. I've been traveling ever since I was fourteen. I was beautiful then.

BROTHER SILENUS. But the things you must have seen! And the things you must have done!

FRANCESCHINA *(musing)*. The things I've seen! And the things I've done!

BROTHER SILENUS. Palaces and the ocean. I've never seen the ocean.

FRANCESCHINA. The ocean! Yes, you're right. I'm glad I've seen the ocean. But palaces? No!

BROTHER SILENUS. And the people you've known!

FRANCESCHINA. And the people I've hated!

BROTHER SILENUS. And loved.

FRANCESCHINA. Hated! No! There was one. In the darkness. In the night. In Seville. Long ago.

BROTHER SILENUS. You see!

FRANCESCHINA. You make me think of my youth. That isn't good, Brother. You are here on business?

BROTHER SILENUS. A message. From the Prior. He wanted to remind you . . . Lent begins at midnight. Your performance must be over by then.

FRANCESCHINA. And tomorrow?

BROTHER SILENUS. And tomorrow you must be gone.

FRANCESCHINA. To the sea!

BROTHER SILENUS. To the sea! And perhaps, dear lady, to Seville. *(He starts to go, turns, and bows.* FRANCESCHINA *applauds silently. He leaves.)*

FRANCESCHINA *(to herself)*. To Seville!

Scene Three

THE KING *is giving* MASTER DUDLEY *a lesson in the proper way to put on armor. He is partly caparisoned.* MASTER DUDLEY *is holding a pauldron in his hands.*

THE KING. No! No! The rerebrace goes on before the pauldron! If you would just look you would see it's the only way that makes sense.

MASTER DUDLEY. I'm sorry, Your Majesty.

THE KING. Don't apologize! Here, let me show you. Oh, how I wish this could be done without assistance! This is the pauldron, and this is the rerebrace. Now watch. They just don't fit together the way you have them. See?

MASTER DUDLEY. I'll never learn!

THE KING. If you're going to be a knight, you'd better learn! You'll have idiot squires to contend with, then, yourself. Now show me the tasset.

MASTER DUDLEY *holds up another piece of armor.*

THE KING. No! No! That's the skirt! It's no use! Go on, back to your studies. If you can't learn something useful, perhaps you can learn to read. *(As* MASTER DUDLEY *goes out.)* And send Terrible Tom to me. He understands these things.

MASTER DUDLEY *leaves.* THE KING *sets up the armor he is not wearing in the form of a figure.*

THE KING. And how are you, my dear other self? My shell? My shadow? My exoskeleton? My hollow friend? How is the world treating you these days? Do you have troubles, too? Is that a cold emptiness inside of you? Do you have to concern yourself with priors and fanatical brothers and harlotry players and idiot squires? Do you have a holy sanctuary to save from infidel kings? An army to feed? A life to redeem? No, my dumb friend, you are at peace. I can see that. In the cold, in the heat, in the day, in the night . . . you are at peace. But why can't you speak? I need your voice, other self. Oh, how I need your voice. And you sit there looking smug, Your Empty Majesty! *(He strikes the helmet, which falls to the ground and rolls to the feet of* TERRIBLE TOM, *who has been listening to the latter part of the speech.*

TERRIBLE TOM. Oh, no, sir!

THE KING. There you are! Help me off with this armor. I'm beginning to itch.

TERRIBLE TOM. Don't hurt him, Your Majesty.

THE KING *(as* TERRIBLE TOM *starts to help him take off the armor).* You're right, Tom. He's served me well. And so have you, my old friend.

TERRIBLE TOM. I've done my best, Your Majesty.

THE KING. Sit here beside me, Tom, and pass the time of day.

TERRIBLE TOM. I couldn't do that, Your Majesty.

THE KING. Sit down. Just this once.

TERRIBLE TOM. Very well, Your Majesty. If you say so. *(He sits.)*

THE KING. I say so, Your Majesty. And how are you enjoying the carnival, Tom?

TERRIBLE TOM. Fine, Your Majesty. But I'm looking forward to the players.

THE KING. And your legs. How are your legs, Tom?

TERRIBLE TOM. Well enough, I suppose, Your Majesty. Except for the cold. The cold gets into the bones something awful. But I expect that'll all go away when we get to the Holy Land.

THE KING. Warmth heals, they say. Your body *and* your soul.

TERRIBLE TOM. I can't speak much about souls, Your Majesty. I haven't rightly thought much about them.

THE KING. You're wise, my friend. Some, they say, think of nothing else.

TERRIBLE TOM. Keeping warm, and keeping fed, and keeping the faith . . . they're enough for me.

THE KING. They're enough for any man. We shall have to get you a horse, old Tom. To give those legs a rest.

TERRIBLE TOM. A horse? If Your Majesty will pardon me . . . I'd rather walk. It wouldn't seem right, after all these years, to ride. And the walking is good for my legs.

THE KING. And our mission, Tom. What about our mission?

TERRIBLE TOM. I just follow my king.

THE KING. And I just follow mine!

SIR GERALD *hurries in.*

THE KING. Sir Gerald?

SIR GERALD. They'll begin soon, Your Majesty. The players. You wanted me to tell you.

THE KING. Thank you, Sir Gerald. Come, Tom, join me at the performance. We'll show them how a king and a wrestler can laugh.

TERRIBLE TOM. They say there's warmth in laughter.

THE KING. That's what they say, Tom. Come along.

THE KING *and* TERRIBLE TOM *exit.* SIR GERALD *follows, shaking his head in disapproval of* THE KING'S *familiarity with a servant.*

Scene Four

BROTHER AMBROSE *is alone. He is studying a chess board, manipulating the pieces to fit his theological argument with himself.*

BROTHER AMBROSE. Now if I make the king God, then the queen will be the Blessed Mother. But who will be the Christ? So I make the king the Christ, but then where is God? God is the more powerful, so the queen will be God, and the king the Christ. But then who will be the Holy Spirit? Dear me! It is so difficult! Suppose I start at the other end. If the pawns are the peasants, then the knights are the knights, and bishops, the bishops, the rooks, the nobles, the king, the king, and the queen, the queen. But now there is no place for Father, Son or Holy Spirit at all. *(He stares at a beam of sunlight.)* Now, take this beam of sunlight. Does it glow? It glows. Does it provide warmth? It provides warmth. Does it illuminate the darkness? It illuminates the darkness. And it descends from Heaven. Therefore, this beam of light is God, for anything that possesses the attributes of God must *be* God. Q.E.D. *(In despair.)* But it isn't! *(He takes up a wisp of straw.)* This wisp of straw! Has it grown? It has grown. From the tiniest of seeds? Yes. Is it complete in itself? It is! It is! But neither is *it* God! Oh, beam of light! Oh, wisp of straw! Oh, kings and queens, knights, bishops, rooks, and pawns. Oh, universe . . . which of you all is God? *(He falls into a fixed staring at the wisp of straw.)*

Scene Five

FRANCESCHINA *is sewing* PULCINELLA'S *costume. She completes the stitch, secures it, and bites off the thread. She stands and calls off stage.*

FRANCESCHINA. Pulci! Pulci! Come here. It's finished. (PULCINELLA *enters.)* Here! Try it on! *(She helps him into the blouse.)* There! Now you are really one of us! Move. Let me see how it is. (PULCINELLA *does a little dance.)* Fine! You would have thought it was made for you in the first place. Come and sit by me, Pulci. *(When he has done so, she continues.)* There. Now you are a player, for sure. And you will be fine tonight. *(She looks at him more closely.)* Pulci! You don't look well. What is it? (PULCINELLA *indicates that he is all right.)* Are you sure? *(He nods.)* Here rest your head in my lap. Rest! Rest! For tonight you will play. On the stage. And the whole world will be watching. *(His eyes are closed.)* That's right, my child. Sleep. Rest. Dream. *(She softly croons a lullaby to him.)*

> When a lamb has lost the flock,
> When the moon is hidden,

Shepherds pray to God above
That he may enter Heaven.
(She continues to hum the lullaby softly as she strokes his head.)

Scene Six

THE PRIOR *and* BROTHER THOMAS *are at prayer on opposite sides of the stage.*

THE PRIOR. O dear God, may the terror in the soul of our erring brother be dispelled by the light of Thy infinite Grace. May the anguish of his nights and the anger of his days find tranquility in Thee. May the sweet passion of Thy love supplant the wrath of Moses in his heart.

BROTHER THOMAS. Most Holy Lord of all the universe, give me the strength to withstand the burden of the mission Thou hast placed upon me. May the doubts in my soul be destroyed in the bringing of Thy holy goodness to the children of men. May the passions of this earth dissolve in the glory of Thy might.

THE PRIOR. Release Thy servant, Thomas, from the pride of his own doubt. Restore the sureness of Thy Being to his soul, that he may abjure the Devil and rejoice in Thee. Return him, Divine Spirit, from the freezing hell of his despair. Allow, O God, this child of Thy own being to live his life in Thy grace, and to pass from it in the eternal spirit of Thy love.

BROTHER THOMAS. The night before the holy season of Thy betrayal is coming. The darkness is descending on the carnival of the world. Masked men are in the streets, and the children cry aloud at demons. Give me the strength, O Lord, to unmask them, to brave their might, to silence their song of the universe, that all may be in a state of Grace for the coming sun of Thy resurrection!

Scene Seven

The costumes and masks of THE CAPTAIN, THE DOCTOR, *and* PANTALONE, *and the mask, alone, of* PULCINELLA *are hanging in a row in a caricature of life. They look like human beings who have been punctured, and from whom all the air has escaped. This is obviously the dressing area of* THE TROUPE. PANTALONE *and* THE CAPTAIN *are heard off stage, arguing.*

THE CAPTAIN. But why *THE CAPTAIN IN LOVE?*

PANTALONE. Why not?

They make their appearance . . . two tired, old men, clothed in rags in comparison with the richness of the costumes. Their walk is a shuffle. Their faces are old and wrinkled. They are weary. During the course of the scene, they dress themselves for the performance. As each item of their regular clothing is removed and each item of costume is put on, they change, bit by bit, to younger, more vital, more exuberant creatures.

THE CAPTAIN. Because it wears me out!

PANTALONE. And *PANTALONE IN LOVE* wears *me* out. What's the difference?

THE CAPTAIN. The difference is that you're Pantalone and *I'm* The Captain.

PANTALONE. Come on, get ready. It's been decided . . . so there's no use complaining about it. Did you see the crowd?

THE CAPTAIN. I don't care. I can't keep up the pace much longer.

PANTALONE. Not since Seville!

THE CAPTAIN. What?

PANTALONE. We haven't seen a crowd like that since Seville. The way they cheered!

THE CAPTAIN. I had a pretty piece in Seville. Small and dark.

PANTALONE. In the love scene they never cheered that way before or since. *(He goes into his part in the love scene.)* "My dear, dear Franceschina. How did you get here in my bed?"

THE CAPTAIN *(feeding him his lines).* "Who are you?"

PANTALONE. "Roll over on your back, and I'll show you who I am!"

THE CAPTAIN. "Why you horrible old man!"

PANTALONE *(leaping around in a rage).* "Old! Old! You come here and I'll show you who's old! Why I have just come from the bed of Venus herself. And in a few days there will be a hundred demi-gods crowding the town." And so on. And they laughed! I'll never hear laughter like that again!

THE CAPTAIN. And the duel! It has never gone as well since. *(Taking on his role.)* "I will show you what kind of weapon *I* have, my little Pulcinella. Come here, my young friend."

PANTALONE *(feeding the lines).* "No! No! Master Captain, Your Honor, not that! I thought we would duel with *swords!*"

THE CAPTAIN. "With this weapon I have conquered the Indies, I have overcome the black savages of Africa. I have become Master of the Universe itself."

THE DOCTOR *(entering).* What's this? *(He begins to dress himself. There is the same transformation in him as in the others.)* It's getting close to time.

PANTALONE. Seville, Doctor. We were just remembering Seville.

THE DOCTOR. I had a wonderful little girl in Seville: small and dark. A *wonderful* little girl.

THE CAPTAIN. Small? And dark?

PANTALONE. Remember, Doctor? The applause? The cheers? They carried us on their shoulders.

THE DOCTOR. Yes. Seville!

THE CAPTAIN. And it was warm there.

THE DOCTOR. It was!

PANTALONE. And there were oranges in the market. And limes.

THE DOCTOR. My speech was longer that night than it has ever been. *(He slips into character.)* "My dear friends. I am here tonight to give you a small bit of my wisdom."

PANTALONE. "Oh! No!"

THE DOCTOR. "Oh! Yes!"

THE CAPTAIN. "Oh! No!"

THE DOCTOR. "Oh! Yes! Yes! Yes! Yes! Yes!"

PANTALONE. "You haven't *got* a *small* bit of wisdom."

THE DOCTOR. "Women are the blessing of mankind."

THE CAPTAIN. "That's true. I remember. . . ."

THE DOCTOR. "The mistresses of our hearths."

PANTALONE. "That's right. I remember. . . ."

THE DOCTOR. "The nourishment of our souls. . . ."

THE CAPTAIN. "Very true. Once I was. . . ."

THE DOCTOR. "The solace of our grief. . . ."

PANTALONE. "That's right. Once upon a time. . . ."

THE DOCTOR. "The joy of our hearts. . . ."

THE CAPTAIN. "Of course! Once I was. . . ."

THE DOCTOR. "And everyone of them is nothing but a monumental whore!"

FRANCESCHINA *(entering in character and picking up her cue, already in her costume and make-up).* "What was that, Doctor?"

THE DOCTOR. "A monumental *bore.* Eavesdroppers, every one of them."

FRANCESCHINA. "I'll eavesdrop you!" *(She beats him during the following part of her speech.)* "You pig, you snake, you cock, you vulture, you sloth, you porcupine. . . ."

PANTALONE. "Porcupine!"

FRANCESCHINA. "You giraffe, you elephant, you . . . you . . . you
. . . hippocampocamelopulus!"
THE CAPTAIN. "Hippo--"
PANTALONE. "--campo--"
THE CAPTAIN. "--camel--"
THE DOCTOR. "--opolus!"

*By now they are in very high spirits. They are having great fun and
are completely transformed. They are costumed completely except for
their masks. At the peak of their delight,* PULCINELLA *enters. He is
completely costumed except for his mask.*

THE DOCTOR. And here he is! We are ready! Put on your masks.
(They do, all except FRANCESCHINA, *who does not wear one.)* Take your
instruments. *(They take up their instruments: tambour, cymbals, bagpipe,
flute, and triangle.)* Let the carnival commence!!!

They begin to play and march out in step with their music.

Scene Eight

THE TROUPE *marches on, continuing the action of the preceding scene.
They are joined by revelers, coming from all directions, until they are
swamped and disappear from our view. The revelers are townsmen and
soldiers, all wearing grotesque carnival mask-heads. They dance, form
chains for crack-the-whip, and generally enjoy themselves. There is much
drinking, wenching, and laughing, and perhaps some fighting. We see*
SIR GERALD *in a rather decorous mask,* MASTER DUDLEY, ARNOLD THE
GOATHERD, TERRIBLE TOM *and* THE KING. *Only* THE KING *is not masked.
None of the monks is to be seen.* THE KING *and* SIR GERALD *find
themselves downstage. They have to shout to make themselves heard
above the din.*

SIR GERALD. Your Majesty! I am surprised you're not masked.
THE KING. A king wears his mask all the time. He doesn't need a
special one for the carnival.

ARNOLD THE GOATHERD *and* TERRIBLE TOM *meet at another place on
the stage.*

ARNOLD THE GOATHERD. Terrible Tom! And how are your legs
tonight?
TERRIBLE TOM. Aching, Arnold, aching!

ARNOLD THE GOATHERD. It's the legs that go first, whatever they say.

TERRIBLE TOM. It's the legs for sure.

MASTER DUDLEY *meets* THE KING.

THE KING. Isn't it late for you to be up, Master Dudley?

MASTER DUDLEY. It's the carnival, Your Majesty. It only comes once a year.

THE KING. Just once, Master Dudley, that's right. Are you enjoying it all?

MASTER DUDLEY. I shall never enjoy myself so much again, Your Majesty.

THE KING. Never again. So, on your way!

The carnival continues until THE TROUPE *appears, still playing their instruments.* THE DOCTOR *finally gets the crowd relatively quiet. But his speech and the performance which follows it are interrupted frequently by cheers, laughter, catcalls, and applause.*

THE DOCTOR. My friends. My friends of the carnival. May I present our troupe. *(As he introduces each, a cheer goes up from the crowd.)* First, the stingiest old man in the world, Pantalone. *(Cheers.)* The biggest braggart from here to Timbuktu, that great warrior . . . Capitano Spavento di Barcelona. *(Cheers.)* And here is the greatest of fools, the master of silence himself . . . Pulcinella. *(Cheers.)* And now, queen of the stage, that loveliest of young ladies, Franceschina. *(Cheers.)* And now, let our show commence. *(Cheers. All leave the stage except* THE CAPTAIN.*)*

THE CAPTAIN. "The beautiful Franceschina is driving me crazy. I don't know what I'm going to do if that old fool of a father doesn't let her be mine. But, shhh! Here she comes. Now I'll find out how my suit is progressing."

FRANCESCHINA *enters, carrying the broom. She doesn't see* THE CAPTAIN.

THE CAPTAIN *(aside).* "Now to put it to her!" *(To* FRANCESCHINA.*)* "My beautiful Franceschina!"

FRANCESCHINA *is startled by this, and turns toward him, swinging her broom and knocking him down as she does so.*

THE CAPTAIN. "Ah! You see, lovely Franceschina, you are so beautiful, you knock me off my feet."

FRANCESCHINA. "I'll knock you off your arse if you don't stop pestering me!"

THE CAPTAIN *(crawling to her on his knees and pleading pitifully).* "Oh, darling Franceschina! How come you treat me so unmercifully, when you know I love you?"

FRANCESCHINA. "You have never given me any token of your love."

THE CAPTAIN. "I'll give you anything you want. Just name it."

FRANCESCHINA. "I don't want very much. . . ."

THE CAPTAIN *(getting more excited as she gets more coquettish).* "Name it!"

FRANCESCHINA. "All I want is a little. . . ."

THE CAPTAIN. "Yes, yes . . . a little. . . ."

FRANCESCHINA. "A little bit of something I know you have a lot of. . . ."

THE CAPTAIN. ". . . I have a lot of . . . yes. . . ."

FRANCESCHINA. "If you'll just come over here a little bit closer. . . ."

THE CAPTAIN. "If I'll just. . . ." *(He is greatly excited by now. He gets set, as a track star might, and runs furiously at her, only to have her step aside. He disappears off stage.* FRANCESCHINA *looks after him as if he had gone a very great distance. Then, from the way she looks, we know that he is coming back. He creeps back on stage, backward, with his hands up,* PULCINELLA *forcing him ahead with his* (PULCINELLA'S) *sword.)*

THE DOCTOR *(appearing).* "That's it, Pulci! Don't let him get away with anything! *(He stalks on.)* So-o-o-o!!! You are trying to steal my beloved from me!"

BROTHER THOMAS *rushes on to the stage. Until now he has not been seen in the crowd.*

BROTHER THOMAS. *Stop!* He must not play! *(He throws his arms around* PULCINELLA.*)*

For a moment everyone is frozen in a tableau; there is not a sound. Then BROTHER THOMAS *speaks. The stillness remains as everyone is hypnotized by the turn of events and* BROTHER THOMAS' *intensity.*

BROTHER THOMAS. He must not play! He is damned. His soul must be saved. All our souls must be saved!

A VOICE FROM THE CROWD. Go away, Brother!

SECOND VOICE. It's carnival. Your turn comes soon enough!

The shouts of the crowd grow louder and angrier.

BROTHER THOMAS. You don't understand! He has been cursed. Ask him.

FIRST VOICE. He don't need to defend himself. It's carnival time.

THIRD VOICE. Wait! (*To* PULCINELLA.) What about it, clown? Are you cursed? (PULCINELLA *tries to speak.*)

SECOND VOICE. Why don't he speak?

THIRD VOICE. What's wrong with him?

BROTHER THOMAS. He must be saved! He must be saved! We must all be saved!

THE DOCTOR (*struggling with* BROTHER THOMAS *to wrest* PULCINELLA *from him, and finally succeeding*). This young man is mad. Let's get on with our show.

There are mixed cheers and boos. THE DOCTOR *signals the others. They take their positions, all except* PULCINELLA, *who simply stands, lost and terrified in the confusion of these events.*

THE CAPTAIN (*taking up the scene where it was interrupted*). "*Your* beloved!"

THE DOCTOR. "*My* beloved!"

There are shouts from the crowd against the performance.

VOICES. Let him speak. Let him have his say.

BROTHER THOMAS (*once more grasping* PULCINELLA *by one arm*). He has blasphemed against God!

THE DOCTOR (*grasping* PULCINELLA *by the other arm*). He is good, I tell you! He is a good man!!!

A VOICE. Let him speak for himself!

BROTHER THOMAS. He can't speak: He has *no tongue!!!*

Sensation in the crowd. PULCINELLA *can stand it no longer. He seems to be literally torn into two parts, by* THE DOCTOR *on one side and* BROTHER THOMAS *on the other. His face . . . that part of it that can be seen below the mask . . . has lost all expression. He stands for a moment, and then he gives a great, silent shriek of anguish until all feeling seems purged from his body. He collapses and is caught by* THE DOCTOR.

THE DOCTOR. Now see what you've done with your damned holiness!

BROTHER THOMAS (*kneeling beside* PULCINELLA). He must be saved!

THE DOCTOR. Too late for that! Too late! Too late! He's dead!

FRANCESCHINA *screams and kneels beside* PULCINELLA, *cradling him in her arms. The great bell of the monastery starts to toll midnight, signaling the beginning of Lent. The crowd disperses, absolutely silent. Only* THE TROUPE, BROTHER THOMAS, *and* THE KING, *off to one side, remain. In the distance the chanting of the monks can be heard. No one has moved among those remaining. When the crowd is all gone,* THE KING *walks slowly to* THE DOCTOR.

THE KING. Come, friend Doctor, Lent has begun. The journey north is a long one. *(Indicating* PULCINELLA.*)* Leave him to his God now.

THE TROUPE *slowly leaves, first* THE CAPTAIN *and* PANTALONE, *then* THE DOCTOR, *gently leading* FRANCESCHINA. *Each takes a final farewell glance as he exits. Finally, only* THE KING *and* BROTHER THOMAS *remain.* BROTHER THOMAS *has not moved. He is still kneeling over the dead* PULCINELLA. *The chanting is growing louder as the monks approach.*

THE KING *(looking down at the dead* PULCINELLA, *and the monk kneeling beside him.)* MEMENTO MORI! *(He shakes his head sadly and leaves.)*

For the first time BROTHER THOMAS *moves. Slowly, as in a trance, he removes the mask from* PULCINELLA'S *face and places it on his own. He gently covers the face of the dead man, rises, and goes off in the direction taken by* THE TROUPE.

Scene Nine

The roadside, as at the beginning of the play, but subtly different. Perhaps there was a growing tree in the first scene . . . a tree that is now barren. Or there may be frost on the milestone. In any event, this is a colder place, more remote, less welcoming. THE TROUPE *enters from the same direction as before, but there is no singing this time.* THE DOCTOR *holds up his hand.*

THE DOCTOR. This will do. *(They stop and put down their burdens.)*
FRANCESCHINA *(pointing to the figure of the Memento Mori).*
Doctor, there's another one of them!
PANTALONE. That's the third one we've seen today.
THE DOCTOR. So what? *(To the figure.)* Hello, Brother! Still not saying anything, eh? *(To the others.)* We can't rest long. The days are getting shorter all the time. *(To the figure.)* I guess you were right last time, eh, Brother? *(He throws back the cowl and speaks to the death's-head, thus revealed.)* Right as rain, you old bag of bones!
PANTALONE. How much farther is it, Doctor? The Captain can't go on much longer.

THE DOCTOR. To the moon, maybe. Maybe farther! *(To the figure.)* How about you? Do you want to join up with us? The cold doesn't bother you, I'll bet. Or the heat. Or the rain. Or the snow. Or women or fleas. Eh?

THE LEPER *of the first scene enters, still with his face hidden, still ringing his hand-bell.*

THE CAPTAIN. Doctor! The leper!

THE DOCTOR. Go away! We don't want anything to do with you.

THE LEPER. Please let me join you?

THE DOCTOR. We've got enough trouble already.

FRANCESCHINA. We'd have less if you hadn't refused the King's money!

THE LEPER. I won't touch anything. I'll keep my distance.

THE DOCTOR. Nothing doing.

THE LEPER. Just close enough to hear your voices from time to time.

THE DOCTOR. On your way.

FRANCESCHINA. Doctor?

THE DOCTOR. What now?

FRANCESCHINA. What more can happen to us?

THE DOCTOR. Wouldn't he be good for business!

PANTALONE. He can leave us before we get to a town.

THE CAPTAIN. Remember what happened the last time we refused!

THE DOCTOR. Still as gutless as ever, the whole lot of you. Worse . . . last time you didn't want him either! *(To* THE LEPER.*)* All right . . . but keep your distance . . . ten paces.

THE LEPER. Thank you. God will reward you.

THE DOCTOR. Not likely! *(To the others.)* All right get off your arses. We've got to be moving. Night's coming on. *(To* THE LEPER.*)* But none of our food, understand?

They gather their things and prepare to leave, but before they can get started THE JEW *of the first scene appears.*

THE JEW. Some bread, for the love of God!

THE DOCTOR. A Jew, and still singing the same tune. We want nothing to do with you, Jew. Be on your way.

THE JEW. For the love of God!

FRANCESCHINA *(going to him and spitting in his face).* There, Jew, that's all you'll get.

THE DOCTOR. Good girl! That'll get rid of him!

But there is a sudden change in FRANCESCHINA. *Puzzled at and troubled by her own action, she takes the edge of her shawl and wipes away the spittle from his face.*

THE DOCTOR. What are you doing now?

FRANCESCHINA. I don't know, Doctor! It suddenly came over me. I don't know.

THE DOCTOR. The whole world's gone mad.

FRANCESCHINA. He's starving! *(She gets some bread for him.)* Here.

THE DOCTOR. Now I've seen everything! Feeding a Jew!

FRANCESCHINA. He must come with us, Doctor. We can't turn him away.

THE DOCTOR. I'll show you who can't! *(He starts for* THE JEW.*)*

FRANCESCHINA. We can't turn anyone away. Not any more. Things are different now.

THE CAPTAIN. They are, Doctor. Things are different.

THE DOCTOR. All right! All right! All right! You've all gone out of your minds. I must be the only sane person in all of Europe. But they must keep behind. Always . . . behind. A Jew and a leper. Good God!

They are about to start off when BROTHER THOMAS *appears. He is still in his robes, but he is wearing* PULCINELLA'S *mask.*

PANTALONE. Doctor! Look!

THE DOCTOR. Well! Well! Well! What have we here!

PANTALONE. It's the monk!

FRANCESCHINA. And wearing Pulci's mask! He's got on Pulci's mask, Doctor!

THE DOCTOR. What do you want, Brother? A leper? A Jew? We're well supplied. Haven't you done us enough harm already? *(He waits for an answer, but none is forthcoming.)* Well, speak up!

BROTHER THOMAS *slowly opens his mouth.* FRANCESCHINA *fearfully goes to him and looks into it.*

FRANCESCHINA. Doctor, his tongue's been ripped out, too! *(To* BROTHER THOMAS.*)* Who did it? The crowd? The soldiers? (BROTHER THOMAS *pantomimes "No."*)

THE CAPTAIN. Not the monks! *("No.")*

THE DOCTOR. Wait! I think I understand. You did it yourself . . . is that it? *(No answer.)* And you want to take his place! *("Yes.")* In the sinful plays we do? In the ungodly plays? You want to take his place? *("Yes.")* All right, my friend.

FRANCESCHINA. No, Doctor! If it wasn't for him Pulci would be here right now.

THE DOCTOR *(pointing at* BROTHER THOMAS*).* Pulci is here right now.

FRANCESCHINA. You can't! You can't let him go with us!

THE DOCTOR. Oh, yes, I can. My monk for your Jew!

THE CAPTAIN. But why?

THE DOCTOR. To carry our burdens. Right, Brother? (BROTHER THOMAS *pantomimes "Yes."*) To listen to my blasphemies without ever talking back. Right? *("Yes.")* To be kicked when we're angry; to be cursed when we're afraid; to be spit on when we want to spit. Right, Brother? *("Yes.")* You see? *(To the others.)* All right. Take up your burdens. Night's coming on, and the north is still far away. And we've a journey to make.

The strange procession goes wearily off. First, THE TROUPE, *then* THE LEPER *and* THE JEW, *and last* BROTHER THOMAS, *carrying the heaviest pack of all. He pauses a moment by the seated figure. Carefully he replaces the cowl left down by* THE DOCTOR, *and then he follows the others.*

The light fades until only the figure is visible against a great panoply of stars, seen now for the first time. A wind rises . . . a cold, northern wind. Finally, the figure dissolves in the darkness, too, and nothing is left but the infinite night.

THE END

APPENDIX

Plays by Student Authors

FOLK-PLAYS *of* *The* CAROLINA PLAYMAKERS

ONE-ACT PLAYS

1918–1968
(In the order of their production)

When Witches Ride, by Elizabeth Lay, Beaufort, N.C., 1919.
The Return of Buck Gavin, by Thomas Wolfe, Asheville, N.C., 1919.
What Will Barbara Say? by Minnie Shepherd Sparrow, Gaston County, N.C., 1919.
Peggy, by Harold Williamson, Carthage, N.C., 1919.
The Fighting Corporal, by Louisa Reid, Gastonia, N.C., 1919.
Who Pays? by Minnie Shepherd Sparrow, Gaston County, N.C., 1919.
The Third Night, by Thomas Wolfe, Asheville, N.C., 1919.
The Hag, by Elizabeth Lay, Beaufort, N.C., 1919.

The heading, above, was used on many of the early playbills. It was designed in 1922 by Julius J. Lankes, noted woodcut artist of Hilton Village, Virginia, and made by him from a piece of apple wood grown in his own orchard. A pirate and a mountaineer flank the stage picture, which shows a scene from *The Last of the Lowries,* Paul Green's first play to be produced by The Carolina Playmakers. That same year Mr. Lankes also designed the Playmakers' emblem, a mask, which appears on the title page of this volume.

The Bell Buoy, by Dougald MacMillan, Wilmington, N.C., 1920.
Dod Gast Ye Both! by Hubert Heffner, Catawba County, N.C., 1920.
The Last of the Lowries, by Paul Green, Lillington, N.C., 1920.
Off Nag's Head, by Dougald MacMillan, Wilmington, N.C., 1920.
The Miser, by Paul Green, Lillington, N.C., 1920.
The Vamp, by William Royall, Goldsboro, N.C., 1920.
The Old Man of Edenton, by Paul Green, Lillington, N.C., 1920.
The Chatham Rabbit, by Legette Blythe, Huntersville, N.C., 1921.
The Reaping, by John Terry, Rockingham, N.C., 1921.
In Dixon's Kitchen, by Wilbur Stout, Burlington, N.C., 1921.
Reward Offered, by Jane Toy, Chapel Hill, N.C., 1921.
Trista, by Elizabeth Lay, Beaufort, N.C., 1921.
Waffles for Breakfast, by Mary Yellott, Chapel Hill, N.C., 1921.
The Lord's Will, by Paul Green, Lillington, N.C., 1922.
Dogwood Bushes, by Wilbur Stout, Burlington, N.C., 1922.
Blackbeard, Pirate of the North Carolina Coast, by Paul Green, Lillington, N.C. and Elizabeth Lay, Beaufort, N.C., 1922.
Wrack P'int, by Paul Green, Lillington, N.C., 1923.
Agatha, by Jane Toy, Chapel Hill, N.C., 1923.
Wilbur's Cousin, by Ernest Thompson, Goldsboro, N.C., 1923.
John Lane's Wife, by Mac Gorham, Rocky Mount, N.C., 1923.
The Berry Pickers, by Russell Potter, Denver, Colo., 1923.
Mamma, by Ernest Thompson, Goldsboro, N.C., 1923.
The Black Rooster, by Pearl Setzer, Hickory, N.C., 1923.
Nat Macon's Game, by Osler Bailey, Raleigh, N.C., 1923.
Gaius and Gaius, Jr., by Lucy M. Cobb, Chapel Hill, N.C., 1923.
Servants of God, by Robert S. Pickens, Albemarle, N.C., 1924.
The Beaded Buckle, by Frances Gray, Chapel Hill, N.C., 1924.
Fixin's, by Erma and Paul Green, Lillington, N.C., 1924.
Nancy's Commencement Dress, by Pearl Setzer, Hickory, N.C., 1924.
The Younger, by Sue Byrd Thompson, Norfolk, Va., 1924.
The Wheel, by Ernest Thompson, Goldsboro, N.C., 1924.
The Honor of Bonava, by Robert Watson Winston, Chapel Hill, N.C., 1924.
Politikin' in Horse Cove, by Martha Boswell, Brevard, N.C., 1924.
The Scuffletown Outlaws, by William Norment Cox, Rowland, N.C., 1924.
Out of the Past, by Frances Gray, Chapel Hill, N.C., 1925.
Yon Side O' Sunk Creek, by Martha Boswell, Brevard, N.C., 1925.
Quare Medicine, by Paul Green, Lillington, N.C., 1925.
The New Moon, by Telfair Boys Peet, Philadelphia, Penn., 1926.
A Carolina Pierrot, by William J. MacMillan, Wilmington, N.C., 1926.
Clay, by David Reid Hodgin, Sanford, N.C., 1926.
Lighted Candles, by Margaret Bland, Charlotte, N.C., 1927.

The Muse and the Movies, by Alice Rodewald, New York, N.Y., 1927.

Mr. Perry Writes a Play, by William DeCatur Perry, Elizabeth City, N.C., 1927.

The Marvelous Romance of Wen Chun-Chin, by Cheng-Chin Hsiung, Nan Chang, Kiangsi, China, 1927.

Mountain Magic, by Edith Daseking, San Francisco, Cal., 1928.

Job's Kinfolks, by Loretto Carroll Bailey, Winston-Salem, N.C., 1928.

The Queen Has Her Face Lifted, by Alvin M. Kahn, Cleveland, Ohio, 1928.

The New Eve, by Mary Dirnberger, Van Wert, Ohio, 1928.

Day's End, by Alice Pieratt, Berkeley, Cal., 1928.

A Shotgun Splicin', by Gertrude Wilson Coffin, Chapel Hill, N.C., 1928.

Blood, by Herbert T. Browne, Palo Alto, Cal., 1929.

The Family, by Catherine Wilson Nolen, Chapel Hill, N.C., 1929.

Graveyard Shift, by Edith Daseking, San Francisco, Cal., 1929.

O Promise Me, by Curtis Benjamin, Kentucky, 1929.

The Lie, by Wilkeson O'Connell, U.S. Army, Plattsburgh Barracks, N.Y., 1929.

Black Water, by Loretto Carroll Bailey, Winston-Salem, N.C., 1929.

Companion-Mate Maggie, by Helen Dortch, Goldsboro, N.C., 1929.

Magnolia's Man, by Gertrude Wilson Coffin, Chapel Hill, N.C., 1929.

Being Married, by Catherine Wilson Nolen, Chapel Hill, N.C., 1929.

In the Shadow of the Desert, by Laurabelle Dietrick, Los Angeles, Cal., 1930.

The White Senorita, by Laurabelle Dietrick, Los Angeles, Cal., 1930.

Saturday Market, by Louise Perry, Greensboro, N.C., 1930.

Lonely Hearts, by Philip Milhous, Elkmont, Ala., 1930.

She's Perfectly Innocent, by Ann Wishart Braddy, Augusta, Ga., 1930.

For Auntie's Sake, by John Patric, Snohomish, Wash., 1930.

Hollyhocks, by Joseph Philip Fox, Andover, Mass., 1930.

Suspended Animation, by Kent Creuser, New York, N.Y., 1930.

Death Valley Scotty, by James Milton Wood, Pomona, Cal., 1930.

Samuel Hinkle, Fireman, by Joseph Philip Fox, Andover, Mass., 1930.

Cloey, by Loretto Carroll Bailey, Winston-Salem, N.C., 1930.

Git Up an' Bar the Door, by Arthur Palmer Hudson, Chapel Hill, N.C., 1930.

Ever' Snitch, by Irene Fussler, Grand Forks, S.D., 1931.

The Blue Remembered Hills, by Theodore Herman, Lancaster, Penn., 1931.

A Very Pale Pink Angel, by Ellen Stewart, Camden, S.C., 1931.

Always a Bettin' Man, by Tom Loy, Hagerstown, Md., 1931.

A Vision of Eugenics, by Maurice Ferber, Westchester, N.Y., 1931.

Old Aus Ramsey, by Charles Elledge, Champion, N.C., 1931.

The Mandarin Coat, by Olive Newell, Greensboro, N.C., 1931.

Those Children, by Osmond Molarsky, Nutley, N.J., 1931.
Whispering Shadows, by Vernon B. Crook, Concord, N.C., 1931.
Patches, by Jo Norwood, Louisville, Ky., 1931.
Penny for Your Thoughts, by Tom Loy, Hagerstown, Md., 1931.
My Business and My Wife, by John Edwards, Baltimore, Md., 1931.
There's a Nigger for You, by Mary Griffin, Nashville, Tenn., 1931.
Love an' Likker, by Irene Fussler, Chapel Hill, N.C., 1931.
The Stray Bullet, by Robert Barnett, Shanghai, China, 1931.
Glenhurst, by Tom Loy, Hagerstown, Md., 1931.
Pleasantly Purple, by Ellen Stewart, Camden, S.C., 1931.
Walnut Boards, by William Long, Seaboard, N.C., 1931.
Doses of Life, by Tom Loy, Hagerstown, Md., 1931.
Immoral Holly, by Closs Peace, Arlington, Va., 1931.
Herbs of Love, by William Long, Seaboard, N.C., 1931.
Spice Cake, by Malcolm Seawell, Lumberton, N.C., 1931.
A Village Tragedy, by Charlotte Hammond, Paris, Me., 1931.
The House of Grief, by Margaret Vale, Chapel Hill, N.C., 1931.
The Last Two Shots, by Irene Fussler, Chapel Hill, N.C., 1932.
Treasures, by Irene Fussler, Chapel Hill, N.C., 1932.
King, Queen, and Joker, by Irene Fussler, Chapel Hill, N.C., 1932.
Birds of a Feather, by Jo Norwood, Louisville, Ky., 1932.
Granny, by Jack Riley, Raleigh, N.C., 1932.
The Golden Lioness, by Reuben Young Ellison, Easley, S.C., 1932.
Proof, by Osmond Molarsky, Nutley, N.J., 1932.
Boardin' Out, by Charles Elledge, Champion, N.C., 1932.
Sleep On, Lemuel, by John W. Parker, Murfreesboro, N.C., 1932.
Bloomers, by Jo Norwood, Louisville, Ky., 1932.
The Common Gift, by Elwyn de Graffenreid, Atlanta, Ga., 1932.
The Loyal Venture, by Wilkeson O'Connell, Chapel Hill, N.C., 1932.
Neighbors of the Dead, by Vernon Crook, Concord, N.C., 1932.
Ol' Honeycutt's Boy, by Jack Riley, Raleigh, N.C., 1932.
The Boss of the House, by Lubin Leggett, Tabor City, N.C., 1932.
Chicken Money, by Winifred Tuttle, Cedar Falls, Iowa, 1932.
The Battle of Shaw's Mill, by Charles Elledge, Champion, N.C., and
    Malcolm Seawell, Lumberton, N.C., 1932.
Election Returns, by Alonzo Hoyle, Shelby, N.C., 1932.
Freights, by Marjorie Craig, Reidsville, N.C., 1932.
A Revolt in the Nineties, by Anne Wilson, Augusta, Ga., 1932.
Playing with Fire, by Thea W. Whitefield, 1932.
A Little Cajun, by Peg Williamson, 1932.
It's Just Too Bad, by James Alfred Stanley, Warrensville, N.C., 1932.
Blessed Assurance, by Evelyn McCall, 1932.
Old Ninety-Seven, by Wilbur Dorsett, Spencer, N.C., 1932.
Nothing Ever Happens, by Elmer R. Oettinger, Jr., Wilson, N.C., 1932.

Gateway, by Eugenia Rawls, Macon, Ga., 1932.
Four on a Heath, by Foster Fitz-Simons, Atlanta, Ga., 1932.
Swamp Creek Nigger, by Harry W. Coble, Doublas, Ga., 1932.
Hell Bent for Honolulu, by William Bonyun, Summit, N.J., 1932.
And They Lived Happily, by Marion Tatum, Raleigh, N.C., 1932.
Stumbling in Dreams, by George Brown, New York, N.Y., 1932.
Davy Crockett, by John Philip Milhous, Elkmont, Ala., 1932.
Coal, by Marguerite McGinnis, Greenville, N.C., 1932.
The State Rests, by Peggy Ann Harris, Rutherfordton, N.C., 1932.
In His Hand, by Betty Bolton, Hendersonville, N.C., 1932.
The Elders Play, by Sue Roberson, Franklinton, N.C., 1932.
Honora Wade, by Eugenia Rawls, Macon, Ga., 1932.
Sour Fodder, by Burdette Kindig, Sioux City, Iowa, 1932.
Back Door, by Wilbur Dorsett, Spencer, N.C., 1932.
Fool's Justice, by Harry W. Coble, Douglas, Ga., 1933.
A Little Boat to India, by Foster Fitz-Simons, Atlanta, Ga., 1933.
Heart Trouble, by Bradford White, Rome, Ga., 1933.
Mumsey, by Sarah M. W. Huntley, New York, N.Y., 1933.
One Every Minute, by Everett Jess, Haddon Heights, N.J., 1933.
Malone, by Marion Tatum, Raleigh, N.C., 1933.
The Last Skirmish, by Marguerite McGinnis, Greenville, N.C., 1933.
Second Edition, by Robert W. Barnett, Shanghai, China, 1933.
Lights in the Sky, by William Bonyun, Summit, N.J., 1933.
Design for Justice, by Elmer R. Oettinger, Jr., Wilson, N.C., 1933.
Comedy at Five, by Martha Matthews Hatton, Chicago, Ill., 1933.
Mihalusek's Wager, by Edward V. Conrad, West Orange, N.J., 1933.
Discontent, by J. M. Ledbetter, Jr., Rockingham, N.C., 1933.
Blow Me Down, by William Bonyun, Summit, N.J., 1933.
And the Poet Laughed, by Burdette Kindig, Sioux City, Iowa, 1933.
Etowah Plantation, by Eugenia Rawls, Macon, Ga., 1933.
Tintagil, by Martha Matthews Hatton, Chicago, Ill., 1933.
Farewell to Glamour, by James P. McConnaughey, New York, N.Y., 1933.
My Son, by Frank McIntosh, Brevard, N.C., 1933.
The Salted Pup, by John Philip Milhous, Elkmont, Ala., 1933.
The Moon Turns, by Elmer R. Oettinger, Jr., Wilson, N.C., 1933.
Beer on Ice, by Harry W. Coble, Douglas, Ga., 1933.
Bull Session, by George Brown, New York, N.Y., 1933.
For Poland, by Edward V. Conrad, West Orange, N.J., 1933.
No Word from the Wise, by Wilbur Dorsett, Spencer, N.C., 1933.
A Mockingbird Singing, by Foster Fitz-Simons, Atlanta, Ga., 1933.
Eternal Spring, by Robert Barnett, Shanghai, China, 1933.
The Queen Was in the Kitchen, by Ellen Stewart, Camden, S.C., 1933.
Burgundy for Breakfast, by Martha Hatton, Chicago, Ill., 1933.

Three Muggy Rooms in the Bronx, by George Brown, New York, N.Y., 1933.

Henna Rinse, by Marion Tatum, Raleigh, N.C., 1933.

Showing at Eight, by Leonard Rapport, Asheville, N.C., 1933.

O Woman, by Carl G. Thompson, Southern Pines, N.C., 1933.

November Night, by Margaret Belle McCauley, Baltimore, Md., 1933.

Hell's Dreams, by Frederica Frederick, New Kensington, Penn., 1933.

Diana, by Kathleen Krahenbuhl, Selma, N.C., 1933.

Shadows of Industry, by Vermont C. Royster, Raleigh, N.C., 1933.

Sing Your Own Song, by Nat Farnworth, Pueblo, Colo., 1933.

Flight Unending, by Robert W. Barnett, Shanghai, China, 1933.

Comedy at Five, by Martha Hatton, Chicago, Ill., 1933.

Everglades and Hickory, by John F. Alexander, New York, N.Y., 1933.

Grand Slam, by James Thompson, Durham, N.C., 1933.

Copper Penny, by Douglas Hume, Monterey, Cal., 1933.

Bought with the Vittles, by Alton Williams, San Francisco, Cal., 1933.

Opposite Poles, by Margaret Siceloff, Asheville, N.C., 1933.

New Rasthenia, by Herman Fussler, Chapel Hill, N.C., 1933.

The Head-Ax of Ingfell, by Anne B. Walters, Philippine Islands, 1933.

Driftwood, by Patricia McMullan, Washington, N.C., 1933.

LaCapilla, by Frederica Frederick, New Kensington, Penn., 1933.

Over the Doorsill, by Harry W. Coble, Douglas, Ga., 1934.

Another Journey, by Virgil Lee, Baltimore, Md., 1934.

Borrowed of the Night, by Kathleen Krahenbuhl, Selma, N.C., 1934.

Moon in the Hawthorne Tree, by Foster Fitz-Simons, Atlanta, Ga., 1934.

Prelude, by Vermont C. Royster, Raleigh, N.C., 1934.

The Stars Are Fire, by Nat Farnwarth, Pueblo, Colo., 1934.

John Brown, by John F. Alexander, New York, N.Y., 1934.

Oh, Hell, by Margaret McCauley, Baltimore, Md., 1934.

Shipmates, by Donald Pope, Highland Park, Mich., 1934.

Cottie Mourns, by Patricia McMullan, Washington, N.C., 1934.

Tomorrow, by Douglas Hume, Monterey, Cal., 1934.

The Lo Fan Joss, by Herman Fussler, Chapel Hill, N.C., 1934.

Pretty, Plump Angel, by Leonard Rapport, Asheville, N.C., 1934.

Never a Second Time, by Leonard Rapport, Asheville, N.C., 1934.

Release, by Jean Smith Cantrell, Winston-Salem, N.C., 1934.

Third Verse, by Wilbur Dorsett, Spencer, N.C., 1934.

Unto the Hills, by Leonard Rapport, Asheville, N.C., 1934.

Strange Interlaken, by Robert Barnett, Shanghai, China, 1934.

Lifeguards and Fish, by Margaret Siceloff, Asheville, N.C., 1934.

Back Page, by Don Shoemaker, Middletown, Ohio, 1934.

The Golden Wedding, by Alton Williams, San Francisco, Cal., 1934.

Rich Man! Poor Man! by Cecilia Allen, Tiro, Ohio, 1934.

When Floosies Meet, by Walter Terry, New Canaan, Conn., 1934.

The Suicide, by Sara Seawell, Chapel Hill, N.C., 1934.
A Beating of Wings, by Foster Fitz-Simons, Atlanta, Ga., 1934.
Beginners, by Bradford White, Rome, Ga., 1934.
Belle, by Patricia McMullan, Washington, N.C., 1934.
When Doctors Fail, by W. A. Sigmon, Alexis, N.C., 1934.
The Skeleton Rattles His Bones, by Douglas Hume, Monterey, Cal.,
   1934.
Spare Ribs, by Donald Pope, Highland Park, Mich., 1934.
Crash, by Milton Kalb, Far Rockaway, N.Y., 1934.
Sea Psalm, by Charles Edward Eaton, Winston-Salem, N.C., 1934.
New Anarchy, by Philip Goddard Parker, Reading, Mass., 1934.
New Nigger, by Fred Howard, Black Creek, N.C., 1934.
Clam Digger, by Jean Ashe, Pittsfield, Mass., 1934.
Hunger, by Ella Mae Daniel, Salisbury, N.C., 1934.
Traficante, by Maxeda von Hesse, Winter Park, Fla., 1934.
The Girl with the White Sweater, by Margaret Siceloff, Asheville, N.C.,
   1934.
Where There Is Faith, by Kathleen Krahenbuhl, Selma, N.C., 1934.
Concealed Aim, by Carl W. Dennis, Lawndale, N.C., 1934.
The Passer-By, by Ralph Lyerly, Granite Quarry, N.C., 1934.
Ancient Heritage, by Philip Goddard Parker, Reading, Mass., 1934.
Octagon Soap, by Nancy Lawlor, Durham, N.C., 1934.
Damned Idealist, by Charles A. Poe, Raleigh, N.C., 1934.
Rations, by Catherine Threlkeld, Asheville, N.C., 1934.
Confidentially Speaking, by Wilbur Dorsett, Spencer, N.C., 1934.
Muddy Jordan Waters, by Mildred Moore, Raleigh, N.C., 1935.
The Villain Gets the Girl, by Charles A. Poe, Raleigh, N.C., 1935.
Pensioner, by Alice A. Truslow, Summit, N.J., 1935.
The Devil's Trampin' Ground, by Sara Seawell, Chapel Hill, N.C., 1935.
Yours and Mine, by Ella Mae Daniel, Salisbury, N.C., 1935.
I Sing Forever, by Mildred Moore, Raleigh, N.C., 1935.
The Settin' Up, by Sara Seawell, Chapel Hill, N.C., 1935.
Tsalagi, by Billy Greet, San Antonio, Tex., 1935.
And So They Grew, by Ellen Deppe, Asheville, N.C., 1935.
Wait a While, by Kenneth Bartlett, Modesto, Cal., 1935.
Goldie, by Wilbur Dorsett, Spencer, N.C., 1935.
Crazy-Patch Quilt, by Anne Hyman Moore, Snow Hill, N.C., 1935.
Metropolitan Feodor, by Philip Goddard Parker, Reading, Mass., 1935.
So It Will Last, by William Howard Wang, Port Chester, N.Y., 1935.
The Best Butter, by Joseph Lee Brown, New York, N.Y., 1935.
Virtue, by Leonard Rapport, Asheville, N.C., 1935.
Hangman's Noose, by Charles A. Poe, Raleigh, N.C., 1935.
Bathroom Echos, by Walter Terry, New Canaan, Conn., 1935.
Dark Journey, by Virgil Jackson Lee, Baltimore, Md., 1935.

There Ain't No Escape, by Ella Mae Daniel, Salisbury, N.C., 1935.
Thou Thief! by Ralph Lyerly, Granite Quarry, N.C., 1935.
Barn Trash, by Mildred Moore, Raleigh, N.C., 1935.
Penny-Wise, by Ellen Deppe, Asheville, N.C., 1935.
Queer New World, by Wilbur Dorsett, Spencer, N.C., 1935.
Debtor's Hall, by Jean Ashe, Pittsfield, Mass., 1935.
The School Teacher, by Kenneth E. Bartlett, Modesto, Cal., 1935.
The Jew, by William Howard Wang, Port Chester, N.Y., 1935.
Across the Tracks, by Frank Durham, Columbia, S.C., 1935.
Cockle Doody Doo, by Patricia McMullan, Washington, N.C., 1935.
Hjemlengsel (Home Longing), by Gerd Bernhart, Sioux Falls, S.D., 1935.
The Red Velvet Goat, by Josefina Niggli, Monterrey, Mexico, 1935.
Take Your Choice, by George Starks, Rochester, N.Y., 1935.
Black Sheep, by Marjorie Usher, Laurel Hill, N.C., 1935.
Election, by Mary Delaney, Angleton, Tex., 1935.
The Other Way, by Lawrence Wismer, Hillsboro, Ore., 1935.
A Most Lamentable Comedy, by Barbara A. Hilton, Savannah, Ga., 1935.
Horses and Mice, by Joseph Lee Brown, New York, N.Y., 1935.
With Onions, by Frank Durham, Columbia, S.C., 1935.
There Is No Guilt, by William Howard Wang, Port Chester, N.Y., 1935.
Transient, by Walter Spearman, Silver Street, S.C., 1935.
The Eternal Comedy, by Mary Delaney, Angleton, Tex., 1935.
Prairie Dust, by Gerd Bernhart, Sioux Falls, S.D., 1935.
Raise a Tune, Sister, by Patricia McMullan, Washington, N.C., 1935.
Soldadera (Soldier-Woman), by Josefina Niggli, Monterrey, Mexico, 1935.
Grandma's Bonnet, by June Hogan, Chapel Hill, N.C., 1936.
Brownstone Front, by William Chichester, Maplewood, N.J., 1936.
Awakening, by Eleanor Barker, 1936.
An Orchid to You, by Jean Walker, Rocky Mount, N.C., 1936.
Cat Alley, by Kenneth Bartlett, Modesto, Cal., 1936.
An Active's Pledge, by William A. Barwick, Raleigh, N.C., 1936.
Frame-Up, by Jane Henle, Cleveland, Ohio, 1936.
Azteca, by Josefina Niggli, Monterrey, Mexico, 1936.
The Cry of Dolores, by Josefina Niggli, Monterrey, Mexico, 1936.
Sunday Costs Five Pesos, by Josefina Niggli, Monterrey, Mexico, 1936.
Country Sunday, by Walter Spearman, Silver Street, S.C., 1936.
Mob-Tide, by John Walker, Chapel Hill, N.C., 1936.
Strike-Breaker, by George Starks, Rochester, N.Y., 1936.
So Spin the Norns, by Gerd Bernhart, Sioux Falls, S.D., 1936.
Fire of the Lord, by Frank Durham, Columbia, S.C., 1936.
Ocean Harvest, by Jean Ashe, Pittsfield, Mass., 1936.

Ugly Hands, by Kate May Rutherford, Hardinsburg, Ind., 1936.
And Things Happen, by Don Watters, Ravenna, Ohio, 1936.
Waitin', by William Peery, Raleigh, N.C., 1936.
The Barren Year, by David Beaty, Anderson, S.C., 1936.
Tidal Wave, by Evelyn Snider, Conway, S.C., 1936.
Cause Unknown, by John Walker, Chapel Hill, N.C., 1936.
Who's Boss? by Lubin Leggette, Tabor City, N.C., 1936.
Widening the Channel, by Sally Wills Holland, Wilmington, Va., 1936.
Six Dollars, by Virginia Peyatt, Liberty, N.C., 1936.
Leavin's, by Janie Malloy Britt, Marion, N.C., 1936.
In the Jungle, by William Peery, Raleigh, N.C., 1936.
Tooth or Shave, by Josefina Niggli, Monterrey, Mexico, 1936.
The Steep Road, by Joseph Feldman, New York, N.Y., 1937.
Funeral Flowers for the Bride, by Beverley DuBose Hamer, Eastover,
  S.C., 1937.
Mrs. Juliet, by David Beaty, Anderson, S.C., 1937.
Rosemary's for Remembrance, by Sally Wills Holland, Wilmington, Va.,
  1937.
Abide with Me, by Walter Spearman, Silver Street, S.C., 1937.
The Sun Sets Early, by William Peery, Raleigh, N.C., 1937.
Near a Spring, by Kate May Rutherford, Hardinsburg, Ind., 1937.
Thank Rotary, by William Peery, Raleigh, N.C., 1937.
Penguin Soup, by Jean Ashe, Pittsfield, Mass., 1937.
Shattered Glass, by Marion Hartshorn, Griffin, Ga., 1937.
Long Sweetenin', by Janie Malloy Britt, Marion, N.C., 1937.
Courtship at Eight, by Charlotte Wright, Raleigh, N.C., 1937.
By Any Other Name, by Marion Hartshorn, Griffin, Ga., 1937.
From Sullen Earth, by Frank Durham, Columbia, S.C., 1937.
Earth Treading Stars, by Manuel Korn, Patterson, N.J., 1937.
The White Doe, by William Peery, Raleigh, N.C., 1937.
Seventy Times Seven, by William Ivey Long, Seaboard, N.C., 1937.
"A-Pinin' and A-Dyin'," by Emily Polk Crow, Dallas, Tex., 1937.
The Ivory Shawl, by Kate Porter Lewis, Tuscaloosa, Ala., 1937.
Drought, by Walter Spearman, Silver Street, S.C., 1937.
Fightin' Time, by Kate May Rutherford, Hardinsburg, Ind., 1937.
Toujour's Gai, by Virginia LaRochelle, Longmeadow, Mass., 1937.
Barge Incident, by Herb Meadow, New York City, N.Y., 1937.
Naughty Boy, by William Chichester, Port Chester, N.Y., 1937.
The Cross of Cannair, by Lynette Heldman, New York, N.Y., 1937.
Uncle Smelicue, by Lois Latham, Rainbow Springs, N.C., 1937.
This Side Jordan, by Lynn Gault, North Jackson, Ohio, 1937.
It Don't Make No Difference, by Joseph Lee Brown, Chapel Hill, N.C.,
  1937.
Hello, Hanging Dawg, by Lois Latham, Rainbow Springs, N.C., 1937.

Kunstbeflissener (Student of Art), by Thad Jones, Chapel Hill, N.C., 1937.

Pennies for Their Thoughts, by Noel Houston, Oklahoma City, Okla., 1937.

Washed in De Blood, by Rietta Winn Bailey, Cochran, Ga., 1937.

Hit's Man's Business, by Lois Latham, Rainbow Springs, N.C., 1937.

And Darling, Do Be Tactful, by Rose Peagler, Homerville, Ga., 1937.

While Reporters Watched, by Rose Peagler, Homerville, Ga., 1938.

Mary Marge, by Ellen Deppe, Asheville, N.C., 1938.

One Man's House, by Gwen Pharis, Magrath, Alberta, Canada, 1938.

The Worm Turns, by Jean Brabham, Batesburg, S.C., 1938.

Murder in the Snow, by Betty Smith, New York, N.Y., and Robert Finch, Dillon, Mont., 1938.

This Is Villa, by Josefina Niggli, Monterrey, Mexico, 1938.

Still Stands the House, by Gwen Pharis, Magrath, Alberta, Canada, 1938.

The Last Christmas, by Noel Houston, Oklahoma City, Okla., 1938.

His Boon Companions, by Lynn Gault, North Jackson, Ohio, 1938.

Where the Wind Blows Free, by Emily Polk Crow, Dallas, Tex., 1938.

Hidden Heart, by Howard Richardson, Black Mountain, N.C., 1938.

Wings to Fly Away, by Rietta Winn Bailey, Cochran, Ga., 1938.

Last Refuge, by Noel Houston, Oklahoma City, Okla., 1938.

Chris Axelson, Blacksmith, by Gwen Pharis, Magrath, Alberta, Canada, 1938.

West from the Panhandle, by Clemon White, Lufkin, Texas, and Betty Smith, New York, N.Y., 1938.

Let the Chips Fall, by Emily Polk Crow, Dallas, Tex., 1938.

Fresh Widder, by Lacy Anderson, Robersonville, N.C., 1938.

Stick 'Em Up, by Gordon Clouser, Roswell, N. Mex., 1938.

Me an' De Lawd, by Jameson Bunn Dowdy, Rocky Mount, N.C., 1938.

Montana Night, by Robert Finch, Dillon, Mont., and Betty Smith, New York, N.Y., 1938.

Triflin' Ways, by Lealon N. Jones, Cape Girardeau, Mo., 1938.

Twilight Song, by Donald Muller, Boonton, N.J., 1939.

Kid Sister, by Wieder Sievers, St. Louis, Mo., 1939.

Pasque Flower, by Gwen Pharis, Magrath, Alberta, Canada, 1939.

Uncle Spence Goes Modern, by William Wolff, Hickory, N.C., 1939.

The Long Ago, by Noel Houston, Oklahoma City, Okla., 1939.

Bad Yankees, by Antoinette Sparks, Birmingham, Ala., 1939.

Wash Carver's Mouse Trap, by Fred Koch, Jr., Chapel Hill, N.C., 1939.

Swappin' Fever, by Lealon N. Jones, Cape Girardeau, Mo., 1939.

Runaway, by Dorothy Lewis, New York, N.Y., 1939.

Design for Stella, by Sanford Stein, Woodmere, N.Y., 1939.

Old Man Taterbug, by Mary Louise Boylston, Crewe, Va., 1939.

The Reticule, by Katherine Moran, Milledgeville, Ga., 1939.
According to Law, by Noel Houston, Oklahoma City, Okla., 1939.
Out from New Bedford, by Frederick G. Walsh, New Bedford, Mass., 1939.
These Doggone Elections, by Fred Koch, Jr., Chapel Hill, N.C., 1939.
Texas Forever, by Emily Polk Crow, Dallas, Tex., 1939.
Lipstick, by Mary Hyde, Athens, Ohio, 1939.
Swamp Outlaw, by Clare Johnson Marley, Cary, N.C., 1939.
Store-Bought Teeth, by Marie Haass, Gander, Ga., 1939.
Squaw Winter, by Frances Langsdorf Fox, Philadelphia, Pa., 1939.
Got No Sorrow, by Caroline Hart Crum, Denmark, S.C., 1939.
Strong Hands for Hurting, by Edward Post, Shelby, N.C., 1939.
New Britches, by Evelyn Dawn Matthews, Asheville, N.C., 1939.
Winter Parade, by Adrian Spies, Newark, N.J., 1939.
Black Tassels, by Frank Guess, Rock Hill, S.C., 1939.
Whipplesnout, by Mary Louise Boylston, Crewe, Va., 1940.
Mist in the Hills, by Evelyn Dawn Matthews, Asheville, N.C., 1940.
Torch in the Wind, by Chase Webb, Tularosa, New Mex., 1940.
Banked Fires, by Constance Smith, Bronxville, N.Y., 1940.
The Devil's Bread, by Edward Post, Shelby, N.C., 1940.
Patches, by Mary Louise Boylston, Crewe, Va., 1940.
Outside De Gate, by William Long, Seaboard, N.C., 1940.
Mi Amigo, by Chase Webb, Silver City, New Mex., 1940.
Taffy, the Tiger, by Mary Louise Boylston, Crewe, Va., 1940.
Come Spring, by William Long, Seaboard, N.C., 1940.
The Woman from Merry River, by Chase Webb, Tularosa, New Mex., 1940.
The Scarlet Petticoat, by Kate Porter Lewis, Tuscaloosa, Ala., 1940.
Truth or Consequences, by Constance Smith, Bronxville, N.Y., 1940.
Billy, The Kid, by Chase Webb, Silver City, New Mex., 1940.
Watermelon Time, by Kate Porter Lewis, Tuscaloosa, Ala., 1940.
Three Links O'Chain, by Kate Porter Lewis, Tuscaloosa, Ala., 1940.
Party Dress, by Kate Porter Lewis, Tuscaloosa, Ala., 1940.
The House in Avondale, by Kate Porter Lewis, Tuscaloosa, Ala., 1940.
June Bug, by Lucy Crenshaw, Oxford, N.C., 1940.
Dark Bayou, by Laurraine Goreau, New Orleans, La., 1940.
August Angel, by Neil Hartley, Boone, N.C., 1940.
Cozy Corners, by Katherine Hill, New Bern, N.C., 1940.
A Daughter to Marry, by Carol Bashore, Schuyllkill Haven, Penn., 1940.
Sho' Nuff Dead, by Herbert Lee, Greenville, N.C., 1940.
Night Run, by Emilie Johnson, Bradenton, Fla., 1940.
Sarah Baske, by Merle McKay, Beverly, Mass., 1940.
The Bridegroom Waits, by Frank Guess, Rock Hill, S.C., 1940.
Sermon on a Monday, by Joseph D. Feldman, New York, N.Y., 1940.

Nine-Hour Shift, by Marian Maschin, Westfield, Mass., 1940.
Swing You Sinner, by Tom Avera, Jr., Rocky Mount, N.C., 1940.
Curse Me These People, by Joe Salek, Chicago, Ill., 1941.
Too Much Paradise, by Sanford Stein, Woodmere, N.Y., 1941.
Uncertain Death, by William L. Maner, Jr., Allendale, S.C., 1941.
Parole, by Robert Bowers, Webster Groves, Mo., 1941.
The Wider Field, by Marian Maschin, Westfield, Mass., 1941.
Union Forever, by Mrs. A. R. Wilson, Durham, N.C., 1941.
First Wave, by George Levy, Paris, France, 1941.
Saint of the Lord, by Elton Parker, Murfreesboro, N.C., 1941.
The Ninth Commandment, by W. T. Chichester, Chapel Hill, N.C., 1941.
Fire Worshipper, by Lelia Allen McMillan, Arkadelphia, Ark., 1941.
Bridal Mist, by Mary Brill, Poughquag, N.Y., 1941.
Hit's Bud's Army Now, by Jane Elizabeth Morrow, Hot Springs, N.C., 1941.
Black Friday, by Barry Farnol, Chicago, Ill., 1941.
Her Star Has Moved, by T'ang Wen Shun, Tienstsin, China, 1941.
Tarantula, by Kai Jurgensen, Copenhagen, Denmark, 1942.
The Cross on the Door, by Kai Jurgensen, Copenhagen, Denmark, 1942.
A Man's Game, by Robert Schenkkan, Brooklyn, N.Y., 1942.
The Hand of Providence, by Selah Richmond, Portland, Me., 1942.
The Red Oak, by Barry Farnol, Chicago, Ill., 1942.
The Wandering Dragon, by T'ang Wen Shun, Tienstsin, China, 1942.
The Vengeance of K'noh, by McCurdy Burnet, Go-Home Bay, Ontario, Canada, 1942.
Got No Misery, by Genie Loaring-Clark, Huntsville, Ala., 1942.
Pen in Hand, by Ellen Mary Pillsbury, Waterville, Me., 1942.
A Motley Assembly, by Marion Gleason, Naples, N.Y., 1942.
Real Trouble, by Ellen Mary Pillsbury, Waterville, Me., 1942.
Boer Commando, by Robert Schenkkan, Brooklyn, N.Y., 1942.
Shee Shih, the Aching Heart, by T'ang Wen Shun, Tienstsin, China, 1942.
Compound Fracture, by Charlotte Stephenson, Covington, Va., 1942.
The Toymaker, by Kai Jurgensen, Copenhagen, Denmark, 1942.
Androboras, by Marion Gleason, Naples, N.Y., 1942.
Flower Gold, by Martha Knight, Deer Lodge, Mont., 1942.
Flora Macdonald, by Clare J. Marley, Cary, N.C., 1942.
The Candle Poppin', by June Randolph, Swannanoa, N.C., 1942.
King in the Kitchen, by Elaine Berg, Grand Forks, N.D., 1942.
De Lost John, by Walter Carroll, Chapel Hill, N.C., 1942.
Pecos Bull, by Russell Rogers, San Antonio, Tex., 1942.
Food and the Student, by Wharton Black, Bluefield, West Va., 1942.
The Sea Wall, by Elaine Mendes, Maplewood, N.J., 1942.

God and the Bishop, by Elizabeth Trotman, Winston-Salem, N.C., 1942.

Park Bench Blitz, by Lucille Culbert, Marion, Va., 1942.

I Shall Not Want, by Kellam Prickett, St. Matthews, S.C., 1942.

And Chewin' Gum, by Albert Lanier, Metter, Ga., 1942.

Tim-Berr! by Doris Marsolais, Coeur d'Alene, Idaho, 1943.

Look Down, Look Down, by Walter Carroll, Chapel Hill, N.C., 1943.

Give Us Time to Sing, by David Hanig, Trenton, N.J., 1943.

Fleas and Figs, by Mary-Averett Seelye, Beirut, Syria, 1943.

My World to Grieve, by Walter Carroll, Chapel Hill, N.C., 1943.

The Right and the Left, by Marcelle Clarke, High Point, N.C., 1943.

Back-Street Blues, by Walter Carroll, Chapel Hill, N.C., 1943.

To the Young, by David Hanig, Trenton, N.J., 1943.

Never Miss a Trick, by Marion Gurney, Gastonia, N.C., 1943.

There Must We Ever Be, by Anne Osterhout, Beaufort, S.C., 1943.

Sackcloth and Sauerkraut, by Ellen Mary Pillsbury, Waterville, Me., 1943.

Muddy Water, by David Hardison, Jr., Dunn, N.C., 1943.

Sunday's Child, by Elizabeth Welch, Asheville, N.C., 1943.

Crusoe Islanders, by Clare J. Marley, Cary, N.C., 1943.

Four in a Room, by Sally Martin, Arlington, Va., 1943.

There's Always Morning, by David Hanig, Trenton, N.J., 1943.

Listen, My Children, by Tom Avera, Rocky Mount, N.C., 1943.

Lovingly, Gay, by Gwendolyn E. London, Charlotte, N.C., 1943.

The Georgian Dandy, by Nananne Porcher, LaGrange, Ga., and Carrington Cross, Richmond, Va., 1943.

Wailers to the Wind, by Anne Bridges, Sumner, Ga., 1943.

Scuttlebutt, by Tom Avera, Rocky Mount, N.C., 1943.

Victory for Sara, by Clyde Register, Henderson, N.C., 1943.

Aunt Aggie, by Emily Mashburn, Asheville, N.C., 1943.

The Valentine Princess, by Elizabeth K. Solem, Oak Park, Ill., 1944.

Strange Sun, by Paul Ramsey, Jr., Chattanooga, Tenn., 1944.

Carnival Cantata, by David Hanig, Trenton, N.J., 1944.

Harp upon the Willows, by Harvey L. Hannah, Camp Butner, N.C., 1944.

Heaven Is What You Make It, by Hyman Levy, New York, N.Y., 1944.

Prologue, by Robert E. Beck, Fort Fisher, N.C., 1944.

Hotel Armageddon, by Carrington Cross, Richmond, Va., 1944.

Thirty Minutes Out of Midnight, by David Hanig, Trenton, N.J., 1944.

Morning Edition, by Kat Hill, New Bern, N.C., 1944.

The Wraith of Chimney Rock, by Clare J. Marley, Cary, N.C., 1944.

Divided We Stand, by Anne Osterhout, Beaufort, S.C., 1944.

The Tale of a Tub, by Myrtle Phaye Proctor, Quahan, Tex., 1944.

Salt Sands, by Virginia Page Spencer, Swan Quarter, N.C., 1944.

Pilgrim's Rest, by Jessie Daniel, Metter, Ga., 1944.

Big Meetin' Time, by Clare J. Marley, Cary, N.C., 1944.
Unshielded Lamp, by David Hanig, Trenton, N.J., 1944.
Rich Man, Best Man, by Mary T. Colones, Selma, N.C., 1944.
The Distances to Go, by Anne Osterhout, Beaufort, S.C., 1944.
Poor Mr. Burton, by Mary Brooks Popkins, Leesburg, Va., 1944.
Wings in the Sun, by Mary Lou MacGowan, Quincy, Fla., 1944.
Deep Roots, by Mary Barker, Asheville, N.C., 1944.
To Defraud the Male, by Frank Echols, Asheville, N.C., 1944.
The Opal, by Frank Echols, Asheville, N.C., 1945.
Crown Me, by Roy Alexander, Fletcher, N.C., 1945.
Heavenly Bound, by Shirley Waters, Pittsboro, N.C., 1945.
From Childhood's Hour, by Randall Brooks, Charlotte, N.C., 1945.
Joyful Noise, by Phyllis Jean Sullivan, New Bedford, Mass., 1945.
Tears of Poison, by Frances Creshire, Kirkwood, Mo., 1945.
Point Chartres, by Robert Adkins, Chapel Hill, N.C., 1945.
Glory Please, by Charles S. Waldman, Long Island, N.Y., 1945.
Through a Glass Darkly, by Elinor Martin, Detroit, Mich., 1945.
The Game, by Elinor Martin, Detroit, Mich., 1945.
Blue Violets, by Richard Kiser, Beverly Hills, Cal., 1945.
To Count Thirteen, by Marion Lipscomb Miller, Aberdeen, Md., 1945.
By Any Name, by Anne Osterhout, Beaufort, S.C., 1945.
Cake Crumbs, by Barbara Rich, Reading, Mass., 1945.
Five Notes in a Bar, by Phyllis Jean Sullivan, New Bedford, Mass., 1945.
The Silver Bell, by Helen Scales, St. Marys, Cal., 1945.
Why, Miss Featherstone! by Helen Elizabeth Eyster, Lewisburg, Penn.,
    1945.
Cornbread, by John Fries Blair, Winston-Salem, N.C., 1945.
Egypt Lan', by Robert Armstrong, Jr., Birmingham, Ala., 1945.
St. Magadelen's Guild, by Mimi MacGowan, Quincy, Fla., 1945.
Niobe in Darkness, by Violet Fidel, Brooklyn, N.Y., 1946.
A New Canaan, by Wayne Bowman, Norfolk, Va., 1946.
The Hollow Man, by Nancy Davis, Durham, N.C., 1946.
A Wise Woman, by Louise Bonner, Staunton, Va., 1946.
Fisherman's Last Supper, by Charles Waldman, Long Island, N.Y., 1946.
Mr. Gabriel, by Lois Warnshuis, Staten Island, N.Y., 1946.
Wherefore Is This Night, by Violet Fidel, Brooklyn, N.Y., 1946.
The Queen Was in the Kitchen, by Charles Waldman, Long Island, N.Y.,
    1946.
Hunter from the Hill, by Violet Fidel, Brooklyn, N.Y., 1946.
Mr. Phipps and the Pink Elephant, by John McKinney, Dallas, Tex.,
    1946.
Habeas Porkus, by Wayne Bowman, Norfolk, Va., 1946.
Down Under, by Paul K. Jones, Salem, Mass., 1946.
The Braggart Captain, by Nell Clark, Tampa, Fla., 1946.

If the Shoe Fits, by Winifred Logan, Akron, Ohio, 1946.

Give Us Pause, by Sam Hirsch, Trenton, N.J., 1946.

If Women Played Cards As Men Do, by Lynn Leonard, Detroit, Mich., 1946.

Never Seek to Tell, by Harold Suits, Liberty, N.C., 1946.

The Mask of the Black Bishop, by John Wills, Newton, Miss., 1946.

If You Know What I Mean, by Winifred Logan, Akron, Ohio, 1946.

To Them in Darkness, by Charles Brockman, High Point, N.C., 1947.

Black Piet, by Robert Schenkkan, Chapel Hill, N.C., 1947.

Subway Rhapsody, by Sam Hirsch, Trenton, N.J., 1947.

Why Don't You Crow, White Rooster? by Wyat Helsabeck, Troy, N.C., 1947.

Althea, by Mark Reece Sumner, Asheville, N.C., 1947.

Flirtin' wid de Cemetery, by Elizabeth G. Savage, Henderson, N.C., 1947.

As Long As There Are Stars, by Emily Chappell, Durham, N.C., 1947.

Phillip Comes Home, by Kermit Hunter, Welch, West Va., 1947.

They Shall Take Up Serpents, by Eugene Wiggins, Nashville, Tenn., 1947.

The Michaels, by Robert C. Eberle, Brooklyn, N.Y., 1947.

The People the Cards Like, by Robert Louis Stevens, Asheville, N.C., 1947.

The Runners, by Arthur Golby, New York, N.Y., 1947.

The Ragged Meadow, by Kermit Hunter, Welch, West Va., 1947.

Nun-Sense, by Louisa Mustin, Augusta, Ga., 1947.

Hunted Men, by Mark R. Sumner, Asheville, N.C., 1947.

Saint Judas, by Eugene Noel Zeigler, Jr., Florence, S.C., 1947.

The Big Pat-Pat, by Quentin Brown, Montreal, Canada, 1947.

Weep into Stones, by Frank Groseclose, Atlanta, Ga., 1947.

The Shiksa, by Sam Hirsch, Trenton, N.J., 1947.

There Are Spirits and Spirits, by Claude Rayborn, Greensboro, N.C., 1947.

The Terrapin Sticks Its Neck Out, by Robert Rolnik, Brooklyn, N.Y., 1948.

Au Fond Du Coeur, by James Geiger, Miami, Fla., 1948.

Morning Dialogue, by John Wills, Raleigh, N.C., 1948.

Spanish Moss, by Robert Barr, Kansas City, Mo., 1948.

The Atom Cantata, by Sam Hirsch, Trenton, N.J., and Harold Schiffman, Greensboro, N.C., 1948.

The Binkle Plan, by Robert Rolnik, Brooklyn, N.Y., 1948.

A Matter of Business, by John Wills, Newton, Mass., 1948.

Of Lucy Wren, by Murray McCain, Newport, N.C., 1948.

The Little Things, by Kermit Hunter, Welch, West Va., 1948.

Channel Fever, by Robert Rolnik, Brooklyn, N.Y., 1948.

Close Quarters, by Catherine McDonald, Chattanooga, Tenn., 1948.
The Word of a Pirate, by Marian Miller, Aberdeen, Md., 1948.
It Is the Night, by Lewis W. Heniford, Loris, S.C., 1948.
The Simple Solution, by Martha Nell Gratton, Durham, N.C., 1948.
The Important Thing, by Edna Dooley, Johnson City, Tenn., 1948.
The Winter's Harvest, by M. David Samples, Joliet, Ill., 1948.
Dearie, Ye're a Dreamer, by Francis Michael Casey, Turners Falls, Mass., 1948.
Snow Falling, by John M. Ehle, Jr., Asheville, N.C., 1949.
A Brighter Star, by Nancy Wallace, Wilmington, N.C., 1949.
Jersey Birt-day, by Ralph Long, Durham, N.C., 1949.
Counterpoint, by Patricia Peteler, Glendale, Cal., 1949.
The Vanishing American, by Anne Martin, Cherokee, N.C., 1949.
Turkeys in the Thirties, by Joseph C. Stockdale, Kalamazoo, Mich., 1949.
The Prisoner, by Alec W. Finlayson, Marietta, N.C., 1949.
False to Any Man, by William Hardy, Durham, N.C., 1949.
A Crystal for Father, by William S. Johnson, Jr., Rocky Mount, N.C., 1949.
Family Heirloom, by Charles H. Williamson, Kennet Square, Penn., 1949.
Five's a Crowd, by Edwin T. Nash, Burlington, N.C., 1949.
The Governor's Lady, by Mary Jo Milburn, Durham, N.C., 1950.
Causes, by Melvin Hosansky, Jamaica, N.Y., 1950.
Of Ladies and Lightning Rods, by Elizabeth G. Savage, Henderson, N.C., 1950.
The Lady Will Jump, by Bradford Arrington, Greenville, S.C., 1950.
The Empty Shoe, by Sam Greene, Mooresboro, N.C., 1950.
Light, by James E. Ginther, Durham, N.C., 1950.
What's a Sauce for the Goose? by Ann Covington, Greensboro, N.C., 1950.
Sure Cure, by Glenn Martin, Chapel Hill, N.C., 1950.
The Long White Pants, by Fred Young, West Monroe, La., 1950.
Here I Am, by Roy S. Waldau, Hartford, Conn., 1950.
A Sea Change, by Nancy Henderson, Wilmington, N.C., 1950.
A Spell for Davy, by Frank Groseclose, Atlanta, Ga., 1950.
The Tiffany Touch, by Albert Klein, Council Bluffs, Iowa, 1950.
From Beneath the Wing, by Reginald Manning, Williamston, N.C., 1951.
Tomorrow and Tomorrow, by Richard Hopkins, Yakima, Wash., 1951.
The Belt, by Emily Polk Crow, Austin, Tex., 1951.
Laura Lee, by Albert Klein, Council Bluffs, Iowa, 1951.
Florida . . . Ain't So Hot! by Philip Bernanke, Dillon, S.C., 1951.
Dinosaur, by John Clayton, Knoxville, Tenn., 1951.
Blue Jean Gal, by Elizabeth Neill, Roanoke, Va., 1951.

In August, by James P. Pretlow, Wilmington, N.C., 1951.
A Brave Man, by Andrew M. Adams, North Hollywood, Cal., 1951.
The Shining Dark, by Elmer Oettinger, Chapel Hill, N.C., 1951.
Pythagoras Bound, by Charles A. Kellogg, Watertown, N.Y., 1951.
Speed, Bonnie Boat, by Nancy Wallace Henderson, Wilmington, N.C., 1952.
Invert Your Advisor, by Lawrence E. Graves, San Diego, Cal., 1952.
When Johnny Comes Marching Home, by Alfred Klein, Chapel Hill, N.C., 1952.
The Overture, by Lynn Neill, Roanoke, Va., 1952.
Hold on to Darkness, by A. Frank Moore, Timmonsville, S.C., 1952.
Tumpkin Tarries, by Louise Lamont, Chapel Hill, N.C., 1952.
Marilyn, My Marilyn, by Donald F. Vincent, Swannanoa, N.C., 1952.
Plain and Fancy, by Louise Lamont, Chapel Hill, N.C., 1952.
Cox-Witch, by Mary Virginia Morgan, Byhalia, Miss., 1952.
Coed Style, by Bradford Arrington, Greenville, S.C., 1952.
Uncross Those Stars, by Emily Crow Selden, Chapel Hill, N.C., 1952.
Silver Birch, by Sydney Z. Litwack, Los Angeles, Cal., 1952.
Buck, by Tommy Rezzuto, Asheville, N.C., 1952.
Hi, Sir, by James Leonard, Trappe, Md., 1953.
The Mute, by Cyril S. Lang, Chapel Hill, N.C., 1953.
Little Wonder, by Donald Deagon, Chapel Hill, N.C., 1953.
Skybow, by Dan Reid, Raleigh, N.C., 1953.
Two's Too Many, by William Waddell, Galax, Va., 1953.
Fellow Immigrants, by Evelyn Bozeman da Parma, Raleigh, N.C., 1953.
The Candy Striped Umbrella, by James Gillikin, Atlantic, N.C., 1953.
The Crowin' Hen, by Mellrose Higginbotham, Princeton, West Va., 1953.
Give Us Our Bread, by Josefa Zotter Selden, Pittsford, N.Y., 1953.
Motion Opposed, by William Waddell, Galax, Va., 1953.
The Other Side of the Mountain, by John Clayton, Chapel Hill, N.C., 1953.
Two Left Hands, by Nancy Murray, Raleigh, N.C., 1954.
The Wrong Invention, by W. David Ashburn, Winston-Salem, N.C., 1954.
The Good Neighbor's Policy, by Walter Creech, Chapel Hill, N.C., 1954.
No Pills for Purcella, by Harold England, Kings Mountain, N.C., 1954.
A Man in the House, by Claire Russell Easty, Chapel Hill, N.C., 1954.
Jezebel Shoes, by Baxter Sasser, Mt. Olive, N.C., 1954.
The Funeral Director, by William O'Sullivan, Chapel Hill, N.C., 1954.
The Last Unemployed American, by William O'Sullivan, Chapel Hill, N.C., 1954.
The Friends, by Joseph Rosenberg, Chapel Hill, N.C., 1955.
Gomennasi, by Christian Moe, New York, N.Y., 1955.

Doris, by Virginia Ferguson, Durham, N.C., 1955.
Johnnie Come Lately, by George Brenholtz, Hellertown, Pa., 1955.
Midland Purple, by Harry Coble, Florence, S.C., 1955.
The Finer Performance, by Christian Moe, New York, N.Y., 1955.
An Angel Came Walking, by Carolyn Kinsey Sumner, Brevard, N.C., 1955.
Board Meeting, by Ruth Hubbard Young, Salisbury, N.C., 1955.
Ladies of Lee, by Norman Booker, Greensboro, N.C., 1955.
Punch and the Parson, by Martha Frazer Rankin, Montgomery, Ala., 1956.
The Walk-In Boots, by Mary Johnston, Europa, Miss., 1956.
The Bereaved, by M. David Samples, Chicago, Ill., 1956.
Prometheus Rebound, by Paul T. Chase, Chapel Hill, N.C., 1956.
To Play the Bear, by Allen Lacy, Dallas, Tex., 1956.
General Alarm, by James Poteat, Charlotte, N.C., 1956.
To a Wild Rose, by Albert Gordon, Greensboro, N.C., 1956.
Children of the Earth, by Robert Chase, Boston, Mass., 1956.
Unlabeled, by Lore Schuller, Wadesboro, N.C., 1956.
The Waiting Room, by Ruth Hubbard Young, Salisbury, N.C., 1956.
Miss Carrie, by Kit Lee Singleton, Florence, S.C., 1956.
Room for Rent, by Marcelline Krafchick, Philadelphia, Pa., 1957.
Portrait of a Dragon, by Josephine Stipe, Chapel Hill, N.C., 1957.
Child of Two Winds, by Peter B. O'Sullivan, Chapel Hill, N.C., 1957.
Lost Goddess, by Christopher Reynolds, New York, N.Y., 1957.
The Spaceman Cometh, by Virginia Page Williams, Fort Thomas, Ky., 1957.
The Thief and the Hunchback, by Leon Rooke, Roanoke Rapids, N.C., 1957.
Big Time Return, by James Poteat, Charlotte, N.C., 1957.
April in the Moon, by Lewis Ennis, Delray Beach, Fla., 1957.
A Midsummer Tonic, by James Poteat, Charlotte, N.C., 1957.
Fairy Beauty, by George H. Hill, Jr., Robbinsville, N.C., 1958.
The Eternal Thread, by Gunsam Lee, Seoul, Korea, 1958.
A White Butterfly, by Gabriela Roepke, Santiago, Chile, 1958.
The Dangers of Great Literature, by Gabriela Roepke, Santiago, Chile, 1958.
Mosell and the Laurel Bush, by George H. Hill, Jr., Robbinsville, N.C., 1958.
The Freudian Years, by Kenneth Callender, Greensboro, N.C., 1958.
Chain of Evidence, by Scott Lett, Charlotte, N.C., 1958.
Once Removed, by Martha Linney, Hiddenite, N.C., 1958.
The Scatterbrain, by Carl Hinrichs, Tryon, N.C., 1958.
Below the Bridge, by Gunsam Lee, Seoul, Korea, 1959.

Fear and Trembling, by Harold Stassel, New York, N.Y., 1959.
The Sisters Gogmagog, by Craven Mackie, Baton Rouge, La., 1959.
With Apologies, Euripides, by Douglas McDermott, San Marino, Cal., 1959.
We Might Become Examples, by Arthur McDonald, Dalton, Ga., 1959.
An Age of Reason, by Robert Merritt, Yonkers, N.Y., 1959.
The Opportunist, by Mary Frances Newton, Winston-Salem, N.C., 1959.
Time of Reckoning, by Timothy L. Jones, Morehead City, N.C., 1959.
Cold Hester, by Parker Hodges, Asheville, N.C., 1959.
Brandon House, by Marjorie Hill, Beaufort, S.C., 1960.
The Return, by Charles R. Nisbet, III, Charlotte, N.C., 1960.
Half Moon, by Shirley Dixon, Greenville, N.C., 1960.
Cakes with White Icings, by Jerome Van Camp, Southern Pines, N.C., 1960.
The Dead Are Quicker, by William Corpening, Hendersonville, N.C., 1960.
Up, by Thomas Turner, New York, N.Y., 1960.
Another Dull Night, by Sally Pullen, Parkton, N.C., 1960.
Penny Tree, by Mary Wideman, Columbia, S.C., 1960.
Footnotes on Salome, by Christine Meyers, Brookneal, Va., 1960.
The Thorn Tree, by Mary Veal Kiser, Winston-Salem, N.C., 1960.
Kiss the Book, by Guilbert A. Daley, Raleigh, N.C., 1960.
Oh, the Mysteries of Love, by William Corpening, Hendersonville, N.C., 1960.
The Taste of Blarney, by Frank Murphy, Hamlet, N.C., 1960.
Unseen Enemy, by Oliver Bloomer, Whitakers, N.C., 1960.
Flatbush Sonata, by Susan Meyer, Greensboro, N.C., 1961.
Eric, by William Corpening, Hendersonville, N.C., 1961.
Token of Esteem, by Wallace Johnson, Forest Hills, N.Y., 1961.
Dark Morning, by A. S. Moffett, Taylorsville, N.C., 1961.
People Are Partial to Peaches, by Sally Pullen, Parkton, N.C., 1961.
The Facade, by Larry Randolph, Fort Smith, Ark., 1962.
The Hands of Ciascuno, by Wallace Johnson, Forest Hills, N.Y., 1962.
Look Down from a Mountain, by Wesley Van Tassel, Kent, Minn., 1962.
Indian Summer, by Gail Place, Bradford, Penn., 1962.
Waiting for Eden, by Douglas M. Young, Chapel Hill, N.C., 1962.
What Did You Learn in School Today? by Wallace Johnson, Forest Hills, N.Y., 1962.
Little Fish, by Larry Warner, Rocky Mount, N.C., 1962.
The Limbo Tree, by H. Bruce Caple, Charlotte, N.C., 1962.
Tight Little Box, by Fred Lubs, Savannah, Ga., 1962.
To Make Men Free, by Jon Phelps, Durham, N.C., 1962.

The Isolate, by George Gray, III, Gastonia, N.C., 1962.
The Voices on the River, by Harry Callahan, Livingston, N.J., 1962.
Mark Eleven at Johnny's, by Robert Malone, Rockville, Md., 1962.
Pity Has a Human Face, by Scott Byrd, Brook Haven, Miss., 1963.
Folly, by Wesley Van Tassel, Kent, Minn., 1963.
Clown for a Day, by Reginald Spaulding, Durham, N.C., 1963.
Rock Quarry, by Richard King, Flat Rock, N.C., 1963.
Where Do You Go When It Starts To Rain? by Richard Parks, Jacksonville, Fla., 1963.
For the Love of a Worm, by Sally Passmore Cook, Bristol, Va., 1963.
Ten Cars before Hope, by Jon Phelps, Durham, N.C., 1963.
I Want So Much: I've Got So Much to Give, by Elizabeth R. Smith, Danville, Va., 1963.
The Button, by George Gray, Gastonia, N.C., 1963.
Sydney, by Richard N. Philp, Vero Beach, Fla., 1963.
A Matter of Distinction, by Tom Benenson, New York, N.Y., 1963.
The Anniversary, by Richard N. Philp, Vero Beach, Fla., 1964.
The Summer Tree, by Randolph Umberger, Burlington, N.C., 1964.
Beast, by Alan Goldsmith, Atlanta, Ga., 1964.
Two Little Tigers, by Lloyd Bray, Charlotte, N.C., 1964.
A Million of Them, by Ben Jones, Chapel Hill, N.C., 1964.
Sister Mae Lies Cold and Dead, by Elizabeth R. Smith, Danville, Va., 1964.
The Love Goddess, by Barbara Hannah, Chapel Hill, N.C., 1965.
Yin Tai and Shan Bwo, by Peter Chang, Taiwan, China, 1965.
". . . And of All the Forgotten Faces," by George A. Gray, III, Gastonia, N.C., 1965.
No Other Gods, by Paul Crouch, Columbia, S.C., 1965.
Purgisnacht, by Millard McDonald, Reidsville, N.C., 1965.
The Woman from Viper, by Paul Byron Baker, Clintwood, Va., 1965.
The Bluff Boxes, by John Irvine, Memphis, Tenn., 1965.
The Ladders or *From Day to Day,* by Roberts Batson, Manzanillo, Dominican Republic, 1965.
Rainbows Are Forever, by Janet Scholz, New Holstein, Wis., 1965.
The Actor, by James Sexton Layton, Chapel Hill, N.C., 1966.
Kilroy Was Here, by William E. Watson, Sanford, N.C., 1966.
The Captain, by Mel Hutto, Birmingham, Ala., 1966.
Fly Away Empty, by Rebecca Ranson Engle, Chapel Hill, N.C., 1966.
Heaven Only Knows, by Betty Atchison Setzer, Durham, N.C., 1966.
Yankee Stew, by Gene Corpening, Granite Falls, N.C., 1966.
Stages, by Gary Weathersbee, Wilmington, N.C., 1967.
A Piece of Flannel, by William E. Watson, Sanford, N.C., 1967.
The Shell Game, by Jeannine van Hulsteyn, Chapel Hill, N.C., 1967.
The Cannon, by Carl F. Thompson, Jr., Falls Church, Va., 1967.

The Sweet-Talking Miracle, by William F. Butler, Bethesda, Md., 1967.
Colonel Starbottle for the Plaintiff, by Jeannine van Hulsteyn, Chapel Hill, N.C., 1967.
The Visitation, by Julian Hartzell, Stony Brook, Long Island, N.Y., 1967.
A Sure Thing, by Jo Mills, Asheville, N.C., 1968.
Bump in the Night, by William E. Watson, Southern Pines, N.C., 1968.
A Homecoming Song, by Joseph W. Walker, Tryon, N.C., 1968.
Mourning Ends at Purim, by Mary Foster Ellis, Hyde Park, N.Y., 1968.
The Grand Piano, by Jeannine van Hulsteyn, Chapel Hill, N.C., 1968.
Gravedigger's Delight, by Gene Corpening, Granite Falls, N.C., 1968.

FULL-LENGTH PLAYS

1918–1968
(In the order of their production)

Job's Kinfolks, by Loretto Carroll Bailey, Winston-Salem, N.C., 1929.
Playthings, by Anthony Buttitta, Monroe, La., 1931.
Rest for My Soul, by Ann Wishart Braddy, Dublin, Ga., 1931.
Strike Song, by Loretto Carroll Bailey, Winston-Salem, N.C., 1931.
Snow White, by Sallie M. Ewing, Mt. Gilead, N.C., 1932.
Sad Words to Gay Music, by Alvin Kerr, Cleveland, Ohio, 1933.
A House Divided, by Frederica Frederick, New Kensington, Penn., 1934.
Water, by Alton Williams, San Francisco, Cal., 1935.
Singing Valley, by Josefina Niggli, Monterrey, Mexico, 1936.
The Fair-God (Malinche), by Josefina Niggli, Monterrey, Mexico, 1936.
Sharecropper, by Fred Howard, Black Creek, N.C., 1938.
Smoky Mountain Road, by Fred Koch, Jr., Chapel Hill, N.C., 1940.
The Marauders, by Noel Houston, Oklahoma City, Okla., 1941.
Remember Who You Are, by Frank Guess, Rock Hill, S.C., 1941.
Cocky Doodler, by William Maner, Jr., Allendale, S.C., 1942.
Behold, the Brethren, by Joseph D. Feldman, New York City, N.Y.,
    1942.
Down to the Sea, by Kai Jurgensen, Copenhagen, Denmark, 1943.
The Twilight Zone, by Tom Avera, Rocky Mount, N.C., and Foster
    Fitz-Simons, Atlanta, Ga., 1944.
Calliope, by Virginia Page Spencer, Swan Quarter, N.C., 1945.
Hear the Hammers Ringing, by Cid Ricketts Sumner, Chapel Hill, N.C.,
    1947.
Call Back Yesterday, by Gene McLain, Sunbury, Penn., 1948.
Egypt Lan', by Robert G. Armstrong, Jr., Birmingham, Ala., 1948.
Inherit the Wind, by Gene A. McLain, Sunbury, Penn., 1949.
Repple Depple, by Sam Hirsch, Trenton, New Jersey, 1949.
The Spirit of Cedarhurst, by Mildred E. Danforth, Berwick, Me., 1949.
October in the Spring, by Joseph G. Stockdale, Jr., Kalamazoo, Mich.,
    1950.
Angels Full Front, by Francis Michael Casey, Turners Falls, Mass.,
    1950.
Spring for Sure, by Catherine McDonald, Chattanooga, Tenn., and
    Wilton Mason, Chapel Hill, N.C., 1950.
First String Concerto, by Martha Nell Hardy, Durham, N.C., 1950.

Lo, the Angel, by Nancy Wallace Henderson, Wilmington, N.C., 1951.
Tempest in a Teacup, by James Ginther, Durham, N.C., 1951.
Hospitality, by Jack Porter, Clinton, Ky., 1951.
Morning in Yellow-Orange, by Agnar Mykle, Copenhagen, Denmark, 1952.
Liberty Flats, by Lawrence E. Graves, San Diego, Cal., 1952.
The Pink Circus, by Gonzalo Estrada, Modesto, Cal., 1952.
A Ballad for Jeannie, by Lynn Neill, Roanoke, Va., 1953.
Judgment Over Daniel, by Frank Groseclose, Atlanta, Ga., 1953.
The Outsider, by Emily Crow Selden, Chapel Hill, N.C., 1954.
Darkening Shore, by Kermit Hunter, Welch, West Va., 1954.
Goodbye, Proud Earth, by Mellrose Higginbotham, Princeton, W. Va., 1954.
Saturday Stranger, by Joseph Rosenberg, Chapel Hill, N.C., 1955.
Cat in Gloves, by Samuel Baxter Sasser, Mt. Olive, N.C., 1956.
Strangers in the Land, by Christian Hollis Moe, New York, N.Y., 1957.
A Little to the Left, by Brock Brower, Princeton, N.J., 1959.
One More Waltz, by Isabella Davis, Chapel Hill, N.C., 1960.
Renegade, by Carl Hinrichs, Tryon, N.C., 1962.
The Summer Tree, by Randolph Umberger, Burlington, N.C., 1965.